The Ful

MW01708013

Endorsements:

The moment you open this book, you know it is different. The subject matter is familiar. But the shape of the discussion, the method of presentation, the tone of the argumentation are arrestingly fresh and attractive.

Most recognized publications about gender issues are written by professional scholars. The style and the format of their books and articles are minutely regulated to look as uniformly stereotypical as possible. By contrast, the presentation of this book is daringly conceived. The style is terse and direct. The method reflects the Socratic pattern of questions raised and answers thoughtfully formulated. The flow of the outline is clearly delineated. The book itself is awash with relevant Scripture references that abound without becoming cumbersome. And, surprise! Photographs of real people dramatically personalize the import of the written text.

Scholars read books authored by other scholars. Lay people, as astute and motivated as they may be to take part in the discussion, are generally left out of consideration.

Because she has done her homework, this text written by a teacher, will appeal to folk happily bereft of the pedantic erudition of the professionals. She has the ability to break down in accessible terms thorny exegetical issues with illustrations such as toes sticking out from under a blanket or the mutilation of a kitchen appliance.

This book goes to prove again that a high view of Scripture entails a high view of women. Common folk will, perhaps for the first time, be able to follow the argument that builds the case. And experts will peek into it for their own edification.

Gilbert Bilezikian

Professor emeritus, Wheaton College.
Author of the classic primer *Beyond Sex Roles* as well as *Christianity 101* and *Community 101* among many others.

The Full Rights of Sons is a readable, simply written book. But don't let that sentence fool you–it is a truly radical book. Something truly radical is not faddish, here today and gone tomorrow. The word radical refers to something that gets to "the root" of a matter. Kathryn Stegall's book is radical because it does precisely that with regard to our equality and full rights in Christ. This is a prudential, sound and well-written book. I heartily commend it to readers who want to understand the biblical message about love and submission.

John H. Armstrong
President, ACT3 Network, Carol Stream, IL.
Author of *Your Church Is Too Small.*

The Full Rights of Sons is a thoroughly researched and scripturally based book. Every thought is drawn from scripture as is seen from the multiple passages on every page. This subject is obviously very close to Stegall's heart, but that does not allow her to get ahead of God's Word in any way. It is a fascinating read for one who truly wants to know what the Bible says about women. This book will have you thinking about it long after you have finished reading. Her scholarship is quite compelling. I highly recommend *The Full Rights of Sons.*

Boni Piper
Marriage and Family Therapist.
Author of *Life Ties, Then They Leave Home,*
and *Relationship Empowering Parenting.*

Kathryn Stegall's book is unique among other books on Christian equality in that it starts with the basic premise that if anyone is in Christ that person is a New Creation (2 Cor. 5:17). The reality of this new life must have profound implications on our ethics, values and relationships. I was personally inspired by what Kathryn had to say about our new life in Christ.

Despite her thoroughness, Kathryn's style is conversational rather than technical, and her writing is accessible to a wide audience. Kathryn's statements are steeped in Scripture. As someone who has read many books on the topic of women in ministry there were new ideas here for me to think about.

Kathryn's high view of Scripture and her devotion to God is evident. Her discussions are thought provoking, compelling and logical, as well as presented in a warm, personal manner. This useful resource is no dry text book.

Margaret Mowczko
Writer at newlife.id.au

I really like Kathryn Stegall's new book, *The Full Rights of Sons.* I remember asking her several years ago when she showed me an earlier draft, "Why do you want to keep the terminology of "sons"? My question, of course, reflected my assumption that her thinking was driven by some form of feminism. I was wrong, and I hadn't read very carefully yet. She patiently responded that that terminology is crucial, essential to her hope as a Christian woman. I believed her, and that has been developmental

Then I began to see Galatians 3:23 through 4:7 as a whole paragraph. Thus, all who are baptized into Christ, including male and female, are now adopted as sons, heirs. There cannot be different layers or categories of sons/heirs, for we are all one through faith in Christ. That is a biblical principle which can and must be received by faith, and it has some far-reaching implications for the church and its life of faith in the world.

Kathryn Stegall is not a feminist, not even a biblical feminist, she is simply a woman pursuing a full-fledged examination of the whole counsel of God on the topic of the place and role of women in Christ's plan for his church. She does this examination thoroughly and reasonably, and her book is very readable. As a pastor, I recommend it highly.

Bruce Hemphill
Pastor, Covenant Fellowship Reformed
Presbyterian Church, Wilkinsburg, PA.

The Full Rights of Sons

by

Kathryn E. Stegall

Publications in the legacy of
Elliott Henry

The Full Rights of Sons

First published by Dog Ear Publishing
4010 W. 86th Street, Ste H
Indianapolis, IN 46268
www.dogearpublishing.net

ISBN: 978-1-4575-2000-6

This book is printed on acid-free paper.

Printed in the United States of America

Dedication

Seventy-two years ago a young couple were planning their wedding. The bride asked, "Shall I promise to obey you?" The groom answered, "No. The Bible says we should submit to one another." And my parents, Howard and Winifred Elliott, did just that for sixty years. They showed me oneness through servanthood. This book is dedicated to them.

And to my husband, who has always loved me as Christ loved the church, giving himself up for me. It is with and through Ron that I have lived oneness through servanthood. His liberation in Christ has allowed me to more fully experience my own liberation.

And to that host of believers throughout all of history, past, present, and future, the body and bride of Jesus, of whom I am a member, with whom I am one.

And to the Reformed Presbyterian Church of North America, that tiny member of that one great body, where I was born and bred, trained and taught, nurtured and molded, challenged and sharpened, supported and loved.

And above all to my maker, redeemer and Lord who has recreated me to be, along with the church, one with him, Jesus Christ, our triune God. He is oneness through servanthood. To him alone be the glory.

These are they from whom I learned it.[1]

They are who I am.

Kathryn Elliott Stegall

Content by Interpretive Principle

The infallible rule of interpretation of Scripture is the Scripture itself; and therefore, when there is a question about the true and full sense of any Scripture, (which is not manifold, but one) it must be searched and known by other places that speak more clearly.

The Westminster Confession of Faith, 1.9

The Clear

Headship: Scripture Interprets Scripture

The Questionable

Contents

Acknowledgments

A tremendous thank you to my dear friend and editor, Karen Olson, for her generous giving of time and skill to this project. Her professional expertise and thoughtful input have improved this study immensely.

I am also deeply grateful to those who were willing to read this manuscript before publication and lend their names in support of *The Full Rights of Sons*: Gilbert Bilezikian, John H. Armstrong, Boni Piper, Margaret Mowczko, and Bruce Hemphill.

Preface

Someone once asked, "Where do you get the nerve?"

The first moment of clarity that remains in my memory came at White Lake Covenanter Camp about 1959. Our Bible study leader instructed us to memorize this verse: "For God hath not given us the spirit of fear; but of power, and of love, and of a sound mind."[2]

Undergirding all my thoughts is the firm conviction of my heart that the following Scripture is true, true for me. It is my experience.

> . . . because those who are led by the Spirit of God are sons of God. For you did not receive a spirit that makes you a slave again to fear, but you received the Spirit of sonship. And by him we cry, "Abba, Father." The spirit himself testifies with our spirit that we are God's children. Now if we are children, then we are heirs—heirs of God and co-heirs with Christ, if indeed we share in his sufferings in order that we may also share in his glory.[3]

God's Spirit continually confirms with my spirit that I am a son of God. That's where the nerve comes from.

January 1993
Larnaca, Cyprus

My husband and I have adopted a child. As a consequence I know about the long list of photos, stamps, signatures, notarizations, certifications, and documents that must be obtained during such a process. It has helped me to imagine my own illustration for the concepts of *sign of authority*, *adoption*, and *full rights* that underlie, permeate, and summarize the contents of this book. My illustration is on the following page.

I have used photos of the women in my family throughout the pages ahead to remind me that the ideas herein discussed are not just theoretical side issues, but real and true and applicable gospel essentials[4] for real people. And, of course, not just real people in my family, but for all people everywhere throughout time and especially every Christian believer and the body of Christ[5] to which all believers belong.

Cover Photo: My grandmother Greeta and mother Winifred~1936. They are my Lois and Eunice.

> I have been reminded of your sincere faith, which first lived in your grandmother Lois and in your mother Eunice and, I am persuaded, now lives in you also. For this reason I remind you to fan into flame the gift of God, which is in you through the laying on of my hands. For God did not give us a spirit of timidity, but a spirit of power, of love and of self-discipline.
>
> 2 Timothy 1:5–7

Certification of Adoption and Full Rights

This is to hereby certify that Kathryn E. Stegall, hereafter known as the Adoptee, has been adopted as a son[1] into the family of God and as a fellow-citizen of his Kingdom[2]. As a consequence the Adoptee is entitled to the Full Rights, privileges and responsibilities of a son of God as exemplified by Our Lord Jesus Christ, Son of God, Our Savior[3].

The attached photograph will act as identity of and security for the adoptee signature below.

The affixed revenue stamp certifies[4] that the price of one indestructible life[5] has been paid for the legalization and implementation of this adoption and the consequent Full Rights conferred.

The signature line and signature of the Creator and Lord of the universe signifies and certifies the ultimate authority for the revenue stamp, the photograph, this document and the consequent Full Rights conferred.

I hereby through faith do acknowledge and certify my acceptance of sonship, conferred on me by God's grace and mercy alone, and all the Full Rights, privileges and responsibilities which accompany this now legal and binding relationship.

Kathryn E. Stegall

Signature of the Adoptee.

This document shall forthwith be viewed by all as a sign of authority[6] and proof of the legal and binding nature of this document and the relationship.

I Am

Creator and Lord of the Universe[7],
the Triune God of the *Holy Bible*.

You are all sons of God through faith in Jesus Christ....But when the time had fully come, God sent his son, born of a woman, born under law, to redeem those under law, that we might receive the adoption[8] and full rights[9] of sons. Because you are sons, God sent the Spirit of his Son in our hearts, the Spirit who calls out, 'Abba, Father.' So you are no longer a slave, but a son; and since you are a son, God has made you also an heir.
(Galatians 3:26, 4:4-7)

ΙΧΘΥΣ

[1] Galatians 4:5.
[2] Ephesians 2:19.
[3] Romans 8:14-17; Hebrews 2:11.
[4] Romans 11:36
[5] Hebrews 7:16; Revelation 5:6, 9-10, 12.
[6] I Corinthians 11:10.
[7] Exodus 3:14-15; John 8:58.
[8] KJV & NASB.
[9] NIV.

All Scripture quotations
are taken from the *New International Version of the Holy Bible, 1984* unless otherwise noted.

All words in ***boldfaced italics*** are my emphasis.

Italics only denotes words being discussed as words, words from quoted text, or foreign words.

Please read with an open Bible before you.
What I say is just that—what I say.
But what the Bible says is God's Word to us.

Examine the Scriptures
to see if these things are true.[7]

My great-great-grandmother Rachel~1868.

Chapter 1

The Interpretation of Scripture: Finding Our Way

I'd thought about it from time to time. Thought about it a lot, in fact. But I had accepted the teaching of my church that women should not be ordained to church leadership. And I accepted the rationale for this as based on the Bible. But I still had questions about little nagging inconsistencies that went unanswered. Somehow this traditional stand on the role or status of women in the church and family just didn't all ring true.

So I quit thinking about it. I said I was bored with all this "women stuff." But the issue kept coming up anyway. It was hard to avoid.

In 1988 the Reformed Presbyterian Church of North America (RPCNA), the denomination to which I belong, appointed a committee to study the role of women in the church. Their report was published in 1990 and recommended to the membership for study.

It's not that there was anything so new in the report. I'd heard most of the arguments before. It's not that I didn't know what the Bible taught. I had been studying it all my life. It's not that the tone of the report wasn't completely respectful toward women. It was. It's not that I wasn't content with my life. I was.

Out of Line with the Gospel

But still . . . something seemed out of kilter. It just didn't all come out square. When some portion of Scripture appears not to conform to the gospel,[1] this should warn us that our understanding may be incorrect and that intense reexamination is necessary.

This report began with a list of rules for how we can find God's truth through the interpretation of the Scriptures. These principles of interpretation lingered in the back of my mind long after I laid the report aside. These principles seemed to get at the heart of the inconsistencies I struggled with and the questions I had harbored for so long.

Thus I was motivated to begin my own study of the Scriptures about the role or status of women in the church, using these principles of interpretation as my guide. I found myself in more than just a theoretical study. It was a very personal study. I sought the answer to a most basic question, "Who am I? What does it mean for me, a woman, to be a Christian?"

The pages before you contain what I found. I pray you will sense the joy and wonder with which I send this forth, the gratitude to the one true God, my Father, my Brother, my Life and the awe I am filled with for his revelation of Scripture, a tapestry of inexplicable beauty and truth.

I have not looked to commentaries or historical/archeological evidence in my study. Important as these things may be to aid and support our understanding of Scripture, they are not my infallible rule for faith and life. We all know a commentary can be found or a piece of archeological evidence exhibited in support of almost any claim.

I am eager to gratefully credit the knowledge and insight I have gained from other Christians who have preserved, studied, and explained the Scriptures throughout the ages. The grace ministered to me through them is of incalculable value. Yet it is the Holy Scriptures alone that must be both my original resource and my final authority. The Scriptures are the standard by which we must evaluate all other evidence. This truth—*sola scriptura*—became the battle cry that galvanized the Reformation of the church.

I am not a scholar. I am an ordinary Christian. I read my Bible in my own English language. I am very thankful for able translators who have given me the Scriptures in a language I can read and understand. Given this, I read God's Word confident that the Holy Spirit will provide all that is needed for true understanding.[2] It is by faith that the eyes of our hearts are enlightened by the Spirit of revelation.[3] My faith is in Jesus, the truth. He is the living Word of God.[4] He is found in the Scriptures.[5] This is where I have turned.

But how can we understand the truth that by faith we know is in the Holy Bible? Or, more pertinent to this particular issue, how do we find the meaning of difficult or conflicting portions of Scripture?

"Women should remain silent in the churches."[6]

That's a pretty confusing statement. Now of course someone might respond that it seems straightforward enough. It means women must be silent in the church.

Well, yes. That's what the words say. Yet, I am still confused. That idea doesn't seem to be in tune with so much else in the Bible. So many biblical injunctions, beginning with the Great Commission itself, cannot be carried out if one is silent. It appears the church is confused also. You wouldn't be reading this book today if people didn't have different ideas about exactly what this scripture means.

I am a woman. But I have not kept silent in the church. I voice myself in many ways, through worship, through teaching, through discussion, through committee work, and through ministry.

Yet I can think of only two times in my experience when I have been reprimanded for not being silent in church: once (or was it many times?) when Joyce and I used to sit together during evening worship when we were in junior high school and once when I led a Bible study/seminar on the word *head*. Even though it may seem rather straightforward, we do not all agree as to the real meaning of "she must be silent."

Discovering Truth in Scripture

Others have faced this question before us. This is not the first passage of Scripture to seem perfectly clear, yet somehow not really so clear.

It also seems pretty straightforward when Paul says of Christ, "He is the image of the invisible God, the firstborn over all creation."[7]

And this passage seems clear enough. "Now if there is no resurrection, what will those do who are baptized for the dead? If the dead are not raised at all, why are people baptized for them?"[8] Paul makes this argument in support of the resurrection of the dead.

What about this scripture? James seems quite plain. "You see that a person is justified by what he does and not by faith alone."[9]

Or this scripture, "Everyone must submit himself to the governing authorities, for there is no authority except that which God has established. The authorities that exist have been established by God."[10]

Paul seems very clear when he says to the Ephesians, "Slaves, obey your earthly masters with respect and fear, and with sincerity of heart, just as you would obey Christ."[11] Peter says that slaves should submit not only to kind masters, but to cruel ones also.[12]

Straightforward as these passages are, orthodox Christianity has not accepted the obvious meaning. We do not believe that Jesus Christ is a created being, but rather God himself. Nor do we believe that one can earn salvation for another who has died in unbelief by being baptized for him. We certainly do not believe that a person can be saved by his own good works. Nor do we believe that everything a king or ruler does or says is from God and is therefore subject to no earthly authority. Nor do we believe that it is right for one person, whether cruel or kind, to own another person as a possession or slave.

Someone might say these examples are contrived, not questionable issues. We all know the truth about these matters.

Yet at one time in history each of these scriptures was under major discussion. Great ecclesiastical battles were fought over these "straightforward" passages. Many were called "heretics" for the positions they took. Some were even burned at the stake or suffered some other form of martyrdom for standing on the "wrong side" of these questions.

But these heretics, martyrs, and reformers stood on the same side of these questions as we stand today. We feel our present interpretation of these passages to be completely scriptural, even though we do not accept the obvious, straightforward meaning.

The early church debated the person of Jesus Christ. After much struggle, the church affirmed that Jesus is God himself, not a created being. We believe he is of the same substance and equal in power and glory to the Father and the Holy Spirit.

At the time of the Reformation, the teaching that one can do anything to help gain the salvation of those already dead was rejected.

Certainly we cling to the great truth rediscovered by the Reformation, salvation by faith alone.

Early Christians living under a Roman emperor, Covenanter martyrs of Scotland, and our Pilgrim forefathers, as well as many other Christians throughout history, have suffered and died because they did not believe in the divine right of kings. They did not believe the actions and words of a king were necessarily God inspired. Nor did they believe absolute obedience to a king was commanded in Scripture.

We look back with awe and admiration to those principled Christians here in America who refused to accept slavery as a God-ordained institution and actively smuggled slaves to the North in the underground railroad, established free states in the West, and gave their lives to free the slaves because this was what their commitment to Jesus Christ demanded.

How did individual Christians and the church as a whole resolve these issues? How have we come to accept as truth something quite contrary to the seemingly obvious meaning of the scriptures I have cited?

We did not become convinced that Jesus is completely God by studying only Colossians 1:15. We examined the entire Scripture, paying special attention to the nature and personage of God and his son, Jesus Christ. We studied common threads of thought and repeated themes from the whole of written revelation. It was the overall unified message of Scripture that led us to believe that Jesus was and is truly, completely, infinitely, and eternally God.

Why do we believe that there may be times when we should not obey governing authorities? Is it in defiance of Romans 13:1? Or is it rather based upon the theme of Scripture summarized by Peter's reply to the governing authorities of Israel: "We must obey God, rather than men."[13]

We did not come to the conclusion that slavery is wrong by studying passages with the word *slave*. Instead, we looked at the whole of Scripture, concentrating on those parts that dealt with the nature of every human being and his or her status before God and relation to other men.

The church has accepted an interpretation for these difficult passages that brings them into unity and conformity with the rest of Scripture, thereby dismissing, or at least modifying, the apparently straightforward meaning.

However, as in the case of Paul talking about being baptized for the dead,[14] I still scratch my head and say, "What on earth did Paul mean?" I simply don't know. Yet I believe that the rest of Scripture is clear that at death our opportunity for repentance comes to an end.

The Infallible Rule—Scripture Itself

What convinced us to take a view different from the seemingly straightforward meaning of these passages? The clear and easily understood passages of the whole Scripture convinced us.

The reformers summarized it this way: "The infallible rule of interpretation of Scripture is the Scripture itself; and therefore, when there is a question about the true and full sense of any Scripture (which is not manifold, but one) it must be searched and known by other places that speak more clearly."[15]

Just as these principles have led to the resolution of problem passages in the past, so they can also guide us to the mind of God on the issue of the role and service of women in the church.

We do not need to flounder about, feeling helpless to discover the truth, pulled first in one direction by our traditions, then in another by a good argument, only to be swayed a little later by yet another explanation. We have a strong commitment to God's Word. We know it is true.[16] And we know the Holy Spirit will lead us into all truth.[17] We *can* discover the truth about this issue.

How to Begin?

I'm a math teacher. But if truth be told, my instincts about mathematics are not very good. Intuition gives me no help in working with number concepts, so I must rely on following the rules. This isn't all bad for a math teacher because most of my students are like this too.

Students come to me with a very complex equation and say they can't figure out the answer. It just all seems far too complicated. Well, I don't know the answer either, but I don't tell them that. What I do know are the rules, the truths, of algebra. I tell them over and over again, "That's the beauty of algebra. Algebra makes it possible for someone even as unmathematically minded as I to figure out very complex problems."

Then I say, "Let's start at the top. Write down the problem. Think about it. What truth can you apply to this equation to make it a slightly simpler problem? Apply it and write down the result. OK, now you have a slightly simpler problem. What else do you know? Not just what do you know to be true, but what can you eliminate because you know it is false? Apply it. Write down the result. Start again." It may take many slightly simpler problems before the final step that reveals the value of the unknown.

We are confronted with a very complex problem or question. What do the Scriptures teach about the role or status of women? It seems like there are numerous arguments going in as many different directions. How can we possibly find the answer?

Well, let's start at the top. What can we do to make this a slightly simpler problem? We can begin by praying for guidance from the Holy Spirit and for his illumination of the Scriptures.

Now what can we do? As a foundation, let's renew our commitment to the basic tenets of our faith, those things enumerated in the Christian creeds and confessions that have been formulated throughout history. We must remember what the Bible as a whole says about the nature of our triune God and the nature of man. What is the essence of our new life in Christ? How are believers to relate to each other in this new life? What is the nature of the church? How is it to be governed? What do we already know to be true? What do we know to be false? Let's apply it and move on.

What else can we do? We can apply the tried and tested rules for biblical interpretation. Let's look for one unified teaching that encompasses all of Scripture. We should allow the clear to shine light on the unclear. When we come to words that seem difficult, let's define them according to their use in Scripture. When something seems very confusing, we can discuss it together, using all the gifts of the body. Let's apply these rules and see if we can get a slightly simpler question.

How will we know that the answers we come up with are right and true? After all, we don't have a teacher's edition with the answers all neatly written in the back.

Well, not exactly, but we do know what the truth looks like. The truth looks like Jesus.[18] The truth will be permeated through and through with the essence of his coming to us, his grace and loving-kindness.[19] The truth will bring freedom.[20]

And finally, after we have summarized what we know to be true and discarded what we know to be false, the very last questions we ask may be, What does 1 Timothy 2:12 mean? What does it mean in 1 Corinthians 14:34–35 that "women should remain silent in the churches. They are not allowed to speak"? But by that time the problem may not seem too complex.

So let's begin. We'll write the question: What should be the status of women in the church?

Now let's look for those clear teachings of Scripture that might relate to our question, a foundation upon which less clear passages can be discussed.

These themes, or threads of thought, are interwoven throughout the fabric of Scripture like the threads of an exquisite tapestry. All of Scripture together reveals one beautiful picture. It may be difficult to see the individual colors or single threads. Yet without them there is no picture.

I will point out just a few glimpses of the red and blue and gold threads as we scrutinize the picture more closely to see just what it is made of. There's a bit of gold. Oh, and look, there is a little larger patch of gold. And over there it is intertwined with the red and a bit of blue.

The Question

What should be the status of women in the family, church and society?

What do we know to be true?

- The truth is available to us through our triune God, the Father, Jesus the Son, and the Holy Spirit.[21]
- God will reveal the truth to those who earnestly seek it.[22]
- The truth is contained in the Scriptures.[23]
- The Scriptures reveal one unified message of truth.[24]
- We can trust the Scriptures to go to the heart of the matter.[25]
- It is imperative for the church to discover the truth because the church is itself "the pillar and foundation of the truth."[26]
- The truth will conform to the gospel.[27]
- The truth will look like Jesus.[28]
- Truth is a partner to grace and mercy.[29]
- The truth will bring freedom.[30]
- The truth will be confirmed through obedience.[31]

What truth can we apply to make this a slightly simpler question?

- If the truth is in God, we can look to him for the answer.
- If God promises to give us wisdom, we can pray.
- If Scripture contains the truth, we can study it.
- If Scripture reveals one unified message of truth, we can look for themes taught through all of Scripture that will have a bearing on our question.

My great-grandmother Nellie~1878

Chapter 2

Oneness: You Are All One

Galatians 3:28

The battle of the sexes.

Opposites attract.

Vive la différence!

A love/hate relationship.

You can't live with them, and you can't live without them.

Who can understand the male/female mind?

You've heard all these and many more. These little bits of folk wisdom about how men and women do and do not get along with each other reflect those confusing feelings that are a part of every culture.

We rely on wisdom from our traditions, experience, stereotypes, and research. We look for help through counseling, quizzes in women's magazines, books, and even Sunday school classes. And yes, there are roles.

Yet the riddle, the mystery, the puzzle, the problem, the conundrum of gender remains.

In the Beginning

How are man and woman to relate to each other? What is to be the nature of their relationship? Does the Bible have anything to say on this?

Of course the obvious place to start is in the beginning . . . when things were good. If we examine the way things were at creation before the Fall, we may learn something about what God originally intended.

The most revealing scripture on God's intentions for Adam and Eve is found in Genesis 2:24, "and they will become one flesh." This was perfection. This was *good.*

We should not be confused about the creation norm. Jesus tells us exactly what it was.

> "Haven't you read," he replied, "that *at* ***the beginning the Creator 'made them*** male and female,' and said, 'For this reason a man will leave his father and mother and be united to his wife, and the two will become ***one flesh***'? So they are no longer two, but one. Therefore what God has joined together, let man not separate."[1]

It's not just that they became one. They quit being two. This is an amazing statement. Jesus is saying that the oneness is so complete that two separate identities cease to exist and are blended into one new identity. This oneness transcends individuality and excludes separation. This oneness is God's doing, and what God has done, man has no business undoing.

A Profound Mystery

When Paul quotes the creation norm from Genesis in his letter to the Ephesians, he adds, "For this reason a man will leave his father and mother and be united to his wife, and the two will become one flesh.' This is a profound mystery—but I am talking about Christ and the church."[2] He admits that it is all a profound mystery, but one that God has chosen to reveal. Still, there remains something about this that we cannot fully know or understand yet.

But hints are given. Jesus tells us that marriage is only a temporary institution that will not continue beyond the resurrection.[3] So perhaps at least part of the purpose of marriage is to picture some greater, more absolute, and eternal truth.

We know what this eternal truth is. Oneness through the first Adam was broken. So God made us all new creations through the second Adam. It is with him that we are now to be one. And not only with him, but with each other. All of us together, ourselves, other believers, and Christ are all to be one, one body, Christ's body. The new creation of humanity is to be one body, just as Adam and Eve were to be one flesh.[4]

We learn a lot about how we are to be one body from Jesus' prayer before his death. In praying for his disciples, he said an astonishing thing: "that they may be one as we are one." He said this twice and defined exactly what he meant, "that all of them may be one, Father, just as you are in me and I am in you."[5]

We are to be one in just the same way that the Father, Son, and Holy Spirit are one. This makes perfect sense since we are made in God's image. "God said, 'Let us make man in our image in our likeness . . . So God created man in his own image, in the image of God he created him: male and female he created them."[6] God is "he"/singular and also "us"/plural. What God created was "man"—"him"/singular and also "male and female"— "them"/plural. The creation mirrors the creator. Man in God's image.

Not Good?

At the end of the sixth day, God found his creation "all . . . very good."[7] Yet there was a point during that sixth day when God saw something was "not good."[8]

The *not-good* thing was that the man was alone. Adam was perfect and without sin. Yet, when there was no other human for Adam to relate to, he felt an unfulfilled need.

If men and women are different in some ways and if it was not good for man to be alone, perhaps the image of God was not completely reflected until after the creation of Eve[9] when God saw that His creation was all very good. Or perhaps it was not the different characteristics of the two that together completed God's image, but the relationship itself. Perhaps two being one was necessary to truly reflect God's image. We believe that God is three in one. One alone could not reflect this triune/oneness aspect of God.

Before the Fall, when things were still good, oneness was complete. There were no barriers between the man and woman. There were no clothes, no shame,[10] no secrets, nothing to divide or separate. There was oneness.

Shattered!

Then humankind fell into sin. Separation was the result of that long-ago disobedience in the Garden of Eden. As soon as Adam and Eve sinned, they realized they were naked, and they were ashamed. On went the clothes. Up went the barriers. They did what we all do. They became hostile toward each other. They began to hurt each other.[11] And suddenly the human race splintered into as many pieces as there were people, maybe more.

Jesus said this separation was completely contrary to God's will.[12] Creation through the first Adam failed and continues to fail to be one— neither one with him nor one with each other, as was God's plan and purpose.

Recreation

So God created again, redeeming oneness through a second Adam.[13] Through Jesus, God took the fragments of his broken creation, drew together what had been separated by sin, and made a new creation—one new man.

> . . . remember that at that time you were separate from Christ, excluded from citizenship in Israel and foreigners to the covenants of the promise, without hope and without God in the world. But now in Christ Jesus you who once were far away have been brought near through the blood of Christ.
>
> For he himself is our peace, who has made the two one and has destroyed the barrier, the dividing wall of hostility, by abolishing in his flesh the law with its commandments and regulations. ***His purpose was to create in himself one new man out of two, thus making peace, and in this one body to reconcile both of them to God*** through the cross, by which he put to death their hostility. He came and preached peace to you who were far away and peace to those who were near. For through him we both have access to the Father by one Spirit.

> Consequently, you are no longer foreigners and aliens, but fellow citizens with God's people and members of God's household built on the foundation of the apostles and prophets, with Christ Jesus himself as the chief cornerstone. In him the whole building is joined together and rises to become a holy temple in the Lord. And in him you too are being built together to become a dwelling in which God lives by the Spirit.[14]

In Christ the hostility is gone. The barriers come down. All the pieces are put together into one. A new creation is made. One new man. And it is good.

Paul mixes his metaphors a little from body to building or temple: body with Christ as the head, or a building in which God delights to dwell. Either way, God wants no separation within this oneness. "Don't you know that you yourselves are God's temple and that God's Spirit lives in you? If anyone destroys God's temple, God will destroy him; for God's temple is sacred, and you are that temple."[15] ". . . what God has joined together, let no man separate."[16]

The creation norm is restored with the recreation norm.

Creation Norm for Man and Woman Matthew 19:4–6	***Recreation Norm*** for the Church Ephesians 2:12–22
"At the beginning the creator made them."	"His purpose was to create in himself."
"The two will become one flesh."	". . . made the two one . . . one body."
"They are no longer two, but one."	". . . one new man out of the two."
". . . let man not separate."	"Remember . . . you were separate."
". . . what God has joined together."	"But now in Christ Jesus . . . the whole building is joined together."

Table 1

In God's Image

The church has been recreated one in God's image, just as man and woman were created one in God's image? All members of the church are needed to express the fullness of Christ.[17] Both male and female are needed to express the image of God.[18] Man and woman are one flesh. The members of the church are one body.

So in order to truly reflect God's character and nature, his church, or body, must be one just as God is one. "The body is a unit, though it is made up of many parts; and though all its parts are many, they form one body. So it is with Christ. . . . Now you are the body of Christ, and each one of you is a part of it."[19]

Imperfection Remains

Does all this mean that the individual person is not made in God's image? Not at all. God cares a great deal about the specific person. Jesus always made things very personal. He addressed individual needs in individual people. Each unique person is created in God's image. But the image of God reflected by one solitary individual is incomplete because oneness cannot be reflected by one person alone. The separation, the aloneness is not good.

What about the single person? Is he or she somehow less in God's image than other people? No. Singleness is a lofty and honored position and can be blessed by God for greater service to and for his church.[20]

All people created by God are in God's image, even those who remain in sin and rebellion against him. Yet all aspects of God's image in each of us are blurred by sin. The oneness of God's image is marred in all of us to the extent that sin has brought aloneness and separation into our lives.

Part of the beauty of Christ's redemption is that we no longer need look only to the temporary institution of marriage for oneness. Through our recreation in Christ, we can be one with him and with all other believers through the church. Of course marriage continues to illustrate this oneness to the world, so it is very important that we keep the institution of marriage as pure and whole as possible.

Our new life in Christ means that the broken aloneness of sin experienced by so many of us through divorce, death, or even plain, ugly lovelessness, is healed as we participate together as parts of the body, members in the church. Through the body of Christ the Christian call to singleness is also fully satisfied. It is in the church that our eternal oneness with God and with each other is experienced. And this experience begins now, not only after we die. As soon as we become believers, we become part of Christ's body.

The imperfections of this life remain. We continually struggle to make the truth of our new life in Christ, our recreation in his image,[21] as pure and full as possible. This includes our oneness in the church. Even though imperfect, it is real.

The Foundation

The foundation of our Christian faith has always been the oneness of our God.[22] The three persons of God are the same. Each is fully God,[23] the one living and true God. This common divinity also makes them equal. None is before or after, over or under, or more or less than another. Yet the persons of the godhead are different as illustrated by their different names, Father, Son, and Holy Spirit.[24] This is the pattern for our oneness. This was Jesus' prayer.[25]

So if we are to be one like God is one, it must mean more than getting along, or even a unanimous vote. It is organic oneness.

However, oneness is foreign to our way of thinking. The concept of the Trinity seems beyond our understanding. Oneness can only be embraced through faith. After we have fully accepted its truth through faith, we begin to see the character of oneness shine throughout all of Scripture, as well as through our own experience. Our understanding is illuminated by faith.

The three persons of God are the same in substance. The three persons of God are equal. The three persons of God are different. We are to be one like that, as God is one. All believers are the same in substance. We are equal. We are different.[26]

"There are different kinds of gifts, but the same Spirit. There are different kinds of service, but the same Lord. There are different kinds of working, but the same God works all of them in all men."[27]

Differences. In this sinful world, differences mean suspicion, quarrels, hatred, murder, tyranny, and oppression. Any difference, no matter how small, can easily become an excuse for the very worst that man does to his fellowman. Just read a little history. Pick up a newspaper.

But in Christ's body, it is different. In the church our differences are all assembled together into one living organism, so there is no division, but rather equal concern for each other.[28] Furthermore, each of our differences is necessary for the common good.[29] This is God's redemption/recreation of oneness.

"There is ***one*** body and ***one*** Spirit—just as you were called to one hope when you were called—one Lord, one faith, one baptism; one God and Father of all, who is over all and through all and in all."[30]

One in Reality

We are one. Not just in theory. Not just in shadow. We are one in reality. Oh, the oneness is not yet perfected, as it will be someday. But it is a fact of the present, the here and now while we pursue its perfect manifestation. The church is the "one new man" in which God lives by his spirit.

Jesus included this amazing fact in his prayer. It is the reality of our oneness which will convince the world that Jesus was sent from God. What a privilege this oneness is. What a mission this oneness has. What a mighty power this oneness must be—to move all the world to recognize Jesus as God.

". . . that they may be one as we are one: I in them and you in me. May they be brought to complete unity to let the world know that you sent me and have loved them even as you have loved me."[31]

The Questions

What does the Bible teach regarding
the nature of the relationship between man and woman?
What does the Bible teach regarding
the nature of the relationship between members of the church?

What do we know to be true?

- God is three.[32]

- God is one.[33]

- We are made in God's image.
  - Humankind was created in God's image.[34]
  - The church is recreated in God's image.[35]

- We are many.
  - Man was created male and female.[36]
    - We are the same.[37]
    - We are equal.[38]
    - We are different.[39]
  - The church has many members.[40]
    - We are the same.[41]
    - We are equal.[42]
    - We are different[43]
      - for the common good.[44]
      - Our differences are all needed.[45]
      - Our differences are all a part of one body
        - by God's design,[46]
        - so there will be no division,[47] and
        - so we will have equal concern for each other.[48]

- We are one.
  - Marriage is the earthly, temporal picture of this oneness.[49]
  - The church is the eternal reality of this oneness.[50]

- Oneness characterizes both God's image and what he has created in his image.
  One God is the foundation of our faith.[51]
  One flesh is the creation norm for man and woman.[52]
  One body is the recreation norm for the members of the church.[53]

- Oneness transcends individuality and excludes separation among the persons/members of
  One God,[54]
  One flesh,[55]
  One body.[56]

The Question

What should be the status of women in the church, family and society?

What truth can we apply to make this a slightly simpler question?

- Oneness is a clear theme taught throughout the whole of Scripture.
- Oneness is the nature of the relationship to which man and woman were created.
- Oneness is the nature of the relationship into which every believing human being is recreated.

My great-grandmother Nancy~1890.

Chapter 3

No Difference: God Does Not Show Favoritism

Romans 2:11

We are all the same . . . but different.

Our differences are only too clear to all of us. Not a day goes by that each one of us does not have to deal with differences. Sometimes we enjoy the differences. But at the root of most controversies is a difference. Most of the time those differences mean that we have to work harder at getting along with other people.

Let's face it. Life would be a lot easier if we were all the same.

Or would it?

Yes, differences can confuse us. We don't know what to think.

Men and women are different. That's why the women's issue is so controversial. The disagreement is about how to handle the difference.

Yet God created us to be one. How does he expect us to cope with all the differences? What is his attitude toward our differences?

Does God Discriminate?

On what basis does God discriminate between people? The Bible is clear in teaching that God's own mercy is the only determining factor in the bestowal of his favor.

Paul gives the example of the twins, Jacob and Esau. Both were children of Abraham through Isaac, the promised seed. Yet God's favor concerning these two boys was not based on anything other than God's mercy. Esau was the elder, who according to custom was the inheritor of the birthright. But Esau was rejected, and instead, God bestowed his favor on his younger brother, Jacob.

"It does not, therefore, depend on man's desire or effort, but on God's mercy. . . . Therefore God has mercy on whom he wants to have mercy, and he hardens whom he wants to harden."[1] Paul repeats this message to Titus. "He saved us, not because of righteous things we had done, but because of his mercy."[2]

This message permeates Scripture. God never discriminates among people: he does not bestow special favor. He is not partial to any person for any other reason than this: because of his mercy.

Of course God welcomes all who come to him. He will never reject anyone who comes. Many scriptures teach this truth.[3] But we should also remember our coming is always the result of God's mercy. In our coming to God, we humbly accept this truth and praise God for it.

Through a dramatic vision on a housetop in Joppa, Peter learned this startling truth. "I now realize how true it is that God does not show favoritism but accepts men from every nation who fear him and do what is right."[4]

What is God's reason for not showing favoritism? For discriminating among human beings only on the basis of his own mercy? The Scriptures give us two reasons:

- "Is he not the One who says to kings, 'You are worthless,' and to nobles, 'You are wicked,' who shows no partiality to princes and does not favor the rich over the poor, for they are all the work of his hands?"[5]

- "This righteousness from God comes through faith in Jesus Christ to all who believe. There is no difference, for all have sinned and fall short of the glory of God."[6]

God made us all. But we all fall far short of the glory that he created us to radiate. All have sinned. These two facts are the same for all human beings. That is why all depend only "on God's mercy."[7]

The Question

On what basis does God differentiate, or discriminate, among people?

What do we know to be true?

- God differentiates among people only on the basis of his mercy.[8]

- God does not differentiate among people on the basis of the following:
  heredity[9]
  human desire[10]
  human effort[11]
  righteous deeds[12]
  wealth[13]
  status and position[14]
  external appearance[15]

- God does not discriminate among people on the basis of these things because
  all human beings are the work of his hands,[16] and
  all have sinned.[17]

Should We Discriminate?

But that is God. What about us within the Christian community? Are we to discriminate among people?

There was Peter on the rooftop. Through a vision God was showing him all kinds of animals, creatures Peter saw as unclean, revolting, disgusting. God told Peter to kill and eat. Peter was aghast. He would never consider such a thing. "'Surely not, Lord!' Peter replied. 'I have never eaten anything impure or unclean.' The voice spoke to him a second time. 'Do not call anything impure that God has made clean.'"[18]

What God makes clean on the basis of his own mercy and grace, we must not judge as impure in any way. Our judgment of others must be based only on what God calls clean. Again the Scriptures are clear: if we discriminate among people on any basis other than those allowed and exhorted in Scripture, then that is favoritism, or partiality.

And since all human beings have sinned, how are we to judge what God has made clean?

Jesus answers, "By their fruit you will recognize them. . . . A good tree cannot bear bad fruit, and a bad tree cannot bear good fruit. . . .Thus by their fruit you will recognize them."[19]

We understand this fruit to be qualities of character and action that reflect God's standard of righteousness. Any judgments we make are to be based only on God's standard of righteousness and sanctification because that is the outward manifestation of God's mercy, and cleansing.[20] But even these judgments must be carried out with great caution, for ultimately, judgment belongs to God alone.[21]

God does not discriminate among people on the basis of wealth,[22] or on status or position,[23] or on external appearance,[24] and therefore neither can we.[25]

Heredity

There is one other area we are not to use as a criteria for discrimination. This is the area that seems most open to abuse by mankind. Perhaps that is why Scripture spends the most time refuting it. This is the criteria of heredity.

Heredity is the thing that determines at the moment of conception whether we are black or white, tall or short, Jew or Greek, brown eyed or blue eyed, male or female. These are all a matter of heredity, genetics, chromosomes, all unconsciously determined by earthly parents. This is heredity.

But the Bible is clear. Discrimination on the basis of heredity has no place in the Christian community.

Or is it clear? At times in the Old Testament, it seemed as if God put a great deal of importance on heredity. He chose a certain people. His blessings were for their descendants. God's people were warned many times against entanglements with other peoples.

No, God's Word is not always easy to understand. Yet the truth is always there. Way back in Genesis, God tells Abram, "'I will make you into a great nation and I will bless you:

. . . and ***all peoples on earth*** will be blessed through you.'. . . Abram believed the Lord, and he credited it to him as righteousness."[26] Just a few sentences to enfold a great truth. The great nation fathered by Abram, later called Abraham, would be composed of and bless all peoples on earth.

Jesus illuminates this truth revealed to Abraham in a conversation with the Jewish religious leaders of his day. Jesus gives us the real scoop on parentage, heredity, genetics, chromosomes.[27] The religious leaders told Jesus, "Abraham is our father . . ."[28] Listen to Jesus' reply.

> "If you were Abraham's children," said Jesus, "then you would do the things Abraham did. As it is, you are determined to kill me, a man who has told you the truth that I heard from God. Abraham did not do such things. You are doing the things your own father does. . . . You belong to your father, the devil, and you want to carry out your father's desire."[29]

With these words Jesus crushed all that these religious leaders had based their lives upon: their values, their philosophy, their morality, their religion. It was all based on the fact that they were Abraham's physical children. They had Abraham's blood in their veins. They were the children of Israel. They were God's chosen people. Now Jesus was saying all this didn't matter. After this conversation, the Jews were so frustrated, angry, and distraught, they picked up stones to kill Jesus.

Peter is the first in the New Testament church to see this startling truth with greater clarity. The vision on the rooftop astounded him. The lightbulb went on. Peter had read the Old Testament. He had probably been there and heard the conversation Jesus had had with the Jews. But now Peter finally understood. "I now realize how true it is that God does not show favoritism, but accepts men from every nation who fear him and do what is right."[30] "Do not call anything impure that God has made clean."[31]

But God chose to reveal this truth most clearly to Paul. Let's go back to Paul's discussion of Jacob and Esau. The truth had been revealed two thousand years earlier to Rebecca. "The Lord said to her, 'Two nations are in your womb, and two peoples from within you will be separated; one people will be stronger than the other, and the older will serve the younger.'"[32] Paul clarifies it: "In other words, it is not the natural children who are God's children, but it is the children of the promise who are regarded as Abraham's offspring."[33]

Flesh and Blood Cannot Inherit

The two nations in Rebecca's womb were none other than the kingdom of Satan and the kingdom of God. The fact that these two brothers had the same human father and mother was of no consequence. The parentage that counts is not of the flesh, but of the spirit.

Does that sound familiar?

> In reply Jesus declared, "I tell you the truth, unless a man is born again, he cannot see the kingdom of God."
>
> "How can a man be born when he is old?" Nicodemus asked, "Surely he cannot enter a second time into his mother's womb to be born?"
>
> Jesus answered, "I tell you the truth, unless a man is born of water and the Spirit, he cannot enter the kingdom of God. Flesh gives birth to flesh, but the Spirit gives birth to spirit."[34]

Well, it was all there. God revealed it through Abraham, through his two sons, Ishmael and Isaac,[35] and through his two grandsons, Jacob and Esau.[36] Jesus taught it. Peter had a vision about it. Paul preached it. Heredity doesn't count. Human parentage makes no difference in Christ's kingdom. Genetics doesn't matter. Chromosomes are of no consequence. All these things are of the flesh.

"I declare to you, brothers, that flesh and blood cannot inherit the kingdom of God, nor does the perishable inherit the imperishable."[37]

Conflicting Scriptures

Yet apparently at the time the early church was struggling with this first great doctrinal crisis, it really didn't seem all that clear. After all, there were other scriptures.

"He did evil in the eyes of the Lord, following the detestable practices of the ***Gentiles***[38] the Lord had driven out before the Israelites."[39]

"You have rebuked the Gentiles and destroyed the wicked: you have blotted out their name forever and ever."[40]

"Behold my servant, whom I uphold; mine elect, in whom my soul delighteth; I have put my spirit upon him; he shall bring forth judgment to the Gentiles."[41]

Jeremiah carried God's message to God's chosen people. "For thus saith the Lord . . . The lion is come up from his thicket, and the destroyer of the Gentiles is on his way . . ."[42] Later Jeremiah identifies himself as "the prophet against the Gentiles."[43]

Declaring God's judgment on the Israelites, Ezekiel said, "And the Lord said, 'Even thus shall the children of Israel eat their defiled bread among the Gentiles, whither I will drive them."[44]

Even Jesus himself seemed to speak against the Gentiles. "These twelve, Jesus sent out with the following instruction: 'Do not go among the Gentiles or enter any town of the Samaritans. Go rather to the lost sheep of Israel.'"[45]

In the Sermon on the Mount, Jesus said, "Therefore take no thought, saying, What shall we eat? or, What shall we drink? or, Wherewithal shall we be clothed? (For after all these things do the Gentiles seek.)"[46]

In foretelling his own death to his disciples, Jesus said, "We are going up to Jerusalem, and the Son of Man will be betrayed to the chief priests and the teachers of the law. They will condemn him to death and will turn him over to the Gentiles to be mocked and flogged and crucified."[47]

No, it was definitely not all that clear.

Not only were there all these scriptures and more, but there was also a language problem.

The Jews had only one word to mean several different things. This one word is translated into the

English as "nations," "heathen," and "Gentiles." Each English word has a different meaning. To the Jew there was only one word, *Gentile.* A Gentile was anyone who was not a Jew. That was its whole meaning to them.

With these seemingly contradicting scriptures plus a very long history of shunning the Gentiles as pagans, how did the early church come to the conclusion that the Gentiles also could be children of Abraham, full and equal members of the church?

Conflict Resolved

Remember Peter on the rooftop. If God called it clean, Peter was not to act otherwise. Peter said he realized God accepted the Gentiles because they feared God and did what was right,[48] the fruit of God's cleansing. Later he said they should be baptized because they had received the Holy Spirit just as the Jews had.[49]

Paul gives more reasons for accepting that there is no difference between the Jew and Gentile.

- The same Lord is Lord of all and richly blesses all who call on him, for, 'Everyone who calls on the name of the Lord will be saved.'"[50]

- Confession is made with the mouth, and belief with the heart.[51] The implication is that we all have hearts and mouths.

- The Jews should accept the Gentiles, because Christ had accepted the Jews.[52]

- Differences among people due to genetics, adherence to the law, appearance, nationality, status, or position make no difference, because "Christ is all, and is in all."[53]

- Paul even considered the Gentile Christians of Rome competent to instruct one another, because they were full of goodness and complete in knowledge.[54]

The Question

On what basis should believers differentiate among people?

What do we know to be true?

- Believers should differentiate among people
  only on the basis of God's work of cleansing mercy,[55] and
  the fruit of their lives,[56]
  which is evidence of God's merciful cleansing.[57]

- Believers should differentiate among people according to their fruits
  only with caution,[58]
  because judgment belongs to God alone.[59]

- Believers should not differentiate among people based on human standards[60] such as the following:
  wealth[61]
  status or position[62]
  ethnicity[63]
  heredity[64]
  physical characteristics or appearance[65]
  race[66]
  gender[67]

- Believers should not differentiate among people on the basis of these things because of the following:
  "Christ is all, and is in all."[68]
  We are all one in Christ.[69]
  God has called us all clean.[70]
  All fear God and do what is right.[71]
  All have received the Holy Spirit.[72]
  All have hearts with which they have believed.[73]
  All have mouths with which they have made confession.[74]
  All have the same Lord.[75]
  Christ has accepted all.[76]

Equality in the Church

Well, so what? We all believe the gospel is for the Gentiles. We all believe the gospel is for women. Why go into such detail about something universally agreed upon?

Yes, we all agree that women receive benefits through the gospel. I am very thankful I belong to a church that values my position before God and in Christ's kingdom. But at this point much of the church says this truth has little to do with church government. And I hear some saying it has little to do with worship either, or service, or . . .

Perhaps men and women will be equal in heaven, but here in the church, they aren't. Here in the church, men are in authority and women are under them.

Peter also realized God didn't show favoritism? He had accepted God's teaching that the gospel was for the Gentiles. But here in the church, there was still plenty of reason to keep some separation. After all, Scripture wasn't that clear about what status the Gentiles have in the church. And considering all those scriptures about the wicked Gentiles, it would probably be better to keep a little distance, just to be on the safe side. Gentiles could certainly become Christians, but they must at least be circumcised. They could be church members, but they should be a bit separate, in a little different category, not exactly the same.

So this was the question for Peter, and for us too: Does equality before God mean equality here in the church?

The question is not an easy one. And there are all those conflicting scriptures.

But Paul felt no confusion. God had made it clear to him. Paul felt that the truth of the gospel and our life here on earth were indeed linked. The truth of the gospel must be lived out here, on the earth, in the church, because that church is the very body of Christ himself.

Paul felt confident enough of his position to confront Peter, who had walked with Jesus from the beginning. Paul recounts what happened.

> When Peter came to Antioch, I opposed him to his face, because he was in the wrong. Before certain men came from James, he used to eat with the Gentiles. But when they arrived, he began to draw back and separate himself from the Gentiles because he was afraid of those who belonged to the circumcision group. The other Jews joined him in his hypocrisy, so that by their hypocrisy even Barnabas was led astray.[77]

So you see, we are not the only ones who find the question difficult. Good, sincere Christians can come to wrong conclusions. Even Barnabas was led astray. How could anyone fault Barnabas's attitude toward the Gentiles? Barnabas had been commissioned with Paul to take the gospel message to the Gentiles and had spent three years doing it.

Acting in Line

Paul went on, "When I saw that they were not acting in line with the truth of the gospel, I said to Peter in front of them all . . ."[78] This is the phrase that jumps out at me. Peter was not acting in line with the truth of the gospel!

What is this truth that must be acted out?

> You are all Sons of God through faith in Christ Jesus, for all of you who were baptized into Christ have clothed yourselves with Christ. There is neither Jew nor Greek, slave nor free, male nor female, for you are all one in Christ Jesus. If you belong to Christ, then you are Abraham's seed, and heirs according to the promise.[79]

We have gone from Abraham to Peter to Abraham again, full circle. Discrimination among men by God or in the church is not dependent on anything but God's promise.

Paul puts the issue of the status and service of women in exactly the same category as the status and service of Gentiles.[80] Neither counts for anything. Only being in Christ through faith counts.[81]

What Counts?

There was only one word from the report my church published on the role and service of women that I took serious issue with, the word *solely*. In commenting on Paul's words from Galatians 3:26–29, the report said this scripture "is concerned ***solely*** with the improvements accomplished through the new administration of the covenant of grace,"[82] implying exclusively, only, or merely my (or any woman believer's) rescue from hell, my justification.

My denomination is not alone in this opinion. In fact, all who hold the complementarian view that women are subordinate[83] to men in family and church seem to agree that these verses speak only of our equality before God and nothing more.

Our equality before God solely. Only that. Nothing more.

Are the improvements accomplished through the new administration of the covenant of grace so little that they really don't have anything to do with my life here on earth in the church? Are these improvements so distant they will only have meaning after I die?

No. A thousand times, no! This is not my experience. I am sure it is not yours. The improvements accomplished through the new administration of the covenant of grace get me out of bed every morning. Through these improvements, I deal with my family. I teach school. I go to church. Through these improvements, I live and move and have my being.[84]

Paul said it so clearly as he confronted Peter. "I have been crucified with Christ and I no longer live, but Christ lives in me. The life I live in the body, I live by faith in the Son of God, who loved me and gave himself for me. I do not set aside the grace of God, for if righteousness could be gained through the law, Christ died for nothing."[85]

Paul is talking about the life he lives "in the body." That probably means his life in his physical body here on earth. Or it could possibly mean the life he lives as part of the church, the body of Christ. Either way, he is talking about his physical life, this side of death. It is here in this life that we are crucified with Christ. It is here in this life that Christ lives in us. It is here in this life that we live by faith.

"Solely" sounds a little like setting aside the grace of God. These improvements of the covenant of grace are not little insignificant things. They are not a side issue to this question, or to our lives in any way. The improvements accomplished through the new administration of the covenant of grace are everything, the whole ball of wax, the sum total, the infinite all.

I am glad Paul did not have a word processor. If he had, he might have been tempted to mail merge some of his epistles. As it is, he often talks about the same subject, but each time he expresses it in just a little different way, enlarging our understanding.

Paul introduces this subject of our human differences to the Colossians by saying that since we have been raised with Christ, our life is now hidden with Christ in God. He goes on to say,

> Put to death, therefore, whatever belongs to your earthly nature: . . . You used to walk in these ways, in the life you once lived. . . . since you have taken off your old self with its practices and have put on the new self, which is being renewed in knowledge in the image of its Creator. Here there is no Greek or Jew, circumcised or uncircumcised, barbarian, Scythian, slave or free, but Christ is all, and is in all.[86]

Did you notice the word *here*? Our human differences do not matter *here*, where we still have to struggle with our earthly nature, so it must be this side of the grave. It is *here* that these differences are of no consequence.

Why don't they matter here? Because "Christ is all and is in all" ***here***. Not just in heaven before God's throne. And not just in God's perceptions of us. Not just in our own individual personal relationships between ourselves and God. But here also. ***Here*** in Christ's body, the church.[87]

The obliteration of these differences of heredity, status, and sex is part of our life in Christ. And I am convinced the Holy Spirit has shined the light of this truth in many of our hearts, perhaps even before our minds have comprehended it. I see it in many homes and marriages. I see it in my own congregation. I see it all across the church. I do not see a hierarchy of authority. I see men and women acting out the truth that there is no male or female, but rather just one in Christ. I see the improvements accomplished through the new administration of the covenant of grace at work every day, in my life, in yours, in the church.

We must act in line with the truth of the gospel just as Paul has said throughout Galatians.

5:1. "It is for freedom that Christ has set us free. Stand firm, then, and do not let yourselves be burdened again by a yoke of slavery." To live under these differences is to subject ourselves again to the bondage of the law, and the yoke of slavery.[88]

5:6. "For in Christ Jesus neither circumcision nor uncircumcision has any value. The only thing that counts is faith expressing itself through love."[89] Neither is there any value in whether you have anything to circumcise or not. We know this because there is only one thing that matters. Along with all other believers, women have the only thing that counts, faith which expresses itself through love.

6:15. "Neither circumcision nor uncircumcision means anything; what counts is a new creation."[90]

Many new believers memorize, "Therefore, if anyone is in Christ, he is a new creation; the old has gone, the new has come!"[91] But perhaps we are not so familiar with the verse just preceding this one. "So from now on we regard no one from a worldly point of view."[92]

Our Differences

Being new creations will not make us all identical. Rather, our recreation makes us one. Our differences will not change. Some of us will continue to be richer than others. Some of us will be Hispanic, and some of us will be Armenian, some Irish, some Jewish, some Korean. Some of us will be tall and some short. Some of us will be leaders in society, even holding positions of power, but most of us will be common people. Some of us will be men, and some of us will be women.

This of course is good for the church, so there will be no division and so we will have equal concern for each other.

In the church we are not all the same. We continue to be different. It's just that our differences make no difference.

We are the same . . . but different.

Value Expressions

Let's go back to algebra class for a minute. Both sides of the equation $(4 + 1) = (8 - 3)$ are exactly equal. Even though the numerical expressions on each side of the equation look different, they both have the same value of 5. If the equal sign were the fulcrum of a scale, the two sides would balance exactly, because each side of the equation has exactly the same significance, value, and weight.

Many numerical expressions such as (–8 + 13), (7 – 2), (10/2), (450 – 445), and (4 x 1.25) also have a value of 5. Each expression is different, yet each has a value of 5. Each expression is exactly equal to every other expression. I could go on all day listing numerical expressions that have a value of 5. In fact, an infinite number of expressions have a value of 5. And each one of those infinite number of unique expressions that has a value of 5 is equal to every other expression that has a value of 5.

Our Sameness

Human beings are like that. Even though each person is unique and different from every other person that has ever or will ever live, we all have the same value, weight, significance. We are all the work of God's hand, and we have all sinned; we are in God's image/short of God's glory.

By faith all who believe have been created and recreated in the image of God. "Christ is all, and is in all."[93] We are "all one in Christ Jesus."[94] "The same Lord is Lord of all."[95] This is our value. We do not make up our own value. Nothing we do can increase or decrease our value. Our value is given to us by our creator. God has made all believers clean.[96]

But our creator God has chosen to express that value in innumerable ways. Yet as different as the various expressions may be, the value remains the same. Therefore, each expression of this image is exactly equal to every other expression.

"***There is no difference***, for all have sinned and fall short of the glory of God, and are justified freely by his grace through the redemption that came by Christ Jesus."[97]

The Question

Does the Bible equate the Gentile question with the women question?

What do we know to be true?

- Women and Gentiles are in exactly the same category, that of the physical: heredity, genetics, chromosomes. No discrimination is to be made on this basis.[98]

- Believing women can be accepted as equals in the church because of the following:

  "Christ is all, and is in all."[99]
  All are one in Christ.[100]
  God has called us all clean.[101]
  All fear God and do what is right.[102]
  All have received the Holy Spirit.[103]
  All have hearts with which they have believed.[104]
  All have mouths with which they have made confession.[105]
  All have the same Lord.[106]
  Christ has accepted all.[107]

The Question

Just because the Gentiles and women are included in the gospel
and receive all the benefits of salvation,
does this have anything to do with our life together in the family
and church here on earth?

What do we know to be true?

- We must act in line with the truth of the gospel.[108]
- To live under our human differences is to subject ourselves again to bondage and slavery.[109]
- The only thing that counts is faith expressed through love.[110]
- The only thing that counts is a new creation.[111]
- The "improvements accomplished through
  the new administration of the covenant of grace"[112]
  have ***everything*** to do with our present life together.[113]

The Question

What should be the status of women in the church, family and society?

What truth can we apply to make this a slightly simpler question?

- "No Difference" is a clear theme taught throughout the whole of Scripture.

- The only basis for God's differentiation among people is his own mercy. God judges on no other basis. Nothing else matters. Everything else makes no difference.

- The only basis for our differentiation among people is fruitfulness, the evidence of God's cleansing mercy. Nothing else matters. Everything else makes no difference.

My grandmother Emma (center) with her sisters May and Lizzie~1890.

CHAPTER 4

Servanthood: Serve One Another in Love

Galatians 5:13

Authority!

When it comes to a discussion of the issue of women in the church, I hear this word all the time. It seems to be central to the question of what exactly is the status of women.

Authority?

Authority and the Bible

What does the Bible say about authority? I thought I should find out for myself. In my search, I discovered that the true biblical authority principle has nothing to do with rank and power over others. Instead, the biblical authority principle is servanthood.

Servanthood is what separates a Christian woman from the secular feminist. In fact this absolute and universal principle of Christ's kingdom is what separates all Christians, men or women, from all other people.

Servanthood is the reason godly Christian women have nothing to do with abortion. We give thanks that God has allowed us women to mirror so clearly his injunction to present our bodies as "living sacrifices, holy and pleasing to God"—which is our spiritual act of worship.[1] The feminists are right in saying that a woman gives up her body to another's use when she becomes pregnant. But for the Christian, it is a privilege to be able to see the principle of servanthood so vividly portrayed through our physical bodies—as living sacrifices.

Jesus has been called the suffering servant. No title could sound less authoritative. Yet he has all authority. What did he teach about authority?

You remember the story of the ultimate stage mother, the mother of James and John. She asked Jesus if her sons could have the highest positions next to Jesus when he brought in his kingdom.

Of course she was not only talking about position and status, but also authority. This is how Jesus understood her request. After telling her that these positions were not his to give away, he immediately began to talk about authority. "You know that the rulers of the Gentiles lord it over them, and their high officials exercise authority over them."[2] He goes on to say that this idea of authority belongs completely to the world.

Sociologists tell us that even in the most loosely organized groups there is always an authority structure. Whether the people are young or old, primitive or highly sophisticated, there is a pecking order. They scramble to see who can be in authority, give the orders, direct the action, lord it over the others. This may not always be done openly and obviously as in the military. In fact, it is usually done through more subtle means. I certainly see this worldly principle of authority at work among my junior high students. I'm sure you have seen it at work within groups you are familiar with too.

Our Prime Directive

The truth of Christ's kingdom is exactly the opposite of how the world thinks things should be. "You know that the rulers of the Gentiles lord it over them, and their high officials exercise authority over them. Not so with you." This is so foreign to our way of thinking that it is even difficult for us believers to accept. Exercising authority is not the way things are done among his followers, nor a guiding principle for the church.

There is a guiding principle for the believers: "Not so with you. Instead, . . . whoever wants to become great among you must be your servant, and whoever wants to be first must be your slave—. . ."[3] It would be difficult to create a directive more at odds with the world's view. In Christ's kingdom, authority is not to be exercised; servanthood is to be exercised. Servanthood is the self-denial required of all who follow Jesus.[4]

Servanthood is the primary directive for how believers are to relate to one another. When

Jesus gave the Golden Rule in the Sermon on the Mount,[5] he said it was a summary of the Law and the Prophets. Servanthood is the second greatest commandment.[6]

Servanthood is the primary directive because it is a reflection of our primary director, Jesus himself.[7] Servanthood is an outgrowth of God's own character. Everything in Christ's kingdom is to be done the way Christ does things. The aim of all the parts, or members of the church, is to become like Jesus.[8]

"You know that the rulers of the Gentiles lord it over them, and their high officials exercise authority over them. Not so with you. Instead, whoever wants to become great among you must be your servant, and whoever wants to be first must be your slave—just as the Son of Man did not come to be served, but to serve, and to give his life as a ransom for many."[9]

The Question

What does Christ teach us about the exercise of authority?

What do we know to be true?

- The authority principle of the world is exercising authority and lording it over others.[10]
- Exercising authority is not the way believers are to relate to one another.[11]
- The way believers are to relate to one another is the opposite of the worldly authority principle.[12]
- Servanthood is the biblical authority principle for the church.[13]
- The servanthood principle is derived from Christ's example, person, and character.[14]
- Servanthood is the prime directive for relating to each other in Christ's church, because we are to be like him.[15]

This worldly concept of authority, that someone must always be on top telling others what to do, must be what leads us to assume that when the Bible talks about submission, it naturally goes hand in hand with the exercise of authority. Contrariwise, when the Bible talks about submission, or directs someone to submit, it is an expansion on the particulars of the servanthood principle.

Submission and Subordination

When we read the word *submit* in the Bible, it often registers as "to be in a God-ordained subordinate position," or "to be under the authority of." With this assumption in mind, no need is seen to define a word according to its normal, ordinary usage.

The words *submit* and *subordinate* are not synonymous. *Submit* means to voluntarily yield oneself to another. It may or may not be to someone in authority. Submission is an attitude of heart, not lines on an authority flowchart. *Subordinate* does not mean acting submissively or one who is submissive. The word *subordinate* as a verb means "to make subject or subservient to; to treat as of less value or importance."[16] As a noun it indicates a position under the authority of a superior. *Submit* comes from within. *Subordinate* is imposed from without. One says, "I will serve you." The other says, "You must do as I tell you."

Submit and *subordinate* may occur together. The patriot soldier freely gives himself to fight for his country. At the same time, he is subordinate to the authority structures of that country and its army.

But *submit* and *subordinate* do not necessarily go together. Sadie, our beautiful purebred Dalmatian dog, is an example. She has given us a lot of pleasure, especially as the mother of eleven wonderful Dalmatian puppies. Everyone in the family knows that Sadie is definitely subordinate to all the rest of us. But Sadie doesn't know this because, subordinate or not, she is not submissive. Any of you who have a dog, or more especially, a cat, may know exactly what I mean.

Most of us can probably think of a circumstance when someone was submissive but not subordinate. It happens all the time in everyday life. Equals submit to equals. Someone simply gives in, yielding his or her will to someone else's. People have lots of reasons for being submissive, and being subordinate is only one of them.

A similar false assumption is often made when we discuss equality for women. We may jump to the conclusion that if there is equality, there can be no submission. It is true that the secular feminist, operating on the worldly authority principle, is often looking for a way to lord it over others instead of being lorded over. But the believer must have a commitment to servanthood. We must serve because Christ came to serve. I believe in submission. I believe women should submit. I believe men should submit. This is what the Bible teaches. Equality does not exclude submission. Equality makes submission the responsibility of every believer.[17]

Jesus is the prime example of one who was submissive, even though not subordinate.[18] The biblical word *submit* is most often ultimately linked to the example of Jesus, and his divine character.

False Assumptions

One example of how we incorrectly assume that the word *submit* goes with an authority structure is in the familiar Ephesians passage that talks about the relationship between husbands and wives.[19] This section is introduced by two restatements of the servanthood principle, which are directed to all believers. "Be imitators of God, therefore, as dearly loved children and live a life of love, just as Christ loved us and gave himself up for us as a fragrant offering and sacrifice to God."[20] "Submit to one another out of reverence for Christ."[21]

Then comes the particular that wives are to submit to their husbands in the same way that the church submits to Christ. The church submits to Christ in humility.[22] Jesus made plain his definition of *submission*: "If anyone would come after me, he ***must deny himself*** and take up his cross ***and follow me.***"[23] The essence of our submission to Jesus is our own death to ourselves so that we can live to God.

At this point, the false assumption is often made that if wives are to submit, then husbands must be in authority over them. But this is not what the passage says. Instead, Paul continues, "Husbands, love your wives, just as Christ loved the church and gave himself up for her."[24]

It sounds to me like the essence of loving your wife is servanthood, just as the essence of Jesus' love was giving himself up. This is verified by Jesus himself: "Greater love has no one than this, that one lay down his life for his friends."[25]

Paul links the servanthood principle to Christ's love for his church in his letter to the Philippians.[26] Speaking of Jesus, Paul says,

> Who, being in very nature God, did not consider equality with God something to be grasped, but made himself nothing, taking the very nature of a servant, being made in human likeness, and being found in appearance as a man, he humbled himself and became obedient to death—even death on a cross![27]

Only One Authority

Jesus is the only one to have authority. He told us, "All authority in heaven and on earth has been given to me."[28] But even in his recognition that he had all authority, it motivated him to serve. John tells us that "Jesus knew that the Father had put all things under his power, . . . so he . . . began to wash his disciples' feet."[29]

Jesus made this very clear when he spoke to his followers about the Pharisees' view of authority.

> But you are not to be called "Rabbi," for you have only one Master and you are all brothers. And do not call anyone on earth "father," for you have one Father, and he is in heaven. Nor are you to be called "teacher," for you have one Teacher, the Christ. The greatest among you will be your servant. For whoever exalts himself will be humbled, and whoever humbles himself will be exalted.[30]

Even though Jesus Christ is certainly in a position to lawfully exercise authority, being God himself, he chose rather to show his love by casting aside his authority and becoming a servant. Jesus is the greatest servant of all because he received all of God's wrath upon himself on our behalf. And because he took this position of ultimate servanthood, God has made him the very first, giving him the most exalted position of ultimate authority. This is a fulfillment of just how Jesus described servanthood to the disciples when he found them arguing about which of them would be greatest. "If anyone wants to be first, he must be the very last, and the servant of all."[31]

Paul introduces the description of Christ's love in Philippians 2 with these words, "Your attitude should be the same as that of Christ Jesus."[32] Just in case we miss the point of what Christ's love is like, he summarizes it for us this way:

> . . . make my joy complete by being like-minded, having the same love, being one in spirit and purpose. Do nothing out of selfish ambition or vain conceit, but in humility consider others better than yourselves. Each of you should look not only to your own interests, but also to the interests of others.[33]

Dying to Self and Living to God

Servanthood means dying to self and living to God. This is how Jesus loved the church: "Christ loved us and ***gave himself up*** for us as a fragrant offering and sacrifice ***to God.***"[34] This is how the church submits to Jesus: "***count yourselves dead*** to sin ***but alive to God*** in Christ Jesus. . . . offer yourselves to God, as those who have been brought from death to life."[35]

Our submission to Jesus always flows from his love for us.[36] He died for us, and thus we die with him so we can also live with him.[37]

Peter says the same thing when he tells both husbands and wives to act "in the same way"[38] as Jesus did. "When they hurled their insults at him, he did not retaliate: when he suffered, he made no threats. Instead, he entrusted himself to him who judges justly. He himself bore our sins in his body on the tree, so that we might ***die to sins and live for righteousness***: by his wounds you are healed."[39] We must all act "in the same way" because "To this you were called, because Christ suffered for you, leaving you an example, that you should follow in his steps."[40]

One Standard for All

The biblical servanthood imperative is universal and absolute for all believers, in all cultures, throughout all history. It is a principle rooted in God's nature, revealed in his word, and summarized in the two greatest commandments, "Love the Lord your God" and "Love your neighbor as yourself."[41]

Most of us learned the Golden Rule as little children. "Do unto others as you would have others do unto you."[42] There is no hierarchy here. This is a statement of complete reversibility, reciprocity, equality, and servanthood.[43]

Reversibility is the whole idea here. What you want is what you must give. Equality is the goal.[44] By following this rule, each of us will have only one standard of treatment for all others, that is, how we want to be treated.

Now all of us may not want to be treated in the same way. So there will be as many standards for treatment as there are people. But if a person follows this rule, he or she will have only one personal standard for treating all other people. This rule leaves no room for an individual to treat one person or group one way, while treating another person or group some other way.

You would think that Jesus might more naturally have said, "Treat other people as they want to be treated" or "as would be best for them to be treated" or even "as they treat you." In fact children, in an attempt to rationalize their mistreatment of others, often misinterpret the Golden Rule with such reasoning.

"Why did you hit Johnnie? Don't you know the Golden Rule?"

"He hit me first so I figured he wanted to be hit."

Another example:

"Why are you making fun of Susie? Would you like it if others made fun of you this way?"

"She likes it. See. She's laughing too."

Kids are sharp. Rationalization starts very early.

The Gentile lords were good at this kind of rationalization too. Listen to what Jesus said about them. At the last supper a dispute began about which disciple was the greatest. Jesus responded, "The kings of the Gentiles lord it over them; and those who exercise authority over them ***call themselves Benefactors***. But you are not to be like that."[45]

When Jesus states the servanthood principle as the second greatest commandment,[46] this strange twist is again there. We are to love each other ***as we love ourselves***.[47] If we do this, it will be very difficult to maintain different standards for different people, different positions for different groups, different status and respect for different brothers and sisters in Christ. Jesus knows that our love for ourselves is so strong, it will always be our best guide for how we should love others.

Modern-day psychology has made much of loving ourselves. Our idea of self-esteem, our love for ourselves, may be muddled. To this present generation at least, "as you love yourselves" may seem a rather confusing standard for how we are to treat others. But when we look at the Golden Rule, our confusion disappears. All of us know how we want to be treated by others. We all recognize bad treatment when we see it, or more accurately, when we receive it. Likewise, we recognize good treatment too. If in doubt about how we want to be treated, we can always consult our fantasies. They will usually tell us how we want others to treat us. It's that simple. That is how we are to treat others. There is only one standard for our treatment of everyone.

Submission, Love, and Authority

In Christ's church, *submission* and *love* are synonymous. They mean the same thing. Submission and love go together to make up servanthood, the primary directive for how we believers are to relate to one another.[48] They both mean voluntarily giving ourselves up to God. Authority doesn't come into this picture. Rather, the exercise of authority is to be put aside as a completely worldly concept.

Authority and submission are not two different sides of the same coin. They are two entirely different coins. One coin is the medium for exchange in the world. The other coin is the medium of exchange in the church.

The Question

When the Bible tells someone to submit,
is it therefore telling someone else to exercise authority?

What do we know to be true?

- *Love* and *submission* both mean dying to self and living to God.
    - Love as Christ loved the church.[49]
        - Jesus is God. He has all authority.[50]
        - Jesus submitted even though not subordinate.[51]
        - Jesus showed his love by choosing to be a servant, rather than by exercising authority.[52]
    - Submit as the church submits to Christ.[53]
        - The church's submission flows from Christ's love.[54]

- The servanthood principle of love and submission is for all believers.[55]

- The servanthood principle is a summary of all the law and the prophets.[56]

- The servanthood principle is the second greatest commandment.[57]

If servanthood, characterized by both submission and love, is the primary directive for all believers, then why are women so often told to submit in the Scriptures? This was a question put to me once. It was a good question. I thought about it a lot. But my own meditation couldn't answer the question. God's Word did.

Authority Instituted among Men

The answer is found in 1 Peter. Peter tells us to "submit yourselves for the Lord's sake to every authority instituted among men."[58] Whether the institution established among men be patriarchy, slavery, or paying the coin to Caesar, our reaction should be one of submission because servanthood is not only the primary directive for God's people as they relate to each other, but also as they relate to the world.[59]

We are not asked to do anything more than Jesus did in submitting himself to the governing authorities that crucified him. Peter goes on to say, "To this you were called, because Christ suffered for you, leaving you an example, that you should follow in his steps. . . . When they hurled their insults at him, he did not retaliate; when he suffered, he made no threats."[60]

Jesus did not submit to the insults, to the whip, to the cross because these were just and right things to exercise authority over him. He submitted because of servanthood. He submitted so he could lay down his life for his friends. And we are to follow his example.[61]

Women are told to submit so often because women are often put under authorities "instituted among men." The woman is the "weaker partner" just as Peter says.[62] The female is in a much more vulnerable position in this sinful world than is the male. Women may live longer than men, but in a physical contest of strength, the woman will usually lose. The woman also endures all the physical consequences of the sexual relationship alone. These two things make her very vulnerable to oppression and "lording over" through sin. Since the fall, the male has usually been in the power position. Thus, as mankind sets up authority structures, women often end up under authority.[63]

The Weaker Partner

Peter calls woman the "weaker partner" in the context of urging husbands to have special respect for their wives because they are especially vulnerable to disrespect. Paul says the same thing: "The eye cannot say to the hand, 'I don't need you!' And the head cannot say to the feet. 'I don't need you!' On the contrary, those parts of the body that seem to be weaker are indispensable."[64]

Women should joy in this weaker position because it demands and forces a greater reliance on the grace of God.[65] Weakness provides the obvious opportunity for God's power to be made known. Here is another principle of the new life that is entirely opposed to the world's view. In Christ's kingdom, weakness is a strength. "For when I am weak, then I am strong."[66]

Peter addresses husbands: "Husbands, in the same way be considerate as you live with your wives, and treat them with respect as the weaker partner and as heirs with you of the gracious gift of life."[67] Husbands, Peter says this weaker partner is your co-heir.[68] If God looks upon your wife as your equal, then you should respect her as such. This is Peter's admonition!

Women of the past, who were held under authority much more than I, may have a greater reward for their submission. Their reward will come not because the authority exercised over them was scriptural or just, but because they followed Christ's example and submitted. Before their oppressors, they did not open their mouths. They suffered and endured for doing good. This is commendable before God.[69]

It is for this very thing that Peter commends the "holy women of the past." He tells us that Sarah did just this and that we can be her true daughters if we do it too, if we submit to "authorities instituted among men."[70]

But submitting to such authorities may not be fun. It may be humiliating and even mean a great deal of suffering because of its ungodly nature. Yet Peter says, "For it is commendable if a man bears up under the pain of unjust suffering because he is conscious of God."[71] He means, "if we continue in what is right and do not give way to fear."[72] How are we to not be afraid?

Trusting the Just Judge

We do this in exactly the same way Jesus did, by not retaliating, but rather entrusting ourselves "to him who judges justly."[73] This is what the holy women of the past did; they "put their hope in God."[74] The ultimate judge and authority is God alone, and we can easily trust ourselves to his justice.[75]

Once Paul felt he was being judged unjustly, so he explained in a little more detail what it means to entrust oneself to God as the final judge.

> I care very little if I am judged by you or by any human court; indeed, I do not even judge myself. My conscience is clear, but that does not make me innocent. It is the Lord who judges me. Therefore judge nothing before the appointed time; wait till the Lord comes. He will bring to light what is hidden in darkness and will expose the motives of men's hearts. At that time each will receive his praise from God.[76]

Men, if God considers women to be heirs with you,[77] if Jesus considers women to be his co-heirs,[78] if God is our final judge "who judges justly,"[79] bringing "to light what is hidden in darkness and will expose the motive of men's hearts,"[80] then what do you think would be the best way for you to consider women?

A question naturally arises about the abuse we know exists in our own society today. Should women just take it if their husbands beat them, humiliate and denigrate them, impoverish them, and hurt their children? Should women be completely silent and never challenge the wrongdoer?

Our modern sensibilities utterly rebel against having to suffer unjustly. We do not believe it is right to allow ourselves to be victimized by evil.[81] Yet this is a difficult question in light of what Peter says to us. But it is a question the church has dealt with before through the issues of submission to governing authorities and slavery.

Here is a similar question. Should we allow ourselves to be sold into slavery, not unknown in our world today, since Peter gave similar admonitions to slaves? No! Peter also told his readers to "Live as free men."[82] Peter is telling us to submit to evil only when we have no other choice, humanly speaking. Slaves had no choice about their submission. They either did it voluntarily, which is true submission in the steps of Christ, or they were forced to do it against their wills, which is subordination. Believing slaves submitted to follow Christ's example rather than because they were under the authority of some human master. This is what made them free people, even though chained by the human institution of slavery.

The holy women of the past sometimes had to submit to evil also. Sarah went along with Abraham's deception that she was his sister, and the resulting adulterous affair with the Pharaoh of Egypt, just because Abraham was afraid his life might be in danger. This happened to her not once, but twice.[83] The wives Peter was talking to often had no choice either. Their society embraced the idea that a woman belonged to her husband, who had absolute say over her life. This was the authority "instituted among men" of that day.

But today our society does not recognize the husband's right to do anything he pleases to his wife. The church must seek through prayer and the Holy Spirit's guidance to know how God wants us to apply Peter's message in view of the "authorities instituted among men" with which we live today.

And let us remember that just as Paul called on Philemon, the slave owner in the position of man-made authority, to accept Onesimus as a brother instead of a slave,[84] so Peter appeals to husbands, the ones in the position of worldly authority, to consider their wives as heirs with them "of the gracious gift of life."[85]

Throughout Peter's entire epistle, he continually contrasts submission to man-made authorities with injunctions for all believers to treat each other with mutual respect and love.

Peter sums up his letter with the servanthood principle:

> ***Finally, all of you,*** live in harmony with one another, be sympathetic, love as brothers, be compassionate and humble. Do not repay evil with evil or insult with insult, but with blessing, because to this you were called so that you may inherit a blessing.[86]

> ***Above all,*** love each other deeply, because love covers over a multitude of sins. Offer hospitality to one another without grumbling. Each one should use whatever gift he has received to serve others, faithfully administering God's grace in its various forms. If anyone speaks, he should do it as one speaking the very words of God. If anyone serves, he should do it with the strength God provides, so that in all things God may be praised through Jesus Christ. To him be the glory and the power forever and ever. Amen.[87]

> . . . ***all of you*** be subject one to another, and be clothed with humility: for God resisteth the proud, and giveth grace to the humble.[88]

Why Care?

If women will receive a greater reward for their submission to these authorities instituted among men,[89] why should I care about the status of women in the church and family? I personally have suffered very little at the hands of man-made authorities. And I know my reward will be proportional to the way I have endured even an occasional humiliation by following Christ's example. Women will not be harmed in any ultimate, eternal sense, no matter what authorities or restrictions are placed on women in the family or church.

Yet, Peter not only tells us to submit to authorities instituted among men, but also to "live as free men."[90] We do not submit because we are under authority. Is that why Christ submitted? No! He submitted because this was how he was going to show his love for us—by dying for us. The reason we submit is to follow Christ's example. The reason we submit is to fulfill the servanthood principle of Christ's kingdom. We are to "live as free men." We are to "live as servants of God."[91] This is why we submit. This is why we should care about the women's issue.

Motivations are complex, and I do not claim that mine are unhindered by sin. But it is my prayer that the reason I am writing today is not because I am a woman of the church, but rather because I am a member of the church. As a woman I have nothing to ultimately fear in submitting to any authority because I entrust myself to the final authority and judge, God.

Who Needs to Fear?

The only one who needs to fear before our holy judge is the one who sets up and promotes an unjust authority to test God, while making it difficult for those turning to God.[92] If a woman will be rewarded for submitting to authority exercised over her, then the one who creates separations in the body of Christ, thus producing cracks in the oneness of the believers by which God has purposed to convince the world that Jesus is from God[93] will also have his reward.[94]

The Question

What does 1 Peter teach us about authorities instituted among men?

What do we know to be true?

- We are all to submit to authorities instituted among men,[95] including:
  governments[96]
  slavery[97]
  patriarchy[98]
  just[99]
  unjust[100]
  kind or cruel[101]

- We submit following Christ's example.[102]
  Christ submitted to authorities instituted among men,
    not because these authorities were just and godly,[103]
    but because of servanthood,[104]
    without fear,[105]
    because he entrusted himself to the just judge, God.[106]

The Question

What should be the status of women in the family, church and society?

What truth can we apply to make this a slightly simpler question?

- Servanthood is a clear theme taught throughout the whole of Scripture.

- Servanthood, characterized by love and submission,
  means dying to self and living to God.

- Servanthood is the primary directive for how all believers are to relate to one another,
  a summary of all the law and prophets,
  the two greatest commandments.

- The servanthood principle comes from God's nature
  and is most clearly demonstrated to us through Christ's example.
  As new creatures, recreated in God's image,
  we are transformed by the servanthood principle as we are to become like him.

My grandmother Greeta (center) with her sister Callie and their mother Nellie~1910.

Chapter 5

The Head of the Body: What Does It Mean?

Colossians 1:18

One can hardly discuss the concept of authority, especially as it pertains to the status of women, without considering *headship*. Two passages that speak about women use this analogy of "the head." Its meaning is critical since this word is used to teach us about the relationship between mankind and womankind,[1] husbands and wives.[2]

"Authority Over" or "Source Of"

Language scholars tell us there are two possible meanings for the Greek word[3] translated "head"[4] in the New Testament. It could mean "authority over" or "source of." The difference is important for our understanding of the status of women.

The most widely accepted meaning for *head* has been "authority over," and the principle of headship has traditionally been built on this definition. It is how we often use the word in English. We all understand that "Mr. So-and-So is head of the Acme Corporation" means he is the boss, the final authority, the one all must answer to, the director of Acme, Inc. The consequence of this definition is women are considered subordinate.

But when the Bible says that Christ is "the head of the body, the church,"[5] does it mean Christ is "the authority over the church" or "the source of the church"? The arguments in support of each definition deal mainly with how this Greek word for *head* is used in other ancient writings, yet none of these arguments are conclusive. However, I believe that by using the interpretive principle—that Scripture is best interpreted by Scripture itself[6]—we can better understand the meaning of *head* that Paul intended.

The Head/Body Metaphor

The *head* that we want to examine is found in Ephesians 5:23: "For the husband is the head of the wife as Christ is head of the church, his body." Here *head* means a physical head, something attached to a body. It's a metaphor. Christ is the "head." The church is "his body."

This passage is really a simile of metaphors: "the husband is the head of the wife " is one metaphor; the other is, "Christ is head of the church, his body." These two metaphors are joined into a simile with the word *as*. So in order to understand how the husband is head of the wife, we must first figure out the meaning of Christ being the head of the church, his body.

The use of a metaphor to describe Christ in Scripture is not at all new. Jesus himself used this technique to describe himself many times. For example he used the phrase "I am" to describe himself as "the gate,"[7] "the way,"[8] "the light,"[9] "the shepherd,"[10] "the bread."[11] John the Baptist called Jesus "the lamb of God."[12] At times we also use the word *lamb* as a metaphor to describe people.

Suppose I were talking with a friend about needing a little extra time away from the office for a special luncheon engagement. I might say of my boss, "Oh, he's a real lamb. He'll let me have the time." Now, is what I described about my boss the same thing that John the Baptist was describing about Jesus? No, not at all.

Then how do we know what John the Baptist meant to tell us about Jesus? We know by studying the rest of Scripture to see how the word *lamb* is used and what meaning it has. We apply the principle of interpretation that Scripture is its own interpreter, giving careful attention to the way one passage of Scripture is used in another, along with the more general principle that each portion of Scripture must be read and understood in light of the whole.[13]

There are two passages using *head* that deal directly with the issue of the status of Women: 1 Corinthians 11 and Ephesians 5. Excluding these two, since they are the controversial and contested passages, there are four other scriptures that talk about Christ as head: Ephesians 1 and 4 and Colossians 1 and 2. Let's take a closer look at these four passages to see if we can discern Paul's meaning.

Fullness

In each of these scriptures where Christ is referred to as the "head" of his body, the church, Paul expands on this idea with the word *fullness*.

"And God placed all things under his feet and appointed him to be head over everything for the church, which is his body, the ***fullness*** of him who fills everything in every way."[14]

> . . . to prepare God's people for works of service, so that the body of Christ may be built up until we all reach unity in the faith and in the knowledge of the Son of God and become mature, attaining to the whole measure of the ***fullness*** of Christ. Then we will no longer be infants, . . . Instead, speaking the truth in love, we will in all things grow up into him who is the Head, that is, Christ.[15]

Fullness describes the body of Christ. The church is pictured as the full expression of all that Christ is. When God's people reach unity in the faith and become mature, they attain the "whole measure," or the complete expression, of the person of Jesus.

"And he is the head of the body, the church: . . . For God was pleased to have all his ***fullness*** dwell in him, and through him to reconcile to himself all things, whether things on earth or things in heaven, by making peace through his blood, shed on the cross."[16]

Here *fullness* describes Jesus Christ as the complete expression of God. Jesus, being the *fullness* of God, carried out the action demanded by God's being, person, and character. This is a repetition of what Paul had said three verses earlier. "He is the image of the invisible God."[17]

This idea was first taught in John: "The Word became flesh and lived for a while among us. We have seen his glory, the glory of the one and only Son, who came from the Father, full of grace and truth. . . . No one has ever seen God, but God the only Son, who is at the Father's side, has made him known."[18] Jesus is the incarnation of God, God made flesh.

In Colossians 2 these two ideas of *fullness* are brought together. "For in Christ all the ***fullness*** of the Deity lives in bodily form, and you have been given ***fullness*** in Christ, who is the head over every power and authority."[19]

Christ is the *fullness* of God, and the church is the *fullness* of Christ. Christ is the full manifestation and expression of all that God is. Likewise, the church is the full manifestation and expression of all that Jesus is. Jesus is the incarnation of God, God made flesh. The church is the incarnation of Jesus, the body of Christ.[20]

Grows From

Fullness is further elaborated on in Ephesians 4 with the concept of growth.

"We will in all things ***grow up into him*** who is the Head, that is, Christ. ***From him the whole body . . . grows*** and builds itself up in love, as each part does its work."[21] Paul repeats this in the Colossians 2 passage: "He has lost connection with ***the Head, from whom the whole body . . . grows*** as God causes it to grow."[22]

The body grows from the head, becoming like the head, becoming the full expression of the head.

Holds Together

Head is also linked to the idea of something that holds everything together.

"Instead, . . . we will in all things grow up into him who ***is the Head, that is, Christ. From him the whole body, joined and held together by every supporting ligament***, grows and builds itself up in love, as each part does its work."[23]

"He has lost connection with ***the Head, from whom the whole body, supported and held together by its ligaments and sinews***, grows as God causes it to grow."[24]

The head is the part of the body that holds all the body together, gives it unity and oneness. The head is what all the parts have in common. Even though there are many parts, there is only one body.[25]

This idea of holding everything together is further reflected in other passages that describe Christ using the Greek word for "head" as in "head cornerstone." The church is described not only as a body, but also as a building. And what holds a building together? The head cornerstone. "Holding together" is the function of a cornerstone.

"The stone the builders rejected has become the capstone."[26] This verse is quoted various times in the New Testament,[27] showing that Jesus Christ is that head cornerstone. This quote is prefaced in 1 Peter 2 this way:

> As you come to him, the living Stone—rejected by men but chosen by God and precious to him—you also, like living stones, are being built into a spiritual house to be a holy priesthood, offering spiritual sacrifices acceptable to God through Jesus Christ. . . . you are a chosen people, a royal priesthood, a holy nation, a people belonging to God.[28]

Jesus holds us together as one building, a temple in which God lives.[29]

> You are . . . God's people and members of God's household, built on the foundation of the apostles and prophets, with Christ Jesus himself as the chief cornerstone.[30] In him the whole building is joined together and rises to become a holy temple[31] in the Lord. And in him you too are being built together to become a dwelling in which God lives by his Spirit.[32]

His Body

Christ is referred to as the head of a body in each of these four Scriptures. He is not referred to as just the head of the church, but rather as the head of the church, which is his body.

"And God placed all things under his feet and appointed him to be head over everything for ***the church, which is his body.***"[33]

". . . to prepare God's people for works of service, so that ***the body of Christ*** may be built up . . . attaining to the whole measure of the fullness of Christ. . . . we will in all things grow up into him who is ***the Head, that is, Christ.***"[34]

"And ***he is the head of the body, the church.***"[35]

"He has lost connection with ***the Head, from whom the whole body***, supported and held together by its ligaments and sinews, grows as God causes it to grow."[36]

Christ is the head of a body. When I think of a head and a body, I don't think of two separate entities. I think of one person, a whole body. If a head and a body are separated, both become useless.

Of course we cannot say that Christ would be diminished in any way without the church. Yet he has chosen to picture himself as head to a body, and that is part of the truth of a head and body. This is certainly Paul's meaning in 1 Corinthians 12, especially verse 21.

In fact, when "one flesh" died, that is, when all humankind died through Adam's sin, this sin was also the cause of Christ's death. Our sin killed Christ. Now of course Jesus chose to die. He allowed himself to be put to death. But it was our sin that necessitated his death[37] if we were to be recreated anew in his image. From the risen Christ has grown the church, his body. All the parts of the body are one together. Christ gives us life, and we fully express and demonstrate who he is. He lives in us and we are his presence.

Where Is Authority?

"Are you saying that Christ has no authority over the church?"

I was asked this question once during a discussion of the meaning of *head.* My answer is, "No! That is not what I am saying. But I am saying that the truth of Christ's authority over the church is not taught through this metaphor.

Of course Christ is the ultimate authority over the church. He is King and Lord of the universe, of all that exists. Jesus Christ is also creator, redeemer, and judge. But husbands are not all these things. We must stay within the metaphor laid down in Scripture. If we do not stay within the confines of the metaphor, given to us so we can better understand how the husband is head of the wife, we may make dreadful assumptions and draw incorrect conclusions about the husband/wife relationship.

The metaphor Paul uses to enlighten our understanding of husbands and wives is "Christ is the head of the church, his body."[38] And as we study the Bible to examine the meaning of this metaphor, we find nothing about the head having authority over the body, or of the head exercising authority over the body. Therefore, authority cannot be applied to the relationship between husbands and wives, or between men and women based on headship.

The Question

What does "Christ is the head of the body, the church" mean?[39]

What do we know to be true?

- In addition to Ephesians 5 and 1 Corinthians 11,
  the two Scripture passages that have a bearing on the status of women,
  there are four passages that speak of Christ as head of the church, his body:
  Ephesians 1 and 4 and Colossians 1 and 2.

- In these four passages, Ephesians 1 and 4 and Colossians 1 and 2:
  The body is the fullness of the head, and
  the fullness is the complete expression of the head.[40]
  The body grows from the head.[41]
  The head holds the whole body together.[42]

My grandmother Greeta and mother Winifred~1918.

Chapter 6

The Head of the Body: 1 Corinthians 11:3–16

Hats, veils, bonnets, shawls, and scarves. Throughout history these have been a part of a woman's clothing, used for protection, for identification of status, for modesty, or just for show.

Today, hats don't seem so important, at least in our part of the world.

The changing attitudes toward hats throughout the centuries tell us that to wear a hat or not to wear a hat is not a point of obvious truth or consequence to all people.

I was taught this attitude toward all outward appearance. "Man looks at the outward appearance, but the Lord looks at the heart."[1] What people look like or what they wear isn't important to God.[2]

Yet in spite of these biblical teachings, at some times and in some places since Paul wrote this letter to the Corinthian church, one item of clothing has prompted more controversy, debate, and schism in the church than any other—a woman's hat!

Is a woman's head covering the crux of this passage? Or is a woman's head where the real meaning lies? Now that we have an idea of what *head* means, perhaps we can gain some insight into the meaning of the head covering too.

Husband/Man

In the passages that we studied in the last chapter, we concentrated on the metaphor, "the head of the body, the church."[3] This same metaphor appears in Ephesians 5:23 preceded by "For the husband is the head of the wife as Christ is . . ." The original Greek words used for "husband" and "wife" in this phrase are the same words used for "man" and "woman" in 1 Corinthians 11:3: "the head of woman is man."[4] Consequently, these two phrases are almost identical, and I will consider them as one, having the same meaning.

Every Man/Mankind/the Church

These two phrases are also very similar:

"The head of every man is Christ."[5]
"Christ is the head of the church, his body."[6]

I will also consider them to have the same meaning because:

1. In Genesis when the creation is recounted, male and female together were created "man."[7, 8]

2. In close context to the phrase "the head of every man is Christ," Paul states, "In the Lord, however, woman is not independent of man, nor is man independent of woman. . . . everything comes from God."[9]

3. Each of these two phrases is parallel to the one phrase that is almost identically stated in both passages, "the head of the woman is man" or "the husband is the head of the wife."

4. The Greek word used for "man"[10] in the phrase "every man" is the same word used in Ephesians 4:13, where the man described is obviously the church, Christ's body, his fullness.

These four reasons taken together indicate that "every man" also refers to the church, which is Christ's body.

Through our study of *head* in the previous chapter, we found three aspects of meaning for Christ being the head of the church, his body: fullness, growth from, and holding together. Now let's apply these to this passage in 1 Corinthians 11.

Applying What We've Learned

It begins with a trio of parallels: "Now I want you to realize that the head of every man is

Christ, and the head of woman is man, and the head of Christ is God."[11]

The idea that man, woman, and Christ are the fullness of their respective heads is fully supported elsewhere in Scripture.

Just as Scripture teaches that Jesus Christ is the fullness of God[12] and that the church is the fullness of Christ,[13] it is also true that woman is the fullness of man. That is exactly what Adam meant when he said of woman, "This is now bone of my bone and flesh of my flesh."[14]

Image and Glory

Paul expands the meaning of *fullness* in verse 7: "A man ought not to cover his head, since he is the image and glory of God; but the woman is the glory of man."[15]

Image and *glory* are words that the Bible also uses to describe Jesus: "He is the image of the invisible God, . . ."[16] and just a few verses later Paul says that Christ is also the fullness of God.[17] Reflecting the image of the head is what fullness is all about.

Jesus is also the glory of God. "The word became flesh and made his dwelling among us. We have seen his glory, the glory of the One and Only."[18] "The Son is the radiance of God's glory and the exact representation of his being."[19]

"Image" and "glory" more completely describe *fullness*. Jesus is the fullness of God. Jesus is the image and glory of God. This new dimension of fullness is also carried out in the parallel of Christ being head of the church.

"And we, who with unveiled faces all reflect the Lord's glory, are being transformed into his likeness with ever-increasing glory, which comes from the Lord, who is the Spirit."[20] The church is the glory and likeness (image) of Jesus.

Now in 1 Corinthians 11, we see this elaboration on the meaning of fullness again in the third parallel of man being the head of woman. "A man ought not to cover his head, since he is the image and glory of God; but the woman is the glory of man."[21]

I have read that "women were created for man's glory."[22] But that is not the biblical phrasing. At the very least, "created for man's glory" has a completely different connotation from "woman is the glory of man." The first sounds as if woman was made just for man's pleasure, for his use, something to make him look good, serve his needs and purposes, belong to him. But the second sounds more like woman is the shining crown[23] of man, something radiating forth from him, his light, his vitality, his energy, a part of him.

Which one of these connotations best describes how Jesus is the glory of God? We must say the second. Jesus is the glory of God, because he is the fullness of God, because everything that God is, Jesus Christ radiates in a visible way because he himself is God. "Anyone who has seen me has seen the Father."[24] They are one.

In the same way, the church is the glory of Jesus, because we explain Jesus to the world.[25] We radiate to the world all that Jesus is, because the church is the very presence of Jesus on earth, his body.[26]

In the Old Testament, Ezekiel had a vision about the restoration of the temple, ". . . and the glory of the Lord filled the temple."[27]

Now we see the fulfillment:

> Consequently, you are no longer foreigners and aliens, but fellow citizens with God's people and members of God's household, built on the foundation of the apostles and prophets, with Christ Jesus himself as the chief cornerstone. In him the whole building is joined together and rises to become a holy temple in the Lord. And in him you too are being built together to become a dwelling in which God lives by his Spirit.[28]

This is what a body is, the physical manifestation of the spirit, the person who dwells within.[29] They are one.

In the same way woman is the glory of man. Everything that man is, she reflects, shows, and demonstrates, because she is man. "This is now bone of my bones and flesh of my flesh: she shall be called 'woman,'"[30] that is, a feminine man. Adam was a masculine man, and Eve was a feminine man. They were one man. Woman is the glory of the man because she was made for the man. "The woman is the glory of man. For . . . neither was man created for woman, but woman for man."[31]

Completion

The Greek word translated "fullness"[32] is related to the idea of completion. In fact, the King James Version translates *fullness* as "complete"[33] in Colossians 2:10: "And ye are complete in him."[34]

Scripture also tells us that Christ came into the world when the times had reached their fullness.[35] Here the meaning of *fullness* is a little bit easier for us to discern, even though it is not speaking metaphorically of a head and body. *Fullness* here means that the time had been completed, brought to fulfillment, accomplished, so Christ came into the world.

I do not find this aspect of completion to be a part of the fullness that is Jesus for his head, God. But as we consider the incarnation of Jesus, the idea of completion is present. Jesus' coming into the world as a man, his life, death, and resurrection, was the completion of God's plan for the redemption of his creation. Many times the actions of Jesus are described as a fulfillment of Scripture. Jesus said,

> Do not think that I have come to abolish the Law or the Prophets; I have not come to abolish them but to fulfill them. I tell you the truth, until heaven and earth disappear, not the smallest letter, not the least stroke of a pen, will by any means disappear from the Law until everything is accomplished.[36]

Through the incarnation of Jesus, God finished his work of redemption. It was completed in Jesus.

All these ideas are found in the first chapter of John's gospel. Jesus was the image[37] and glory[38] of God, revealing all that God is, the visible representation of God.[39] Through the incarnation of Jesus, God's plan for the redemption of his people was completed.[40] Jesus was God.[41]

John later tells us that God's love is made complete in us. "But if anyone obeys his word, God's love is truly made complete in him. This is how we know we are in him: Whoever claims to live in him must walk as Jesus did."[42] If we have God living in us, if we are like Jesus, then God's love will be made complete in us. Again John says, "No one has ever seen God: but if we love one another, God lives in us and his love is made complete in us."[43] The church, those who love him and love each other, makes God visible to the world because it is God who lives in us, and this is a completion of God's love.

"God is love. Whoever lives in love lives in God and God in him. In this way, love is made complete among us so that we will have confidence on the day of judgment, because in this world we are like him."[44] Again, completion is the result of God living in us and us being like him.

"I have brought you ***glory*** on earth ***by completing*** the work you gave me to do."[45] Jesus brought glory to God by completing his work. Woman is the glory of man by completing him.

Woman Is Man

Why was the aloneness of man the only thing in creation that was "not good"?[46] Man was incomplete. Something was lacking. Woman's creation was necessary to complete man. "Neither was man created for woman, but woman for man."[47] This "for man" does not mean that God created woman for man's pleasure, or his use, a possession. God created woman for man's completion, so he could be whole, so God's creation would be finished and be "very good,"[48] so that man, both the male and female of humankind, could be the fullness of God, his image and glory.[49] Woman does not belong to man; she is man.

Woman makes man visible by radiating forth his light, his energy, his life, just as the church makes Jesus visible by radiating forth his light, his energy, and his life,[50] just as Jesus makes God visible by radiating forth his light, his energy, and his life.[51]

Image, Glory, and Completion of the Head

The fullness completely manifests the head by radiating forth its glory.

Fullness	in relationship with	Head
Every man, the church	Col. 2:10; Eph. 1:22–23, 4:12–13	Christ
Woman	Gen. 2:23	Man
Christ	Col. 2:9, 1:19; 2 Cor. 4:4–6	God

Fullness	is the image of the	Head
Every man, the church	1 Cor. 11:7; 2 Cor. 3: 17–18; Gen. 1:27, 5:1–2	Christ
Woman	Gen. 2:23	Man
Christ	Col. 1:15	God

Fullness	is the glory of the	Head
Every man, the church	John 17:9–10; 1 Cor. 11:7; 2 Cor. 3:17–18	Christ
Woman	1 Cor. 11:7	Man
Christ	John 1:14; Heb. 1:3	God

Fullness	is the completion of the	Head
Every man, the church	1 John 2:5–6, 4:12, 16–17	Christ
Woman	1 Cor. 11:9; Gen. 2:18, 1:27, 31	Man
Christ	Matt. 5:17–18; Eph. 3:10–11; Acts 3:18; John 1:29, 41, 45, 17:4	God

Table 2

From

Do man, woman, and Christ grow from their respective heads? This growth aspect, of the fullness from the head, is emphasized in this passage. The word *growth* is not used, but where people "come from" is mentioned five times.[52] "A man ought not to cover his head, since he is the image and glory of God; but the woman is the glory of man. For man did not ***come from*** woman, but woman ***from*** man."[53]

Isn't this similar to "grows from"?[54] Isn't "Now I want you to realize that the head of every man is Christ, . . . and the head of Christ is God"[55] parallel to "and you are of Christ, and Christ is of God"?[56]

In fact "growth from" or "coming from" is why woman is the glory of man, the visible manifestation of fullness.[57] Why did Adam say that Eve was "bone of my bones and flesh of my flesh"? Because she came from man, "she shall be called 'woman.' for she was taken out of man."[58] The result of this coming from man was not authority over the woman, but rather becoming "one flesh" with the woman.[59]

Paul tells us that the new self is "renewed in knowledge in the image of its creator."[60] Not only is the new believer recreated in God's image, but the logical reason for this is that God in Jesus Christ created the "new self." The new self comes from Christ himself, so of course it will be in the image of Christ, his fullness.[61]

> For in Christ all the fullness of the Deity lives in bodily form, and ***you have been given fullness in Christ***, . . . ***In him*** you were also circumcised, in the putting off of the sinful nature, not with a circumcision done by hands of men but with the circumcision ***done by Christ***, having been buried ***with him*** in baptism and raised ***with him*** . . . ***God made you alive with Christ***. . . . the Head, ***from whom the whole body*** . . . ***grows*** as God causes it to grow.[62]

Compare this with Matthew 10:40: "He who receives you receives me, and he who receives me receives the one who sent me." The sending one is the head, the sent one is the fullness, the visible reflection of the sending one. Jesus relates the ideas of "comes from" and "sent from" when he said, "If God were your Father, you would love me, for I ***came from*** God and now am here. I have not come on my own; but ***he sent me.***"[63] Later Jesus prays to his Father, "As you sent me into the world, I have sent them into the world."[64] No Scripture passage speaks more eloquently than John 17 of the fact that Jesus was sent from God, is the visible glory of God, and is God[65] and that the church is sent from Jesus, is the visible glory of Jesus, and is Jesus.[66]

Fullness: John 17:11, 21, 26
Glory: John 17:4–5, 22
Grows, comes, is sent from: John 17:18

These concepts are integrated so thoroughly throughout John's writings that it is difficult to sift out specific references, but here are a few:

Fullness..................grows, comes, is sent from........................Head
John 6:57, 7:29, 8:42, 17:18, 20:21; 1 John 4:6
...............visible glory and image of..................
John 1:14, 18, 14:5–14, 17:22; 1 John 2:29, 3:1–3, 4:7–12
................is..............
John 1:1, 6:57, 17:20–23; 1 John 4:13–17, 5:20

Table 3

A Clear Summary

Our main interest in the passage of 1 Corinthians 11:3–16 at this point is what it says about the status of women in the church.

We've now learned that woman is mankind's full manifestation, the visible glory and image of man. All that mankind was meant to be was completed in the creation of woman. Woman was made for man, from man. Woman was man. They were one: the male and female of humankind.

Woman in relation to man is all of these things, just as the church in relation to Christ Jesus is all of these things, just as Christ in relation to God is all of these things. Being the fullness is no subordinate or lowly position. This is an exalted position. Mankind, created and recreated in Christ, male and female, is the fullness of Christ himself, his very presence on the earth. These parallels loudly proclaim the equality of woman with man.

This is precisely Paul's clear summary: "In the Lord, however, woman is not independent of man, nor is man independent of woman. For as woman ***came from*** man, so also man is ***born of*** woman. But everything ***comes from*** God."[67] Where everyone comes from seems to be central to Paul's message. Paul inserts these verses to be sure his readers understand his meaning. Oneness transcends individuality and excludes separation, regardless of who comes from whom.[68]

Verse 11 begins, "In the Lord, however." *In the Lord* implies that a spiritual truth that goes beyond the temporal and physical is about to be revealed, so there will be no misunderstanding. *However* implies that the equality and interdependence between man and woman spoken of here is more fundamental than the differences spoken of in the preceding verses.

Fullness from the Head

Fullness is repeatedly described as "from" the head. Fullness is never described as "over" the head. Attention to the exact words is important.

Fullness	grows from the	Head.
every man, church	Eph. 4:15–16; Col. 2:9–10	Christ
Fullness	comes from the	Head.
every man, church	Col. 3:10; 1 Cor. 11:12	Christ
Woman	1 Cor. 11:8; Gen. 2:23	Man
Christ	John 1:14, 8:42, 7:29, 6:32–33	God
Fullness	is sent from the	Head.
every man, church	John 7:29, 17:18, 20:21	Christ
Christ	Matt. 10:40; John 17:18, 20:21	God

Table 4

Head and Fullness Are One

Our study of *head* in the previous chapter showed that Christ as head of the church, his body, held all the body together and gave it oneness. This is obviously true in the relationship between Jesus and the church, because the church has so many distinct individual members, all needing to be held together as one. But I do not see this aspect of headship so clearly taught for the parallel relationships between God and Christ or between man and woman.

Likewise, I do not find the fullness of God, which is Jesus, described as the "body" of his head, even though we often refer to Jesus as the incarnation[69] of God himself because he is God made flesh.[70] The wife is only once described as the body of her husband in Scripture.[71] Perhaps this is because both Jesus and woman as fullness do not seem to have so many distinct parts either to be compared to a body or to be held together as a body must be. And even though the Trinity has three distinct persons, individual members are not tainted by sin that divides and separates. Holding together is not really necessary for the Godhead since God's oneness is a perfect reality undiminished by sin.

Yet, even though holding together is not emphasized concerning the relationship between Christ and God or between woman and man, both Christ and woman are definitely referred to as one with their respective heads, just as Jesus is one with his body, the church.

Three aspects of the meaning of head described throughout Scripture are (1) fullness, (2) growth from, and (3) held together by. All of these concepts lead us directly to the truth that the head and its fullness are one.

The Question

What does
"the head of every man is Christ,
and the head of the woman is man,
and the head of Christ is God"[72]
mean?

What do we know to be true?

- The church, woman, and Christ are the fullness of their respective heads.
  - The church:[73]
    - image and glory[74]
    - completion[75]
  - Woman:[76]
    - image and glory[77]
    - completion[78]
  - Christ:[79]
    - image and glory[80]
    - completion[81]

- The church, woman, and Christ grow, come, and are sent from their respective heads.
  - The church:[82]
    - Both man and woman come from God (growth)
      - and are not independent from each other.
      - In the Lord they are interdependent, equal, one.[83]
  - Woman[84]
  - Christ[85]

- A man ought to honor his head because he is the image and glory of God (fullness).[86]

- A woman should honor her head because she is the glory of the man (fullness).[87]
  - She comes from the man (growth).[88]
  - She was created for the man (completion).[89]

Two Signs

This phrase "sign of authority"[90] has been one of the foundation stones for the subordination of women.

But those who hold this view may fail to consider that there are two types of signs. One is exemplified by the number tattooed on the arm of a Nazi concentration camp victim. It clearly symbolized to everyone that the person was not his own but rather under the control of the one who branded him. The number showed that the bearer had no authority of his own and that all authority belonged to his Nazi jailers. The number was a sign of authority.

A very different sign is a policeman's badge. When the officer stops a lawbreaker, he must show his badge to verify that the community has authorized him to stop lawbreakers and to exercise that authority. The badge is a sign of authority.

Which type of sign is Paul referring to in 1 Corinthians 11? Complementarians believe he was referring to the first type. Of course they would say that the authority of man over woman was never meant to be as extreme as the Nazi concentration camp example. Yet they would say that a woman's head covering is a sign that the man has authority over her.

But this interpretation does not seem to align with the scriptural themes we have discussed so far, or with the teaching concerning "head," the immediate context of this verse.

Privilege and Right

Instead, the sign of authority Paul is talking about here is a sign of privilege, right, position, and status equal to that of the man.[91] The whole point of this passage is what is appropriate when men and women pray and prophesy.[92] Paul assumes that women will pray and prophesy right along with the men. This point is never questioned or even discussed. It is a given. All believers will pray and prophesy together equally.

But since the Fall, men and women have experienced the separation caused by sin. Their interdependence and oneness were ruptured by their disobedience. The curse of that separation has meant that man would rule over woman and her desire would be for her husband.[93] Consequently, equal status for woman is not generally accepted by the world. Therefore, a woman may need a sign, or badge, to demonstrate the authority, privilege, and right that God through Christ has bestowed on her.

The Greek word translated "authority"[94] in the NIV can also be translated "right" or "privilege." Just a few chapters earlier, Paul uses this word to speak of his ***rights*** as an apostle. The word translated "right" in verses 9:4, 5, and 12 is the same word that has been translated "authority" in 11:10. Perhaps it would help us understand what type of sign of authority Paul is referring to if we thought of the phrase as meaning "a sign or visible symbol of right, privilege, or even power," as the KJV translates it.

Freedom

Maybe we would understand it even better if it were translated a sign of "freedom," as translated in 1 Corinthians 8:9. This is the translation I think best fits the meaning and context of this passage. New freedom comes to all through faith. Women could now participate in worship alongside men. "In him and through faith in him ***we may approach God with freedom*** and confidence."[95]

Angels and Spies

Verse 10 also contains the most difficult phrase of the entire passage. Complementarians have been unable to find a credible interpretation of "and because of the angels." Some scholars of ancient Greek suggest that the word used for "angels" may also mean "spies."[96] Both angels and spies are agents who act on behalf of another. Both watch in secret.

When I learned that the Greek word used for "angels"[97] in this verse literally means "messengers,"[98] I began a search for times when it was translated "messenger" in the Bible.[99] I found that this same word is used in James 2:25: "In the same way, was not even Rahab the prostitute considered righteous for what she did when she gave lodging to the ***spies*** and sent them off in a different direction?" There can be no mistaking the meaning in this context. It was the Israelite spies, human beings who watched others secretly to get information to use against them, whom Rahab hid and later helped to escape.[100]

As far as I know, James 2:25 is the only instance in the Bible of this word being translated "spies." Only one time. Can we attach any significance to that?

Yes. It indicates at least one very important thing. It tells us that if someone using ancient Greek wanted to talk about human spies, people who watched others covertly, they could use this particular Greek word and others would understand the meaning.

It also enables us to reasonably explain the phrase, "and because of the spies." In fact, translating this word as "spies" was the key that unlocked the meaning of this entire passage[101] for me. It told me this passage is about freedom. If we translate 1 Corinthians 11:10 as "because of the *spies*, the woman ought to have a sign of *freedom* on her head," then the meaning of the whole passage becomes clear and resonates as the same message Paul wrote to the Galatians in Galatians 2:3–5 when he refused to allow the truth of the gospel to be blurred by requiring circumcision for the Gentiles.

The possibility that there might have been unbelievers who spied on the Christians is supported in Paul's letter to the Galatians: "This matter arose because some false brothers had infiltrated our ranks ***to spy on the freedom we have in***

Christ Jesus and to make us slaves. We did not give in to them for a moment, so that the truth of the gospel might remain with you."[102] Here again spies are being linked to the new freedom believers find in Christ. Jesus himself also had spies from the opposition watching him.[103]

Paul expands on this subject in the Galatian letter:

> It is for freedom that Christ has set us free. Stand firm, then, and do not let yourselves be burdened again by a yoke of slavery. . . .You, my brothers, were called to be free. But do not use your freedom to indulge the sinful nature; rather, serve one another in love. The entire law is summed up in a single command: "Love your neighbor as yourself."[104]

The freedom that Christ gives is not to be given away. But neither is it a weapon to "indulge the sinful nature"[105] or hurt others.

Spies and Freedom

What would these spies have to do with head coverings and headship? Women had found a new place of right, privilege, and freedom among Christians. They were considered as equals among the believers, all being "sons of God"[106] and "fellow citizens" in God's household, the church.[107] The women were now included as active participants in the worship of God, praying and prophesying along with the men.

But this freedom[108] was not to be used to hurt others or to indulge a sinful nature. The women should still show proper respect for the men in the company of believers, giving no one any reason to think they were acting improperly. If they came to worship immodestly dressed, even if the immodesty was only in the eyes of possible spies, it might give an excuse to the watching world for their unbelief. No, the new freedom we find in Christ should not be abused.

Nor should the women give away their freedom,[109] or allow it to be taken away.[110] They should exercise their new right and privilege by continuing to pray and prophesy together with the men, not giving way to anyone suggesting their equal participation was inappropriate in any way. The evidence and demonstration of this new freedom would be their modesty and respect towards the believing men, which is proper since man is woman's head, symbolized by an inoffensive covering of the head.

The Issue and the Principle

A woman's head covering was the issue Paul was addressing with the Corinthians, but the principle was about being "the Lord's freedman."[111]

"In him and through faith in him we may approach God with freedom and confidence."[112]

"Am I not free?"[113]

"For why should my freedom be judged by another's conscience?"[114]

"Be careful, however, that the exercise of your freedom does not become a stumbling block to the weak."[115]

"Though I am free and belong to no man, I make myself a slave to everyone, to win as many as possible."[116]

So . . . whatever you do, do it all for the glory of God. Do not cause anyone to stumble, whether Jews, Greeks or the church of God . . . For I am not seeking my own good but the good of many, so that they may be saved. Follow my example, as I follow the example of Christ.[117]

Issues may change, but not biblical principles.[118]

Today we face the issue of the status of women in the family and church. The principle remains the same.[119] The overarching principle of 1 Corinthians 11:3–16 is very clear. "In the Lord, however, woman is not independent of man, nor is man independent of woman. For as woman came from man, so also man is born of woman. But ***everything comes from God.***"[120]

The Question

What does "because of the angels" mean in 1 Corinthians 11:10?

What do we know to be true?

- The Greek word translated "angels" in 1 Corinthians 11:10 (NIV)
  can also be translated "spies," as it is in James 2:25 (NIV),
  where it refers to the human spies sent by Joshua to spy out the promised land.[121]

- Spies sometimes tried to infiltrate Christian groups to destroy their freedom.[122]

- In Galatians Paul teaches certain principles about our freedom in Christ:
  We should not allow it to be taken away from us.[123]
  We should not give it away.[124]
  We should not use it as an excuse to "indulge a sinful nature."[125]
  We should not use it to hurt others.[126]
  If we allow any of these things to happen,
    it would be an insult to Christ, who suffered to give us this freedom;[127]
    it would hide the truth of the gospel;[128]
    it would return us to slavery.[129]
  Our freedom should always be used to fulfill the law of servanthood:
    "Love your neighbor as yourself."[130]

The Question

What does "sign of authority" mean in 1 Corinthians 11:10?

What do we know to be true?

- Paul assumes that the women will pray and prophesy along with the men in worship.[131]

- The Greek word translated "authority" in 1 Corinthians 11:10 (NIV)
  can also be translated "right" or "privilege,"
    as in 1 Corinthians 9:4, 5, 12, 15, 18 (NIV),
  or "freedom," as in 1 Corinthians 8:9 (NIV).

Such or *Other*

In verse 16 we have a conflict between the translations. The KJV says, "But if any man seem to be contentious, we have no ***such*** custom, neither the churches of God." But the NIV says, "If anyone wants to be contentious about this, we have no ***other*** practice—nor do the churches of God."[132]

The Greek word which the KJV translates "such"[133] is always translated *such.* In no other passage is it ever translated "other." Only here in 1 Corinthians 11:16 do the NIV and NASB translate it "other." The two words really give exactly opposite meanings to the sentence.

If someone asks me, "Is Ron Stegall your husband?" I can answer, "I have no such husband." The listener will understand that Ron Stegall is definitely not my husband. But if I answer, "I have no other husband," the listener will understand that indeed Ron Stegall is my husband and that he is the only husband I have. The listener will understand exactly opposite meanings just by my changing one little word.

So is the case in 1 Corinthians 11:16. To say that Paul observes "no ***such*** custom, neither the churches of God," (KJV) indicates that Paul did not observe this head covering practice as a strict rule of worship, or even as a custom practiced for the sake of the weaker brother or the unbeliever. The churches of God had not made this a rule for their gatherings either. Instead, Paul means that if someone is unhappy about having to wear a head covering or having to enforce this custom within the circle of believers, not to worry about it, because this is not a law of Christian behavior. The head covering is simply an issue of Christian liberty.

However, if Paul is saying "we have no ***other*** practice—nor do the churches of God" (N1V), the listener understands that if some are unhappy about these directives from Paul, they should silently submit to them anyway, because this is Paul's practice as well as that of the churches of God. It's the way things should be done, the only way.

Paul's Personal Conviction

So this word is very important. It clarifies Paul's position on a woman's head covering, as well as the position of the churches of God. Since the word translated "such" in the KJV is never translated any other way in the Bible, and certainly never with such an opposite meaning as "other," I can only assume that the use of *other* is mistaken here. In fact, the NASB Bible has a footnote for the word *other* in verse 16, saying that its literal translation is really "such." Different Greek words are used for *other* throughout the New Testament that do not seem to be related to the word for *such* in any way.

Therefore, when we use *such* to express Paul's personal conviction concerning a woman's use of a head covering, we see that even though modesty and respect for one another are the fruit of a redeemed life and new freedom in Christ, the head covering, as a demonstration of that fruit, may or may not be needed. Paul presents it here simply as food for thought, perhaps a good idea, but certainly not an absolute rule of Christian behavior that must always be enforced. The churches of God had the same attitude. This puts the issue of a woman's head covering into the realm of Christian liberty, something on which believers are free to decide differently, not an issue worthy of conflict, tension, or disagreement.

The Question

Is wearing a head covering an absolute rule of worship for women?

What do we know to be true?

- The Greek word translated "other" in the NIV and NASB actually means "such."[134]

Summary

In summary, these verses in 1 Corinthians 11:3–16 are about the new freedom the believers, especially women, have in Christ. This freedom means they can openly and equally participate in the worship of God along with the men.

But the women must be careful not to abuse their new freedom with the slightest appearance of impropriety or disrespect toward the believing men. One way to do this would be by covering their heads during worship because some might view the absence of a head covering as immodest or presumptuous and arrogant. They should be willing to show this respect for the men because man is woman's head. They may also want to wear a head covering to deprive any unbelieving observer of any reason to assert that a woman's full participation was inappropriate, or to accuse them of wrongdoing.

In fact, a woman's head covering would be a visible sign to those watching that indeed women do have the recognized freedom in Christ to fully participate in worship as equals with the men. And since the equality and interdependence of men and women are really a more fundamental and significant truth than who comes from whom, because both come from God, the issue of a head covering is not something that Christians should make rules about or allow to be a reason for conflict among themselves. Rather it should be an issue of Christian liberty with each believer having the freedom to decide what is best before God and her own conscience.

Context

One way to cross-check any interpretation of a particular passage is to read it as a part of a whole. Does this interpretation of 1 Corinthians 11:3–16 fit into, or make sense with, the rest of this letter to the Corinthians?

The verses immediately preceding this verse are all about the freedom we have in Christ and how we should use it properly. In 1 Corinthians 10:23–11:2, Paul clearly tells us that our freedom is to be used but not abused. He sums up his attitude toward these issues of Christian liberty this way:

> So whether you eat or drink or whatever you do, do it all for the glory of God. Do not cause anyone to stumble, whether Jews, Greeks or the church of God—even as I try to please everybody in every way. For I am not seeking my own good but the good of many, so that they may be saved.[135]

Actually, Paul began discussing the subject of our freedom in Christ in chapter 7, verse 12 and on through chapter 11. Here Paul brings up several things about which no absolute rules can be made: to marry or not,[136] to eat food sacrificed to idols or not,[137] how Paul as an apostle should use his freedom,[138] whether head coverings should be worn in worship or not,[139] and how this freedom affects the fellowship of the Lord's Supper.[140]

Paul concludes his remarks about the Lord's Supper with this exhortation: "wait for each other."[141] I love that phrase because it seems to sum up Paul's attitude toward our new freedoms in Christ and how we as a church should deal with them. To wait for each other is certainly to treat others as we wish to be treated. From childhood on through old age, the cry, "Wait for me!" is a familiar one.

The whole of 1 Corinthians deals with the problem of divisions within the church.[142] Paul condemns these divisions brought on by immaturity in the faith,[143] sectarianism,[144] immorality,[145] selfish pride that produces quarrelling,[146] and the issues of Christian liberty.[147] Paul deals directly with these church division problems in the first eleven chapters of this letter.

Beginning with chapter 12, Paul enunciates the truths concerning Christ's church, his body, which are foundational to the healing of these divisions: the spiritual gifts to the church;[148] the organic oneness of the church that is one body yet many members;[149] the law of servanthood as epitomized in the action of love;[150] the gospel center, or fulcrum, which is found in the reality of resurrection;[151] and loving fellowship.[152]

Oneness through Servanthood

1 Corinthians is about the oneness of the church lived out day to day in real life through servanthood. Paul teaches that this oneness must be demonstrated over differences of personalities, of gifts, of conscience, of maturity in the faith. These differences must be overcome through fleeing the sinful old life, through the use of spiritual gifts, through humility and love, and above all, through faith in the gospel of Jesus Christ, which assures us of victory.[153] All this is so that our witness to the world will be not one of words only. "For the kingdom of God is not a matter of talk but of power."[154]

The Question

Does interpreting 1 Corinthians 11:3–16 as
upholding women's equal status with men in the church,
fit into its context?

What do we know to be true?

- Immediately preceding these verses, Paul speaks about the believer's attitude toward issues of Christian liberty and conscience.[155]

- In the chapters preceding this passage, Paul speaks of the many specific issues of freedom and Christian liberty that were causing division within the Corinthian church.

    These issues were as follows:

    To marry or not[156]
    To eat food sacrificed to idols or not[157]
    Paul's personal use of freedom[158]
    To wear head coverings in worship or not[159]
    How our freedom affects the Lord's Supper[160]

- Paul sees these issues of Christian liberty as one of the problems causing the many divisions in the Corinthian church in chapters 1–11 of his first letter to the Corinthians.

    These divisions were the result of the following:

    Immaturity in the faith[161]
    Sectarianism[162]
    Immorality[163]
    Selfish pride that produced quarreling[164]
    Issues of Christian liberty[165]

- In the last part of this letter, chapters 12–16,

    Paul teaches the Corinthians how these divisions within the church can be healed through the following:

    Spiritual gifts[166]
    The oneness of the body[167]
    Servanthood[168]
    Worship[169]
    Faith in the gospel[170]
    Fellowship and servanthood[171]

- Divisions within the church and how they can be healed is the theme of 1 Corinthians.[172]

My grandmother Greeta and mother Winifred~1927.

Chapter 7

The Head of the Body: Ephesians 5:22–33

Even though Ephesians 5 is used as one of the chief supports for the position that women should be under the authority of men, I believe it is this passage that has elevated the women of the church to the position in which they find themselves today. Slowly but surely, the beauty of these familiar verses has brought the equality of women with men into sharper focus.

Nowhere do women receive greater everyday respect and honor from men than in the Christian church. I believe this. I observe this. I live this.

We may talk about Christ's authority over the church, but when we look at Jesus, we see just what Paul saw—his love, sacrifice, and servanthood. The inescapable clarity of Christ's example has led Christian men into conformity with his image. Not seeing many examples of Christ exercising his authority over the church, men have not made that an important part of their behavior, even though they may be intellectually committed to a husband's authority over his wife. Instead, Christ living in them has led them to respect their wives as fellow heirs. Christ in them has molded their behavior with attitudes of humility, gentleness, and love.

As the woman's offspring crushes the serpent's head, the curse is lifted.[1] I praise God for his word.

A Life Worthy of the Calling

Since the whole book of Ephesians flows together as one message, it is difficult to know just where Paul takes up the subject we focus on in chapter 5:22–33. But at the beginning of chapter 4, Paul introduces the specific issue of how to live the Christian life. His subject is this: since we are one with Christ, how can we make that a greater reality in our daily lives?

Having just finished a prayer requesting God to fill the Ephesian believers with all his fullness, Paul begins, "As a prisoner for the Lord, then, I urge you to live a life worthy of the calling you have received."[2] Then Paul goes on to describe "a life worthy of the calling."

"Be imitators of God, therefore, as dearly loved children and ***live a life of love***, just as Christ loved us and gave himself up for us as a fragrant offering and sacrifice to God."[3] This restatement of the servanthood principle is addressed to all believers.

What is love? The Scriptures answer:

> This is how we know what love is: Jesus Christ laid down his life for us. And we ought to lay down our lives for our brothers.[4]
>
> This is love: not that we loved God, but that he loved us and sent his Son as an atoning sacrifice for our sins. Dear friends, since God so loved us, we also ought to love one another. No one has ever seen God; but if we love one another, God lives in us and his love is made complete in us.[5]
>
> God is love.[6]
>
> Love is patient, love is kind. It does not envy, it does not boast, it is not proud. It is not rude, it is not self-seeking, it is not easily angered, it keeps no record of wrongs. Love does not delight in evil but rejoices with the truth. It always protects, always trusts, always hopes, always perseveres. Love never fails. . . . And now these three remain: faith, hope and love. But the greatest of these is love.[7]

After we are told to love, we find another restatement of the servanthood principle, "***Submit to one another*** out of reverence for Christ."[8] Once again, we are to exercise servanthood through submission out of respect for the servanthood that Christ exercised on our behalf. We should submit because Christ submitted.

The meaning of both *love* and *submission* is "dying to self and living to God."

> ***Your attitude should be the same as that of Christ Jesus: Who***, being in very nature God, did not consider equality with God something to be grasped, but ***made himself nothing***, taking the very nature of a servant, . . . he humbled himself and became obedient to death—even death on a cross![9]

This is how Christ loved us. He "gave himself up . . . to God."[10] This is how we are to submit to him. We "offer *our* bodies as living sacrifices . . . to God."[11] Jesus did it. We must do it because he did it.

Submit and Love

This confirmation of the servanthood principle as the path for all Christians is Paul's introduction to his directives to husbands and wives. "Wives, submit to your husbands."[12] "Husbands, love your wives."[13]

Are these two commands meant exclusively for those addressed? Are only wives to submit? Are only husbands to love? Can we assume wives are not to love and husbands are not to submit? No. Paul has already made it clear that all believers are to both love and submit to one another.[14]

Because of Christ

Why are believers, specifically husbands and wives, to love and submit? Let's go over it again—because Paul goes over it again. Wives are to submit to their husbands because "the husband is the head of the wife as Christ is the head of the church, his body."[15] The truths we found in our study of *head* can now be applied to this passage.

1. The church, Christ's body, is the "fullness" of Christ, the head. The church radiates forth Christ's glory, his image.
2. The church, Christ's body, grows from Christ, the head.
3. The head, Christ, holds all the body, the church, together as one.

These things are beginning to seem obvious now. Taken together, the transcending theme of oneness emerges. These verses confirm that the head/fullness relationship is oneness.

Here Paul completely intermingles and parallels a discussion of these two head and fullness/body relationships: Christ as head of the church, his body, and a husband as head of the wife. The second mirrors the first.

Wives are to submit for the same reason that all believers are told to submit, "out of reverence for Christ."[16] ". . . and the wife must respect her husband."[17] Since Jesus is our savior, we naturally want to display great gratitude and reverence toward him by acting like he acted. Wives are not told to submit because they are under the authority of their husbands, but because they love the Lord. Self-denial is our worship response to Christ's self-sacrifice on our behalf.[18] He submitted[19] so all believers should submit to each other,[20] and wives should submit to their husbands.[21]

Husbands are to love because Christ loved the church. It is for this same reason we are all commanded to love in imitation of God.[22] Jesus loved us,[23] so we are to love each other,[24] and so husbands are to love their wives.[25]

Giving Everything

How are wives and husbands to fulfill these commands?

"Wives, submit to your husbands . . . as the church submits to Christ, so also wives should submit to their husbands ***in everything***."[26] We aren't to submit just when we feel like it, or when it is convenient. Submission is complete, not halfhearted. It is not giving your fair share. It is giving your all. Submission must be "in everything."[27]

"Husbands, love your wives, just as Christ loved the church and gave himself up for her."[28] This does not mean authority. Neither does it mean leadership, nor even administration. This means death!

Loving as Christ loved means giving your all, all you are and all you have. It means giving until there is nothing more left to give, because you have given your very life. Love means giving up your superior position of strength and power.[29] This is how Jesus loved. This is how husbands are to love.

Wives are to submit and husbands are to love. But also wives are to love and husbands are to submit. Both love and submission mean giving ourselves up for another,[30] considering others as better than ourselves[31] and their good above our own,[32] honoring others above ourselves,[33] treating others as we wish to be treated,[34] loving others as we love ourselves.[35]

One Flesh

This complete giving and reciprocity leads Paul to the central truth of the head and fullness/body relationship. "'. . . and the two will become one flesh.' This is a profound mystery—but I am talking about Christ and the church."[36] The oneness of Adam and Eve was the focal point of their relationship at creation. This is the point Moses chose to comment on,[37] the point Jesus chose to comment on,[38] the point Paul has here chosen to emphasize as the essence of the relationship between the head and his body in marriage and the head and his body in the church. The simile of metaphors points to oneness.[39] It is a mystery, something we can see only by God's revelation, but nevertheless real and true.

> For the husband is the head of the wife as ***Christ*** is the head of the church, ***his body***, . . . In this same way, ***husbands*** ought to love their wives as ***their own bodies. He who loves his wife loves himself.*** After all, no one ever hated ***his own body,*** but he feeds and cares for it, just as Christ does the church—for ***we are members of his body.*** "For this reason a man will leave his father and mother and be united to his wife and the two will become ***one flesh.***" This is a profound mystery—but I am talking about Christ and the church. However, each one of you also must ***love his wife as he loves himself*** . . .[40]

One Body

Marriage pictures a far deeper eternal truth for the world, the oneness of the church. Just

as a man and his body are one,[41] so is Christ and his body.[42] The phrase, "He who loves his wife loves himself," is not talked about much in this passage. Yet to me it is very telling. A man should love his wife because his wife is him. The woman is man. They are one.

And if Paul is building a parallelism here between Christ and the church and husbands and wives, then this adds evidence to what we have already found. The church is then Christ himself, in the sense that the church is the dwelling place of God.[43] Jesus is the life of the church.[44] If we consider the reference to God being the head of Christ in 1 Corinthians 11:3, we conclude that Christ is God himself! All three of these concepts are supported throughout the rest of Scripture. All this is but one more confirmation of the oneness of Christ and the church, man and woman, and God and Christ.

1 Corinthians 11:3–16 points the word *head* to where the fullness comes from. Ephesians 5:22–33 points the word *head* toward oneness. This takes us right back to creation and the creation norm.[45] "The man said, 'This is now bone of my bones and flesh of my flesh: she shall be called "woman" ***for she was taken out of man.' For this reason*** a man will leave his father and mother and be united to his wife, and ***they will become one flesh.***"[46] Paul says it again here in Ephesians, ". . . just as Christ does the church—***for we are members of his body. 'For this reason . . . the two will become one*** flesh.' . . . ***I am talking about Christ and the church.***"[47]

Christ and the Church

Since Paul's foundational message is about Christ and the church, this helps us understand

what Paul says about Christ giving himself up for the church: ". . . to make her holy, cleansing her by the washing with water through the word, and to present her to himself as a radiant church, without stain or wrinkle or any blemish, but holy and blameless."[48]

A human husband cannot atone for his wife's sin or purify her by giving himself up for her. Other clear scriptures teach that Jesus alone, because of his perfect life without any blemish, can redeem sinners through his own death and resurrection.[49]

But here we again see the idea of glory, the visible manifestation of fullness. Christ atoned for the sin of the church and purified it so the church could be his glory, radiating forth his fullness, the essence of his own being. Jesus, the second Adam, is creating a bride from himself,[50] suitable for himself.[51]

Husbands cannot atone for and purify their wives, but they can give themselves up for their wives and care for them, just as they care for themselves, so their oneness will radiate the completion of humankind, the essence of what "man" was created to be. As husbands and wives, indeed all believers, love and submit to one another, they radiate the true expression of the "new creation," the "one new man,"[52] oneness through servanthood.

If a spouse can act as a catalyst for sanctification, that responsibility is not based on gender, but on the spouse's relationship to Christ, whose grace it is that really sanctifies.[53] In Christian marriage, both husband and wife must promote godliness in themselves and each other.[54]

Oneness through Servanthood

What a beautiful and joyful discovery our study of *head* has revealed! Through this Ephesians passage, we see that the clear teachings of oneness and servanthood go hand in hand. Servanthood is the vehicle through which oneness is expressed.

Once discovered, this wonderful truth began jumping out at me from many pages of Scripture, beginning with Paul's introduction to this very passage,

> Live a life worthy of the calling you have received. Be completely humble and gentle: be patient, bearing with one another in love. Make every effort to keep the unity of the Spirit through the bond of peace. There is one body and one Spirit—just as you were called to one hope when you were called—one Lord, one faith, one baptism: one God and Father of all, who is over all and through all and in all.[55]

	Oneness
Christ and the Church	Husband and Wife
"his body" (Eph. 5:30)	"their own bodies" (Eph. 5:28)
"a dwelling in which God lives by his Spirit" (Eph. 2:22)	"himself" (Eph. 5:28, 33))
"one body" (Eph. 2:15–16, 4:4)	"one flesh" (Eph. 5:31; Gen. 2:24; Matt. 19:4–6)
"for we are members of his body." (Eph. 5:30–31)	"for she was taken out of man." Gen. 2:23–24)
	Through Servanthood
The Head	The Fullness/Body
Christ	The Church
love (Eph. 5:2, 25)	submit (Eph. 5:21, 24)
"gave himself up" (Eph. 5:2, 25)	deny ourselves (Mark 8:34)
"carrying his own cross" (John 19:17)	carry our cross (Luke 14:27)
"fragrant offering and sacrifice" (Eph. 5:2)	"living sacrifices" (Rom. 12:1)
"to God." (Eph. 5:2)	"to God." (Rom. 12:1)
The Husband	The Wife
love (Eph. 5:25, 33)	submit (Eph. 5:22, 33)
"just as Christ" (Eph. 5:25)	"as the church" (Eph. 5:24)

Table 5

Marriage Is a Witness

In marriage the first "man" became one flesh, imaging our creator, the One Triune God.[56] But that first man fell into sin. Oneness disintegrated into separation, and self-interest replaced servanthood, the modus operandi for oneness. In the church the "one new man" is one body, redeeming and fulfilling the creation ordinance that "the two will become one flesh."[57]

If Jesus Christ is the second Adam,[58] then the church is the second Eve. The first Adam was of the flesh, but the second Adam of the Spirit.[59] The bride of Christ is his body, the church.[60] The church is one with all its different members and with Christ himself.[61]

Marriage then stands as a witness both backwards to creation, telling the world about its creator as it reflects the creator's nature, and forward as it shadows the marriage of the lamb and his bride[62] made perfect in the new heavens and the new earth. "No longer will there be any curse."[63]

The sanctity of marriage as an institution, then, is very important. Marriage reveals a mystery to the world,[64] at least in part. Christian marriage must mirror both the oneness of our triune God-Creator and the oneness of Christ and his church. Therefore, nothing should be allowed to taint Christian marriage, blurring or marring the clarity of this picture.

This revelation of oneness is so important that God has devoted one entire book of the Bible to it, the exotically, erotically, yet mysteriously beautiful Song of Songs.[65]

There is complete reciprocity: "How handsome you are, my lover! Oh, how charming!

And our bed is verdant."[66] "All beautiful you are, my darling; there is no flaw in you."[67]

Complete love: "His banner over me is love."[68] "I found the one my heart loves."[69]

Complete submission: "My lover is mine and I am his."[70]

Complete perfection: "I belong to my lover, and his desire is for me."[71]

> For love is as strong as death. Its jealousy unyielding as the grave. It burns like blazing fire, like a mighty flame. Many waters cannot quench love: rivers cannot wash it away. If one were to give all the wealth of his house for love, it would be utterly scorned.[72]

Summary

In summary, the central message of Ephesians 4 and 5 is the eternal truth of the oneness of Christ and his church through servanthood.

The verses of Ephesians 5:22–33 are just one example of how this oneness is to be lived out and made visible. Marriage is the temporal union of male and female into one flesh that pictures the broader eternal truth of the union of Christ and his church into one body. This oneness is realized through the love and submission of servanthood.

These verses are indeed beautiful. Here the believer is raised to the lofty heights of being one with Jesus Christ and all other believers in one body. Here we learn that the institution of marriage has been endowed with the privilege of picturing this oneness. Through it all the beauty of servanthood shines as men and women renewed in the likeness of their creator[73] become like Jesus and "live a life of love."[74]

The Question

What does Ephesians 5:22–33 mean?

What do we know to be true?

- What Paul is foundationally talking about in these verses is the oneness of Christ and his church.[75]

- This oneness is to be realized and demonstrated through servanthood.[76]
  - One body, the church:[77]
    - All believers are to love.[78]
    - Love is complete, even to the giving of one's life,[79]
      - because Christ loved by giving his life.[80]
    - All believers are to submit.[81]
    - Submission is complete, in everything,[82]
      - because the church submits in everything.[83]
  - One flesh, marriage:
    - Husbands are to love,[84]
      - like Christ,[85]
      - giving themselves completely.[86]
    - Wives are to submit,[87]
      - like the church,[88]
      - in everything.[89]

Context

Now we must check this interpretation against our most basic hermeneutic rule. Does it fit the context of Paul's overall message to the Ephesian church?

Does it fit? That seems like the wrong question. It doesn't just fit. The message of these few verses addressed to husbands and wives ***is*** the message of the entire letter. We've heard it from 5:22–33; now let's hear it from the letter as a whole.

The message of Ephesians is the oneness of the church. 1 Corinthians was about the oneness of the church as opposed to divisions caused by disagreements. Ephesians is about the oneness of the church, meaning that everyone who believes is a part of that oneness; all belong on equal footing with all others.

This oneness is a mystery. The Gentiles can be absolutely sure of the truth that they are included in the gospel. But more than that, they are also included in the church with all other believers.

This theme is introduced in the first chapter.

> And he made known to us the mystery of his will according to his good pleasure, which he purposed in Christ, to be put into effect when the times will have reached their fulfillment—to bring all things in heaven and on earth together under one head, even Christ. . . . ***And you also were included in Christ.***[90]

In the second chapter Paul explains this mystery in greater detail, reviewing the separation from God the Gentiles had experienced before Christ came, and now their inclusion in the gospel and in the church with the Jews. "But now in Christ Jesus ***you who once were far away have been brought near*** through the blood of Christ."[91] "***His purpose was to create in himself one new man*** out of the two, thus making peace, and in this ***one body*** to reconcile both of them to God through the cross, by which he put to death their hostility."[92]

What is this "one new man" like?

> Consequently, you are no longer foreigners and aliens, but ***fellow citizens with God's people*** and ***members of God's household***, built on the foundation of the apostles and prophets, with Christ Jesus himself as the chief cornerstone. In him the whole building is joined together and rises to become a holy temple in the Lord. And ***in him you too are being built together to become a dwelling in which God lives*** by his Spirit.[93]

The mystery is most clearly defined in the third chapter: "This mystery is that through the gospel the Gentiles are heirs together with Israel, members together of one body, and sharers together in the promise in Christ Jesus."[94] The mystery is that all believers, the "one new man,"[95] share membership in the church in the same way they all share together in the gospel.

The theme of the first half of this letter is oneness. The message of the second half is servanthood, dying to self and living to God. The central theme of the whole letter is oneness realized through servanthood. Our calling is to "one body." "A life worthy of the calling" is servanthood. Because we have "one God and Father of all, who is over all and through all and in all."[96]

Specific examples of oneness through servanthood are addressed to husbands and wives, children and parents, slaves and masters. Servanthood is enjoined to all six. The conclusion of these examples is a reminder of God's attitude of no difference. "And masters, treat your slaves in the same way. Do not threaten them, since you know that he who is both their Master and yours is
in heaven, and there is no favoritism with him."[97]

The Mystery of the Gospel

Paul's final words are a call to arms. "Finally, be strong in the Lord and in his mighty power."[98] Paul wants us to be ready to withstand all evil assaults. He closes his letter by requesting that the Ephesians pray for him, that he also will be strong to "fearlessly make known the mystery of the gospel, . . . that I may declare it fearlessly, as I should."[99]

This is the mystery that Paul needs the courage to preach: that all believers are members together in the church, Christ's body, in exactly the same way we all share together in the promise of the gospel.[100]

The mystery is oneness. The demonstration of the mystery is servanthood. "Live a life of love . . . Submit to one another."[101] Thus we express the fullness of Christ, making plain "the unsearchable riches of Christ" to everyone, even "rulers and authorities in the heavenly realms."[102]

> For this reason I kneel before the Father, from whom his whole family in heaven and on earth derives its name. I pray that out of his glorious riches he may strengthen you with power through his Spirit in your inner being, so that Christ may dwell in your hearts through faith. And I pray that you, being rooted and established in love, may have power, together with all the saints, to grasp how wide and long and high and deep is the love of Christ, and to know this love that surpasses knowledge—***that you may be filled to the measure of all the fullness of God.***[103]

"Everything exposed by the light becomes visible."[104]

Ephesians 5:13

The Question

Does interpreting Ephesians 5:22–33
as using the husband/wife relationship
to illustrate the greater truth of the oneness of Christ and his church through servanthood fit into the context of the rest of Paul's letter to the Ephesians?

What do we know to be true?

- This is the calling we have received[105]
  to participate in the mystery of the gospel.[106]
  The mystery of the gospel is
  that the Gentiles,[107]
  indeed all believers, those faithful in Christ Jesus,[108]
  are included in the gospel[109]
  and in the church[110]
  on equal footing[111]
  with all other believers[112]
  because the church is one[113] and
  because God is one.[114]

- This is a life worthy of the calling:[115]
  to demonstrate the oneness of the church through servanthood[116]
  by acting in love and submission toward one another[117] and
  by living in unity as one.[118]

- We are to be like this because
  this is what God is like.[119]
  We are to be like him[120]
  because Christ is our head[121] and
  we are his fullness.[122]

- All this is different from the old life of the past.[123]
  It is completely new.[124]

•

We are called by one God
from the old life to the new,
redeemed by our head, Jesus,
becoming his fullness, one body,
in the church as in the gospel,
through servanthood,
like God himself.

My sisters Esther, Nancy, and Margaret Ann and me~1951.

Chapter 8

The Head of the Body: Oneness through Servanthood

A chip off the old block!

That seems like a less than reverent way to refer to God and us, his offspring. But we all understand the meaning. We are like God because we are his children.[1]

We just can't miss the point! The similes, the parallels, and the obvious statements. Even aside from those mentioned in our study of *head,* there are still many more. The apostle John especially chose to report these in his gospel. They are spread throughout other books also, but John provides more than enough to make the point.

Jesus says that what is true of the Father is also true of himself: "I tell you the truth, the Son can do nothing by himself; he can do only what he sees his Father doing, because whatever the Father does the Son also does."[2] That's just one example. Thus "the head of Christ is God."[3] And "I and the Father are one."[4]

In addition Jesus says that the believers are to be like him: "I tell you the truth, anyone who has faith in me will do what I have been doing."[5] Thus "the head of every man is Christ,"[6] and "you are all one in Christ Jesus."[7]

Hidden with Christ in God

Jesus also tells us that we, the believers, are to be like him because he is like the Father.

> As the Father has loved me, so have I loved you. Now remain in my love. If you obey my commands, you will remain in my love, just as I have obeyed my Father's commands and remain in his love. I have told you this so that my joy may be in you and that your joy may be complete. My command is this: Love each other as I have loved you.[8]

It is Jesus who is both a member of the Godhead and a member of the church. Jesus is both God[9] and human[10]—and the link between. Just as he said, "I am the way and the truth and the life. No one comes to the Father except through me."[11] Jesus is the "new and living way."[12] "For there is one God and one mediator between God and men, the man Christ Jesus, who gave himself as a ransom for all men."[13]

"Your life is now hidden with Christ in God."[14]

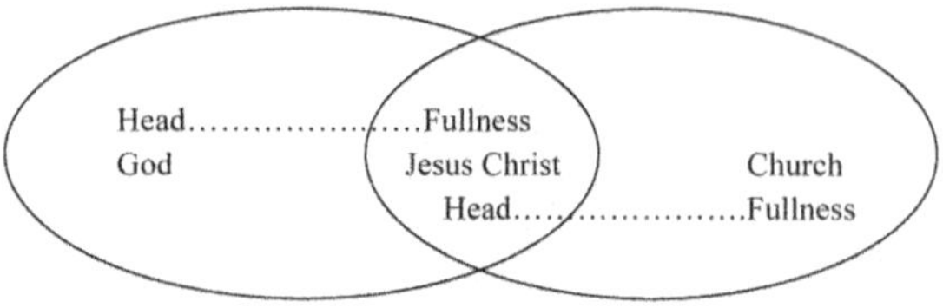

Figure 1

All of these statements culminate in the great truth Jesus revealed in his prayer for us:

> . . . that all of them ***may be one***, Father, ***just as you are in me and I am in you. May they also be in us*** so that the world may believe that you have sent me. I have given them the glory that you gave me, ***that they may be one as we are one***: ***I in them and you in me***. May they be brought to complete unity to let the world know that you sent me and have loved them even as you have loved me.
>
> Father, I want those you have given me to be with me where I am and to see my glory, the glory you have given me because you loved me before the creation of the world. Righteous Father, though the world does not know you, I know you, and they know that you have sent me. I have made you known to them, and will continue to make you known in order that the love you have for me may be in them and that I myself may be in them.[15]

"The head of every man is Christ, and the head of the woman is man, and the head of Christ is God."[16] It means oneness. The fullness and the head are one. Oneness is the essence of who God is and who we, his creation, are.

God is one God. "Hear, O Israel: The Lord our God, the Lord is one."[17] The body is one body. "The body is a unit, though it is made up of many parts; and though all its parts are many, they form one body."[18]

Man is one man. "He who created them from the beginning made them male and female. and said, 'For this cause a man shall leave his father and mother, and shall cleave to his wife: and the two shall become one flesh.' Consequently they are no longer two, but one flesh."[19]

Jesus said, ". . . that they may be one as we are one."[20] We are one because he is one. "There shall be one flock and one shepherd."[21]

One God

In order to understand our oneness together as members of a body or as man and woman, we must first understand the oneness of God.

In Scripture we are told about three persons who are God. Yet there are not three gods. There is only one God. So we have come to call these three persons members of the Godhead, the Father, the Son, and the Holy Spirit. Each is spoken of in Scripture as somewhat different from the others, different names with somewhat different tasks, functions, or work.

Let's take a closer look at the Trinity from this economic point of view. Each person of the Godhead works in a specific way, carrying out specific tasks. The Father has formulated the plan for our redemption. Jesus Christ is the instrument to accomplish the Father's plan. The Holy Spirit makes the work of Christ real in the human heart.

Yet in all this, we must remember that there is but one God.

This oneness seems beyond our understanding, especially when we see these differences. Complementarians may use these differences within the Trinity to support their position. They may assume that because there are differences, there must also be a hierarchy of authority. They say that the Father is the ultimate authority and that the Son and the Spirit are subordinate to the Father.

This is a very complex issue and one for which there are no easy proof texts. Yet I do not believe that this is what orthodox Christianity has believed through the centuries about the nature of God.

God is one. If the Father is in authority and the Son and Spirit are subordinate, then how can we be talking of just one God. Instead, we begin to think of three Gods. How can Jesus be subordinate to the Father when he himself is God? How can they be equal in power if the Father is in authority over the other two? We begin to see God in our image, rather than ourselves in God's image. In our efforts to make the Trinity more understandable, we tend to think three become one through authority. This is our human mentality of separation, individualism, and authority rather than his divine mentality of oneness through servanthood.

But this is natural for man in his fallen state. Our minds are darkened. We are blind. There is something here that we cannot fully grasp. Only through faith can we begin to perceive the truth.[22] God is one God in three persons.

Unity in Trinity

The relationship between Christ and God is one of the first questions, perhaps ***the*** question, with which the early church wrestled. The mystery of the Trinity was not immediately apparent to the early church leaders. And what they accepted by faith had to be enunciated and clearly set forth in writing so there would be unity in church belief and teaching. Many varying ideas and heresies were proposed. But with the consideration of each idea, the church clarified its definition of exactly what the nature of God is, what the Trinity is.

These controversies over the nature of God as he is revealed in the Trinity through Scripture finally came to an end with the formulation of the Athanasian Creed in about AD 450.[23] The statements of this creed have since represented the belief of orthodox Christianity to this day. Even though the Reformation, a thousand years later, uprooted and reformed many unbiblical doctrines within the church, the doctrine of the Trinity remained the same.

The Athanasian Creed says in part,

> So likewise the Father is almighty:[24] The Son almighty: and the Holy Ghost almighty.
>
> And yet there are not three almighties: but one almighty.
>
> So the Father is God: the Son is God: and the Holy Ghost is God.
>
> And yet there are not three Gods; but one God.
>
> So the Father is Lord: the Son Lord: and the Holy Ghost Lord.
>
> And yet not three Lords; but one Lord.
>
> For like as we are compelled by the Christian verity to acknowledge every Person by himself to be God and Lord:
>
> So are we forbidden by the catholic religion to say, there are three Gods, or three Lords.
>
> . . . In this Trinity none is before or after another: none is greater or less than another. But the whole three Persons are co-eternal together, and co-equal.
>
> So that in all things, as aforesaid, the Unity in Trinity, and the Trinity in Unity is to be worshipped."[25]

The reformational creeds, confessions, and catechisms all reiterate the doctrine of the Trinity as set out in the Athanasian Creed and sum up the above ideas by saying that the three persons of the Godhead are equal in power.

This word *power* does not just mean ability, but also authority to carry out that ability, the authority to get it done. This is how the word *power* was used when the Athanasian Creed was formulated, when the reformational catechisms were written, and how we use it today. The dictionary on my computer has as its definition of *power*: "possession of control, authority, or influence over others."[26] Of course God's power ultimately includes all definitions of power.

All three persons of the Godhead are omnipotent. Yet, there is only one omnipotent, all-powerful God. The Father is God. The Son is God. The Spirit is God. There is one God and all three persons of the Godhead are equal in power.

These reformational creeds, confessions, and catechisms guide and articulate our own belief. This is the catechism I studied as a child:

Question:	Are there more Gods than one?
Answer:	There is but one only, the living and true God.
Question:	How many persons are there in the Godhead?
Answer:	There be three persons in the Godhead, the Father, the Son, and the Holy Ghost: and these are one true, eternal God, the same in substance, equal in power and glory; although distinguished by their personal properties.[27]

The Incarnate Son—Trinity in Unity

One of the personal properties of the Son is that he became God incarnate. The Son became flesh, a human being. This adds another dimension to an already very complex definition of God. The Athanasian Creed goes on to say that Jesus Christ the Son is "Equal to the Father as touching His Godhead: inferior to the Father as touching His Manhood. And although He be God and Man: yet He is not two, but one Christ."[28] Of course humanity is under the authority of divinity. And even so, the Son came under the authority of the triune God by becoming human of his own free will.[29]

But the relationship between God the Father and the incarnated humanity of the Son Jesus cannot be compared to the relationship between men and women. Jesus was both God and human. Women are only human. Men are only human too. Women are not human in addition to some other species that is inferior to humans. Christ's humanity, as a part of the economic relationship within the Trinity, cannot apply to the relationship between man and woman because between man and woman there is only the ontological relationship of shared humanity.[30] It is the ontological relationship that denotes the essential being of one common divinity that yields the perfect equality that is God,[31] just as the ontological relationship of one common humanity yields perfect equality for all humankind.

This creed also reflects one aspect of our study of *head*, that Jesus came from God and was sent by God.

> The Father is made of none; neither created; nor begotten.
>
> The Son is of the Father alone: not made; nor created; but begotten.
>
> The Holy Ghost is of the Father and the Son: not made; neither created: nor begotten; but proceeding.
>
> Thus there is one Father, not three Fathers: one Son, not three Sons: one Holy Ghost, not three Holy Ghosts.
>
> And in this Trinity none is before or after another: none is greater or less than another.
>
> But the whole three Persons are co-eternal together, and co-equal.

> So that in all things, as aforesaid, the Unity in Trinity, and the Trinity in Unity is to be worshipped.[32]

We must wrestle with all of these things, difficult as they are, as we try to understand the God we serve. Yet, in the end, we come to what the theologians call the incomprehensibility of God. It is only by faith that we can know this God and accept and trust what he has revealed of himself to us.[33]

God has revealed his triune personhood in oneness, a oneness that has no hierarchy or authority. God's oneness transcends individuality and excludes separation.[34] It is a oneness demonstrated through servanthood, which is of the very nature of God. Yet, the one God I serve is omnipotent.

Trinity in Hierarchy?

But what I hear often today is that the Trinity is a hierarchy of authority with the Father at the apex.[35] It is not my intention here to write a treatise rearguing this aspect of the Trinity. The church has already done this, and it took five hundred years. I will leave that to others. But I do reject the idea that the Trinity is a hierarchy of authority. This is not what the church has believed. This is not what I have been taught. This is not the defined doctrine of orthodox Christianity.

Completely apart from the issue of the status of women, the church must either renew its commitment to belief in the Trinity as the church has defined it in the past, or we must again address the question, debate it openly, and change the creeds and confessions if need be. But no fair judgment can be made if the issue of subordination within the Trinity is dealt with at a glance, while our full attention is really with the subordination of women. We cannot allow our beliefs to be eroded through unchallenged statements of assumption just because they are confidently stated numerous times.

Subordination in Trinity?

I have been very hesitant to state my thoughts as boldly as in the preceding paragraphs. Yet I can come to no other conclusion. Subordination within the Trinity is being proclaimed as a given, a tenet of Christianity. I hope that as arguments are put forward to keep women subordinate, the great truths the Christian Church has fought so hard to make clear will not be abandoned.

Let's be careful! We dare not revert to denying Christ's equality with God as integral to a rationale that denies woman's equality with man.

The Mystery of Oneness

God is one. This is the most fundamental truth of Christianity. And after that comes Jesus Christ is God. The pronoun for God is *he*, not *they*. And the *he* refers to the triune God, not God the Father only or alone. It is the same mentality of separation that has led us to understand *male* when the Bible says "man" and that also leads us to think "Father" when the Bible says "God."

As an example, let's look at Ephesians 1:3–14 where all three persons of the Godhead are spoken of in connection with the eternal purpose and plan of God's will. Yet the three persons of the Godhead are so intermingled that it is difficult to say exactly which person is being referred to as *he*. In verses 3–6, *he* seems to refer to the Father, who has chosen "us to be adopted as his sons." In verses 7–8, *him* seems to refer to the Son, through whose blood we have received forgiveness of sins. In verse 9, *he* seems to refer to the Spirit, who reveals to us the mysteries of the gospel.[36] Yet those are all somewhat incorrect assumptions. The mentality of oneness infers that *he* refers to God, the Triune God who is One God.

These verses in Ephesians eloquently speak of the oneness of the Trinity—each person carrying out certain functions, but at the same time, so intermingled in plan and work that it seems impossible to say one function belongs specifically to one person completely exclusive of the other two. Romans 8:30 sums up all these tasks described in Ephesians 1:3–14 as done by God.

> For those God foreknew he also predestined to be conformed to the likeness of his Son, that he might be the firstborn among many brothers. And those he predestined, he also called; those he called, he also justified; those he justified, he also glorified.[37]

God is one.

The Question

What is the nature of the relationship between the head and its fullness?

What do we know to be true?

- The head and its fullness are one.
  Christ and the church are one—one body.[38]
  Man and woman are one, one man—one flesh.[39]
  The Father and Christ are one—one God.[40]

Differences

But what about those differences? How can there be differences and oneness at the same time without authority?

The Father, Son, and Holy Spirit do not maintain their oneness through a hierarchy of authority. This is not what the church has believed the Scriptures teach us. Rather, these differences in the work of each person of the Godhead provide an opportunity for submission and love toward one another within the Trinity as there is also to be within the church.

The persons of the Godhead love and submit to each other. The persons of the Trinity love each other as they love themselves because the others are themselves. The persons of the Trinity esteem each other more highly than themselves.[41]

The Father: "The Father loves the Son and has placed everything in his hands."[42]

The Son: "But the world must learn that I love the Father and that I do exactly what my Father has commanded me."[43]

The Spirit: "But when he, the Spirit of truth comes, he will guide you into all truth. He will not speak on his own; . . . He will bring glory to me by taking from what is mine and making it known to you."[44]

We do not feel comfortable using the words *submit* and *submission* with reference to God. But when we remember the biblical usage of *submit* as voluntary, self-denying service to others, rather than obedience compelled by authority, then we realize that God is the ultimate example of that very thing. "This is how we know what love is: Jesus Christ laid down his life for us."[45] If the love and submission of servanthood are such a central characteristic of the person of Jesus Christ, then we must assume that it is central to the person of God because Jesus is God's revelation of himself to us. The Father sent Jesus to explain God to us. What Jesus is, God is. "No one has ever seen God, but God the One and Only, who is at the Father's side, has made him known."[46]

God the One and Only

The persons of the Godhead submit to each other and love each other because this is the nature of God, and consequently, the law of the kingdom of which He is the creator.[47] "God is love."[48]

Some may interpret Christ's words "not my will but yours be done"[49] to mean that Christ was against the plan for redemption, but since he was outvoted in the Godhead, he went along with it anyway. But this is not what we believe. This phrase from Jesus' prayer in Gethsemane did not show his disagreement with the plan, or even his bowing to a plan in which he had no say. Rather this prayer showed Christ's human side, that he was indeed vulnerable to the pains and sorrows of being human and that Satan's temptations for shortcut redemption were real. Yet he remained without sin.[50]

Gave Himself Up

Christ's submission was freely given and completely voluntary, not compelled through the authority of his Father. He "***gave himself*** up," "***made himself*** nothing." The plan of redemption came from his very own nature, and so he would steadfastly submit to it. This is apparent from John's account of this prayer in John 17:1–5.[51]

But does Christ also submit to the church? Remember it is Christ who is the mediator, the go-between, the way between us and God. Christ is both a member of the Godhead and a member of the church. He is God and he is human. This is the beauty of the incarnation. "The Word became flesh and made his dwelling among us. We have seen his glory, the glory of the One and Only, who came from the Father, full of grace and truth."[52]

Servanthood is the essence of the love he has for the church: he gave himself up for her. Jesus Christ submitted his life to the dictates of our needs. "The Son of Man did not come to be served, but to serve, and ***to give*** his life as a ransom ***for many***."[53]

But Christ, as he submits to the needs of the church, will never act outside of the plan of redemption, his eternal decrees and purposes, which the Triune God determined before time. This is always the case with all submission. None of us are to submit to anything that is outside of that plan. Christ will not be a puppet whose strings can be pulled by the church. Instead, he continually gives himself for our welfare, ultimately by taking a human form and dying.[54]

Christ not only gave himself in that ultimate sacrifice but in other ways too. When Christ realized his authority and power, his reaction was a very submissive one. Is washing someone's feet a submissive action or an exercise of authority?[55] Is carrying out someone's request submission or an exercise of authority?[56] Christ's service to the church is a natural result of his oneness with the Father.[57]

Differences—An Opportunity for Servanthood

The persons of the Trinity use their differences as an opportunity for servanthood. The members of the Godhead do submit to one another as they carry out their unique work, or "role," if you will. These differences within the Godhead are reflected in the gifts that have been given to individual believers to serve the whole church.[58] We have been given different personal properties,[59] which we must also deal with through servanthood,[60] like God does.[61]

But when the first man fell into sin, he lost oneness and no longer lived by servanthood. Now authority indeed seemed necessary if there was to be any sort of unity or working together. It was certainly necessary in order to get others to serve one's own needs, since self-interest was now the driving force of mankind, rather than the other-interest that God intended.

But we who believe have become the "one new man."[62] We are again motivated and compelled by servanthood, and the exercise of authority is gone with the old life.[63] Our differences are now an opportunity to "serve one another in love."[64]

Serve One Another in Love

The message of Ephesians 5:22–33 is that husbands and wives can also deal with their differences through servanthood. These verses say nothing about Christ being under the authority of God the Father, or about the wife being under the authority of the husband. Nor can authority be inferred through the metaphor of *head* or the word *submit*. Nothing is said about the task-related differences or distinctive roles in the Trinity, in the church, or in marriage. Instead, Ephesians 5 talks about the oneness of a husband and wife and of Christ and his church made visible and real through the self-giving attitudes and actions of servanthood.

The world understands authority and sameness. But the way of the kingdom of God is completely different and entirely new.[65] It is a mystery[66] to the world, understandable only through God's revelation.[67] The way of the kingdom is oneness through servanthood.

This is a life worthy of the calling we have received.[68]

The Question

How do the head and the body demonstrate their oneness?

What do we know to be true?

- God as Trinity demonstrates his oneness through the submission and love of servanthood.
  The Father[69] demonstrates oneness through servanthood.
  The Son[70] demonstrates oneness through servanthood.
  The Spirit[71] demonstrates oneness through servanthood.
  God is love.[72]

- We are to be like God.[73]

- Christ and the church demonstrate their oneness through servanthood.[74]
  Christ serves the church.[75]
  Christ submits
    his life to the church,[76]
    his power to the church,[77] and
    his oneness with the Father to the church.[78]
  Christ loves the church.[79]
  The church submits to Christ.[80]
  The church loves Christ.[81]
  The members of the church, his body, are to submit to each other.[82]
  The members of the church, his body, are to love each other.[83]

- The two different partners in marriage demonstrate their oneness through servanthood.[84]
  Wives are to submit to their husbands in everything.[85]
  Wives are to love their husbands.[86]
  Husbands are to love their wives, giving themselves up for them.[87]
  Husbands are to submit to their wives.[88]

Margaret Ann, me, Nancy, and Esther~1962.

Chapter 9

The Head over Everything: You Have Only One Master

Matthew 23:8

Perhaps you noticed!

We haven't really covered all the references to *head.* In Ephesians 1 and 4 and Colossians 1 and 2, the four passages we originally studied to determine the meaning of *head of the body, head* is also used to describe Christ's relationship to everything.[1] Is Christ's relationship with everything the same as his relationship with his body, the church? Let's go back to these four passages and see.

I believe it is important to pay attention to the little words. Sometimes they say a lot more than their size would indicate. Christ is the "head of the body"[2] and "head over everything."[3]

Did you catch it? Did you hear the two different little words? Does it make a difference?

I recently read this, "God created man to be head over the woman."[4] That's not what the Bible says. The Bible says that man is the "head of" the woman.

"Of" and "over." So what! Does it really make a difference?

Over/Under

". . . to bring ***all things*** in heaven and on earth together ***under one head***, even Christ."[5] "And God placed all things under his (Christ's) feet and appointed him to be ***head over everything***."[6]

"And you have been given fullness in Christ, who is the ***head over every*** power and authority."[7]

The phrase *head over everything* has much in common with *head of the body.* Jesus created all things.[8] Created seems similar to *grows from.* Jesus also holds all things together,[9] just as he holds every part of his body together. But Christ's body is one with him, and this is never said of "all things." Jesus "fills everything in every way,"[10] and yet everything is never referred to as the "fullness" of Jesus or as his "body."

Over Everything

However, the phrase *head over everything* seems to point most clearly to Christ's firstness. Christ is the firstborn over all creation because he created everything.[11] Christ is before all things,[12] and all things are under him.[13] Jesus is the first in time and the first in position among everything else in existence. Jesus is "head of the body, his church" because he was the first one raised from death to life.[14] In fact, Jesus Christ has the "supremacy" (NIV), the "preeminence"(KJV), "the first place in everything." (NASB)[15]

Everything means "all creation,"[16] including all rule, authority, power, dominion, title, and thrones[17] of this present age and the age to come.[18] It encompasses things that are both visible and invisible, in heaven and on earth.[19]

Everything also includes the unjust and evil powers and authorities that have tried to thwart the work of Christ throughout the ages. Even though God's good creation has been perverted by sin, Christ has disarmed even these powers and authorities and triumphed over them by the cross.[20]

Thus, *everything* includes the church, but also far more than the church, the body that Christ is "head of." As "head over everything," Jesus is first among all reality, all that exists, everywhere, at all times, in all dimensions.

Over Everything for the Church

The subtle difference between "head of the body, the church" and "head over everything" is clarified as the two ideas are brought together. "And God placed all things under his feet and appointed him to be ***head over everything for the church, which is his body***."[21] Christ is "head over" everything, good and evil. But everything is not Christ's body. Only the church is Christ's body.

Paul never confuses the two. He always uses "head of the body" to describe Christ's relationship to the church, and "head over" to describe Christ's relationship to everything. And even though the two phrases have similar aspects, they are not interchangeable.

We must remember that the *head* in the phrase *head of the body* has a body. The entire phrase is a metaphor used to describe the relationship between Christ and his church, and then further compared to a husband and wife. But "head over everything" is not a metaphor. There is no mention of a body in connection with this "head."

Under His Feet

"Everything" or "all things" are put under Christ's feet.[22] Well, what are Christ's feet?

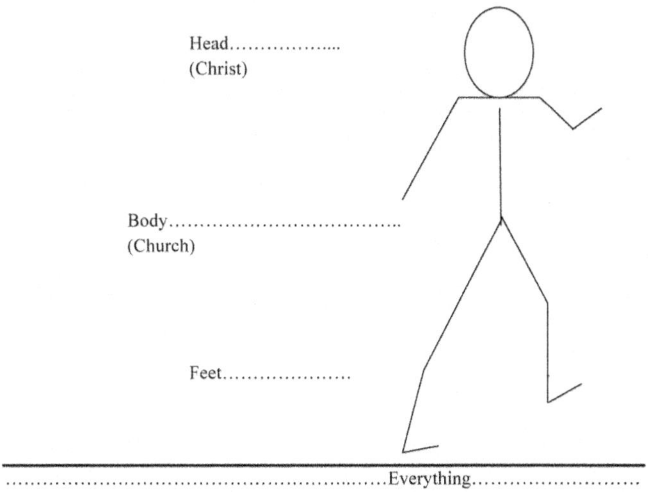

Figure 2

Christ's feet are a part of Christ's body, the members upon which Christ's body stands. So everything is not only under Christ, but under Christ's body as well. Paul says it again in a different way: Christ is "***head over everything for the church.***"[23] Paul told the Romans, "The God of peace will soon crush Satan under your feet."[24] His feet or our feet, they are all the same feet, because we are one body.

God has seated Jesus at his right hand above every rule, authority, power, and dominion.[25] And God has raised us up with Christ and seated us with him.[26]

Can this be?

Is Paul saying that we, the believers, are over everything along with Christ? It seems like too much. It seems too great, too fearfully wonderful to even consider.

With Christ

Yet Paul prays "that the eyes of your heart may be enlightened in order that you may know the hope to which he has called you, the ***riches of his glorious inheritance*** in the saints. and his incomparably ***great power for us who believe.***"[27] Paul goes on to tell us exactly what "power for us" God has. It is the same power God used to raise Jesus from the dead and to seat him at his own right hand.[28] It is "the power of an indestructible life."[29]

Indeed it is a rich and glorious inheritance. Too great for us? Not in God's eyes. Not according to his plan. But our eyes must be enlightened with God's Spirit before we can see this.[30] "Such knowledge is too wonderful for me, too lofty for me to attain."[31] But when we remember that we are now in Christ, members of his body, which is his fullness, we must believe it. It is part of our new identity. God has made us "alive with Christ."[32] This is the glorious richness of the mystery Paul proclaimed to the Gentiles: "Christ in you, the hope of glory."[33] We are one with Christ, so we sit with him in his first place over everything.

Jesus Is First

It is because Jesus is first that he sits at the right hand of the throne of God.[34] This infers a position of power over all things.

The implication of Jesus Christ being the first over all things, including "every power and authority,"[35] is that he is in control. As "head over everything," Jesus is the first and ultimate instigator, creator, source, and sustainer of everything; and consequently, he is the first and ultimate power, authority, ruler, judge and King over all things, both in heaven and on earth, "so that in everything he might have the supremacy."[36] Our God, Jesus Christ, is "the only Ruler, the King of kings and Lord of lords."[37]

And since we are one with Christ and sit with him in his first place over everything, we also rule with him.

Christ is *over* everything, along with the church, but he is *of the body*, the church. This idea is further verified when Paul speaks of the church as God's family. We have been adopted into the household of God and receive God's rich and glorious inheritance.[38] We, the church, have been made sons, heirs, and joint heirs with Christ, our brother.[39]

Rule through Reconciliation

How does Christ exercise his supremacy, his preeminence, his first place over everything?

"For God was pleased to have all his fullness dwell in him, and ***through him to reconcile to himself all things***, whether things on earth or things in heaven, by making peace through his blood, shed on the cross."[40]

Christ exercises his supremacy through reconciliation.

And when Jesus Christ comes again, he will also exercise his supremacy by judging the living and the dead with justice.[41]

Paul explains Christ's reconciling work of peacemaking on our behalf. "For he himself is our peace, who has made the two one . . . one new man out of the two, thus making peace, and in this one body to reconcile both of them to God."[42]And now the church, the *one new man*, is to join Christ in this exercise of supremacy through the work of reconciliation.[43] This was always God's plan.

> So God created man in his own image, in the image of God he created him: male and female he created them. God blessed them and said to

> them, "Be fruitful and increase in number; fill the earth and subdue it. Rule over the fish of the sea and the birds of the air and over every living creature that moves on the ground."[44]

> All this is from God, who reconciled us to himself through Christ and gave us the ministry of reconciliation: that God was reconciling the world to himself in Christ. And he has committed to us the message of reconciliation. We are therefore Christ's ambassadors, as though God were making his appeal through us. We implore you on Christ's behalf: Be reconciled to God.[45]

Christ has all authority.[46] In fact his last words on earth were on this very subject. "All authority in heaven and on earth has been given to me." The consequence of this authority is that the church, his body, must go forward ministering reconciliation until all things are reconciled to God, under his/our feet. "Therefore go and make disciples of all nations, baptizing them in the name of the Father and of the Son and of the Holy Spirit, and teaching them to obey everything I have commanded you. And surely I am with you always, to the very end of the age."[47]

Agents of Reconciliation

Christ finished his work on the cross.[48] Since then the work of reconciliation is to be done through his body, his church.[49]

We are to be the agents of Christ's rule. Just as Jesus Christ rules through reconciliation,[50] bringing everything into submission to God,[51] so it is our assigned task, as Christ's body, to carry out his supremacy and rule through reconciliation. We have been given the ministry of reconciliation.[52] We seek to reconcile all things to God through proclamation of the gospel, and by being a demonstration model of Christ's reconciling power.[53] By our oneness through servanthood,[54] we tell the world that Christ has raised us from the dead and reconciled us to God.

Why does Christ's work of reconciliation become our work? Why do we become ministers of reconciliation? Because we are one with Christ.

And when Christ comes again, we will also judge and reign with him.[55]

The Question

What does "head over everything" mean?[56]

What do we know to be true?

- Jesus Christ has the first place in everything.[57]
  He is before all things.[58]
  He is over everything.[59]

- Everything includes:
  All creation;[60]
  All rule, authority, power, dominion, every title,[61] and thrones;[62]
  Things in this present age and the age to come;[63]
  Things visible and invisible;[64]
  Things in heaven and on earth;[65] and
  Things unjust and evil.[66]

- Jesus Christ has the first place over everything because of the following:
  He is the image of the invisible God.[67]
  All things were created by him.[68]
  All things were created for him.[69]
  In him all things hold together.[70]
  He is the head of the church.[71]
  He is the beginning and firstborn
  over all creation[72]
  from among the dead.[73]

The Question

How does Christ exercise his first place over everything?

What do we know to be true?

- Christ reconciles all things to God[74]
  by making peace through his shed blood.[75]

- Christ will judge the world with justice on the day that God has set.[76]

- Through Christ's atoning sacrifice, we are reconciled to God:[77]
  Becoming one with Christ[78]
  Receiving new life[79]
  Receiving the Holy Spirit[80]
  Receiving the same power from God that Jesus has[81]
  Joining his kingdom[82]
  Joining his family[83]
  Receiving his riches[84]
  Sharing his inheritance[85]

- Since we are one with Christ, his work becomes our work.[86]
  The church rules with Christ[87]
  by proclaiming reconciliation through the gospel,[88] and
  by demonstrating reconciliation through the life of the church.[89]
  The church will judge the world with Jesus.[90]

Whatever You Do

What does Christ's first place over everything mean for the life of the church? Paul goes on to tell us exactly what it means.

> ***Since, then, you have been raised with Christ***, set your hearts on things above, where Christ is seated at the right hand of God. Set your minds on things above, not on earthly things. For ***you died, and your life is now hidden with Christ in God. When Christ, who is your life, appears, then you also will appear with him in glory.***
>
> Put to death, therefore, whatever belongs to your earthly nature: sexual immorality, impurity, lust, evil desires and greed, which is idolatry. Because of these, the wrath of God is coming. You used to walk in these ways, in the life you once lived. But now you must rid yourselves of all such things as these: anger, rage, malice, slander, and filthy language from your lips. Do not lie to each other, since you have taken off your old self with its practices and have put on the new self, which is being renewed in knowledge in the image of its Creator. Here there is no Greek or Jew, circumcised or uncircumcised, barbarian, Scythian, slave or free, but Christ is all, and is in all.
>
> Therefore, as God's chosen people, holy and dearly loved, clothe yourselves with compassion, kindness, humility, gentleness, and patience. Bear with each other and forgive whatever grievances you may have against one another. Forgive as the Lord forgave you. And over all these virtues put on love, which binds them all together in perfect unity.
>
> Let the peace of Christ rule in your hearts, since as members of one body you were called to peace. And be thankful. Let the word of Christ dwell in you richly as you teach and admonish one another with all wisdom, and as you sing psalms, hymns and spiritual songs with gratitude in your hearts to God. And whatever you do, whether in word or deed, do it all in the name of the Lord Jesus, giving thanks to God the Father through him.[91]

Paul writes this same basic message to the believers many times.[92] The themes from this passage, repeated so often throughout all of Scripture are:

1. Oneness with Christ.[93] No longer do we live our own lives, but having been brought back to life from death and reborn, we now live new lives, Christ's life.
2. Shunning the old life and all its characteristics such as immorality, selfishness, and idolatry.[94] This includes giving up old ways of relating to each other, which are mostly characterized by hatred. Among other

things, we are to put aside judgments of each other based on anything other than oneness with Christ.[95]

3. Embracing the new life, which is characterized by love.[96] New ways of relating to each other in love always include humility, self-denial, and servanthood as we minister to each other through the use of our gifts[97] and through our worship.[98] It can always be summed up by the Golden Rule and the second greatest commandment, which is repeated so many times in Scripture[99]—Love one another.

The New Life

How do these things govern the church? They do it, not through autocratic means, chains of command, or through authority flowcharts. Rather, it is done through means of the Spirit. After all, it is a new life, which works on principles quite different from the old life.[100]

First, these principles govern, or rule, through the indwelling of the Holy Spirit,[101] which makes our oneness with Christ a reality in every moment of time, in every place in space, in every spiritual or physical dimension.

Second, we are governed by these laws of the new life because they are written in our hearts and minds,[102] rather than in law books or other official documents. And all the laws are summed up in the greatest law, love God. "And whatever you do, whether in word or deed, do it all in the name of the Lord Jesus."[103]

Perfect Unity

Of course the two great commands are defined in the Holy Scriptures as they are written in the Bible. It is by this standard of the written word that we must always judge our hearts and actions, as individuals and as a church. But God's Word does not ultimately control or govern because it is written in the Bible, but because it is written in our hearts. Only insofar as it is written in our hearts will we become Christ's fullness, his body, one whole held together by Jesus through love.[104]

I have heard the argument that authority is necessary in the church because without it everything would fall apart. We couldn't function as a church without a clear chain of command. But this is not what Scripture teaches.

What holds everything together? Jesus does.[105] How does he do it? Through love.[106] Christ's love compels us.[107] Christ's peace rules us.[108] And love binds everything together in perfect unity.[109]

The Question

How does Christ exercise his first place over, or rule of, the church?

What do we know to be true?

- Christ rules the church:
  - Through our oneness with him,[110]
    - He has made us his body, his fullness.[111]
  - Through his peace[112]
  - Through his word in our hearts[113]
  - Through his Spirit[114]
  - Through each other
    - in the servanthood of love and submission,[115]
    - in the use of our gifts,[116] and
    - in worship.[117]

My daughter Christina, mother Winifred, and grandmother Greeta~1978.

Chapter 10

Brothers: You Are All Brothers

Matthew 23:8

I've never had a brother. I have three sisters, but no brothers. My sisters and I are all different, yet very much the same. People outside the family say we look alike. We don't think we do at all. We love each other deeply, yet we have a long history of disagreements.

Would we be friends if we weren't in the same family? I don't know. That's really beside the point. We are more than friends. We are sisters. An indefinable bond, not of our own making, ties us together. The bond is what we have in common, the same parents, the same home, the same experiences.

When I looked up the word *brother* in my concordance, I found that it literally means "of the same womb"[1] in the ancient Greek. That is exactly what my sisters and I are. We have shared the same womb. So, in that sense, my sisters are my brothers.

Of the Same Womb

What a beautiful definition for the word Jesus used to describe all believers. "You are all brothers."[2] Nicodemus asked Jesus if he had to enter his mother's womb a second time in order to be born again. Jesus answered, "I tell you the truth, no one can enter the kingdom of God unless he is born of water and the Spirit. Flesh gives birth to flesh, but the Spirit gives birth to spirit."[3]

All believers are of the same womb of the Spirit. We share the same parent, God, our Father.[4] We are all brothers.

As brothers we have many things in common. Remember the list of reasons that convinced the Jewish Christians to accept the Gentile Christians as brothers?

- "Christ is all, and is in all."[5]
- All are one in Christ.[6]
- God has called us all clean.[7]
- All fear God and do what is right.[8]
- All have received the Holy Spirit.[9]
- All have hearts with which they have believed.[10]
- All have mouths with which they have made confession.[11]

- All have the same Lord.[12]
- Christ has accepted all.[13]

A Collective Term of Direct Address

Peter's first words of address to the New Testament church begin with the recognition that all believers, men and women, are brothers.

> When they arrived, they went upstairs to the room where they were staying. Those present were Peter, John, James and Andrew; . . . They all joined together constantly in prayer, along with the women and Mary the mother of Jesus, . . . In those days Peter stood up among the believers (a group numbering about a hundred and twenty) and said, "Brothers, . . ."[14]

The other New Testament writers followed Jesus' example[15] and continued to use the term *brothers* to refer to all believers. The epistles were written to be read aloud to an assembly of believers. So educational level or the ability to read made no difference since each believer heard these letters in exactly the same way. Certainly these assemblies included many women. In fact, about 30 percent of those specifically mentioned or directly addressed in the New Testament epistles are women.[16]

These New Testament letter writers define what a brother is by using it as a term of address. When we see who the New Testament books are addressed to, we see who the writers include in the term *brothers.*

"To the church of God in Corinth, to those sanctified in Christ Jesus and called to be holy, together with all those everywhere who call on the name of our Lord Jesus Christ—their Lord and ours: . . . I appeal to you, brothers."[17] Paul also addresses as "brothers" those loved by Go[18] and faithful in Christ Jesus.[19]

> To God's elect, strangers in the world, scattered throughout Pontus, Galatia, Cappadocia, Asia and Bithynia, who have been chosen according to the foreknowledge of God the Father, through the sanctifying work of the Spirit, for obedience to Jesus Christ and sprinkled by his blood . . . you have sincere love for your brothers.[20]

A Common Appellation Denoting Equality

All these verses, and many more, tell us what a brother is. Even a person with some special office in the church is still a brother. "To all the saints in Christ Jesus at Philippi, together with the overseers and deacons: . . . Now I want you to know, brothers, . . ."[21]

Paul also interchanges the term *brothers* with *saints,*[22] which he defines as those "called to belong to Jesus Christ . . . who are loved by God."[23] Paul addresses the believers as saints eight times in Romans, including 16:1–2 where he relates the term directly to Phoebe.[24]

A Relationship

"You are all brothers."[25]

Jesus said that.

He said it amid his scathing critique of the Pharisees and the teachers of the law. He didn't try to be tactful or to soften the blow. He said very plainly that they stood condemned.

In spite of their super religiosity, they still didn't know God and even kept others from knowing him too.[26] They intimidated others with their show-off religion[27] and supposed knowledge of the Scriptures and the ways of God,[28] burdening them with loads no one could carry.[29]

These teachers were interested only in their own position and status.[30] Jesus affirmed the scriptural teaching that God is interested in the heart, not in outward appearances.[31] Nor was God interested in the Pharisees' legalistic maneuverings so that they could seem religious while still having their own way.[32]

According to Jesus, these teachers of the law had widely missed the mark and fallen far short of what it really meant to be a child of God. Despite appearances, these people were actually hostile to God, even seeking to overthrow God's rule.[33]

When Jesus finished his condemnation of these religious leader imposters, he wept. He wept for those he longed to love. He wanted to give them life, comfort, and freedom from such tyranny, yet they refused to come.[34]

Tucked inside this harsh condemnation of the Pharisees and teachers of the law is Jesus' message to his own, those who are willing to come to him:

> But you are not to be called "Rabbi," for you have only one Master and ***you are all brothers***. And do not call anyone on earth "father," for you have one Father, and he is in heaven. Nor are you to be called "teacher," for you have one Teacher, the Christ. The greatest among you will be your servant. For whoever exalts himself will be humbled, and whoever humbles himself will be exalted.[35]

The message to the believers is clear. Jesus does not want his disciples to be anything like those counterfeit religious leaders. Jesus wants his followers to be equal with each other before God and among each other. Only one is a father. Only one is a teacher. That one is God, the one triune God. All others in God's family are brothers, all having the same relationship with God, all having the same relationship with each other. The way to greatness in God's family is through humility and servanthood. Exaltation is God's business, no one else's.[36]

Related by Grace

Remember when Jesus was told that his mother and brothers wanted to speak to him. "He replied to him, 'Who is my mother, and who are my brothers?' Pointing to his disciples, he said, 'Here are my mother and my brothers. For whoever does the will of my Father in heaven is my brother and sister and mother."[37]

Doing the will of God through the righteousness and sanctifying grace of Christ is what makes us a brother. In addition there is one amazing and outstanding item Jesus includes in this definition of *brother*. Jesus is not just defining any brother; he is defining "***my*** brother."

Not only are all believers brothers, but they are brothers with Jesus Christ himself. No matter what our stature or position may be in the world's eyes, if we have been redeemed by Jesus, we are his brother.[38] We are brothers to the King, who is over everything!

Both of the Same Family

The writer to the Hebrews makes this all so clear.

> In bringing many sons to glory, it was fitting that God . . . should make the author of their salvation perfect through suffering. ***Both*** the one who makes men holy and those who are made holy are ***of the same family. So Jesus is not ashamed to call them brothers***. . . .
>
> Since the children have flesh and blood, he too shared in their humanity so that by his death he might destroy him who holds the power of death—that is, the devil—and free those who all their lives were held in slavery by their fear of death. . . .
>
> For this reason he had to be made ***like his brothers*** in every way, in order that he might become a merciful and faithful high priest in service to God, and that he might make atonement for the sins of the people. Because he himself suffered when he was tempted, he is able to help those who are being tempted.
>
> Therefore, ***holy brothers, who share in the heavenly calling***, fix your thoughts on Jesus, the apostle and high priest whom we confess.[39]

Once again God reveals the awesome splendor of our oneness with Christ. He is our brother.

All Brothers

The common things all these brothers share fall into three main categories:

All stand before God clothed in Christ's righteousness.[40]
All have access to the truth through the Holy Spirit.[41]
All rule with Christ[42] through the ministry of reconciliation.[43]

God has forgiven the sins of all brothers through Christ's atoning death on the cross.[44] We have all died with him.[45] We have all been raised to new life with Jesus also.[46] Now we all stand before God clothed in Christ's righteousness.[47] Consequently we all have perfect access to God.[48] None of us has a better line to God than any other.[49] We all have the same access. We all have equal access. We all go through Jesus, our brother, our life.[50]

We brothers have all been given the Holy Spirit to make our oneness with Christ a living reality of energy and vitality.[51] The presence of the Holy Spirit affirms our union with Jesus, our brotherhood with him.[52] Through the power of the Holy Spirit, we are raised with Jesus to a new life, a sanctified life.[53] It is the Holy Spirit who reveals God's truth to us.[54] He enlightens our study of the Scriptures.[55] We have only one teacher, the Christ,[56] and the Holy Spirit reveals him[57] and makes us like him.[58]

We brothers have all been given the honor and privilege of sitting with Jesus in the heavenly realms because we are one with him, his brothers and fellow heirs, sharing his glory.[59] We reign with Jesus[60] through the ministry of reconciliation.[61] We seek to bring reconciliation through the proclamation of the gospel to the world.[62] We live a life of reconciliation through servanthood within the body,[63] which demonstrates to the world the reality of Christ's reconciling power and the truth about who Jesus Christ really is.[64]

The Question

Who are brothers?

What do we know to be true?

- Those addressed as brothers in the New Testament are the following:

    Men and women[65]

    Jesus' disciples and followers[66]

    Those sanctified in Christ and called to be holy[67]

    Those everywhere who call on the name of the Lord[68]

    Those loved by God[69]

    The faithful in Christ[70]

    Those who love Jesus[71]

    God's elect[72]

    Those cleansed by Christ's blood[73]

The Question

What do all brothers have in common?

What do we know to be true?

- All have been forgiven through Christ's shed blood.[74]
- All have complete access to God through the righteousness of Christ.[75]
- All have been justified.[76]
- All have the Holy Spirit living within them.[77]
  The Holy Spirit guides believers into all truth.[78]
  The Holy Spirit writes God's law on the hearts and minds of believers.[79]
- All are being sanctified.[80]
- All are now brothers to King, Jesus.[81]
- All are co-heirs with Jesus.[82]
- All rule with him[83]
  through the ministry of reconciliation.[84]
- All are adopted.[85]

The Question

What should be the status of women in the church?

What truth can we apply to make this question slightly simpler?

- All believers are brothers.

- Each believer has the same relationship to Christ as every other believer: brothers with Christ.

- All believers have the same relationship with each other: brothers with each other.

My daughter Elizabeth~1979.

Chapter 11

The Head over Everything: Rule through Reconciliation

All this would seem to say that there is no authority within the church other than Christ himself. Can this be true?

Yes. That is exactly what the Scriptures teach. Jesus Christ is our only Lord and teacher. Yet in his loving-kindness he has made us righteous. He has made us children of God. He has made us his brothers and fellow heirs. He has made us his body, his fullness. He has made us one with him. Our oneness with Christ allows his peace and love to bring unity through our consequent servanthood, making one of many. Thus we become one with each other through our oneness with him.

Since he is one with each of us, Christ uses each one of us to bring order to the church. We govern each other through servanthood, through gifts, and through worship.

Ouch!

Did you ever stub your toe? Most of us have. Remember what it feels like? The pain is excruciating. Immediately the whole body is affected. Muscles leap into action. Emotions electrify. The mouth, tongue, and vocal cords, way off at the other end of the body, give expression. Liquid secretions may spring into the eyes.

Once cleared, the eyes examine the damage. Fingers probe with the gentlest of touch.

The pain, swelling, and invading discoloration are evidence that injury has been inflicted. Testing is done: Is walking still possible? The brain begins to calculate: Will the nail be lost? The toe is held. The body rocks. Comfort is given. A mournful peace returns.

But even as all that happens, other parts of the body are rushing to heal. The blood begins to clear away the mess. Nutrients are brought for repair. Compensation is provided by other parts, so the injured part can rest. The brain chooses the best shoes. The nerves have veto power. Maybe if each part does its job, the scheduled tennis match can proceed.

All the parts have their unique function. Yet they all work together. Each part serves the others.

Through Each One of Us

So it is with Christ's body. "But in fact God has arranged the parts in the body, every one of them, just as he wanted them to be. If they were all one part, where would the body be? As it is there are many parts, but one body."[1]

Organization is not the same as authority. *Organization* means "order rather than chaos, harmony rather than confusion, one rather than many." Every body needs order. A living body has systems, organs, and tissues, all organized to sustain its life and to carry out its work. The body as a whole carries out one unified task through the different and unique functions of the many parts.

Even a very elementary study of the human body makes clear the intricate organization, yet complete interdependence of the many distinct parts. We may be amazed at how badly we feel when only one small part is not functioning correctly and how many other parts may be affected by that one malfunction. Consequently, we become more aware of how well all the parts work together when we are healthy. The intricate organization and cooperation are beyond our comprehension.

Organization can be achieved through authority. That is one common way we achieve organization in our worldly institutions from the military to corporations to families. But God has chosen a different way to achieve order. God has chosen servanthood as the means to accomplish order within his body.

Servanthood is the beautiful blend of love and submission that Jesus Christ is and we are in the process of becoming. Through servanthood the attitude of each individual part is love for and submission to every other part. Each part esteems the others above himself, looks out for the good of others, loves others as he loves himself because the other parts are himself. They are one together in one body. This was the attitude of Jesus, and it must be the attitude of the church, his body.

All this we have discussed in detail already. So for now let's only be reminded that servanthood is the mode of action through which the organization of the church, the body, takes place. Servanthood is the means by which Christ governs us through our gifts and through our worship.

The Organization of the Body

Chapter 12 of 1 Corinthians, which talks about the organization of the body of Christ, is primarily about how the church's life is ordered through the gifts given by the Spirit to each member. Interwoven throughout this chapter is the attitude of servanthood.

The spiritual gifts must all be viewed through the spectacles of servanthood. In fact, Paul says that love is the "greatest" gift, the "most excellent way."[2] Love is greater than prophesy, tongues, knowledge, or even faith.[3] Without love all the other gifts become useless.[4] It is through love that we are bound together in perfect unity.[5]

So, love is the primary attitude and action of order, organization, and government. Love is the pathway to be followed for the proper use of the gifts. "Follow the way of love and eagerly desire spiritual gifts."[6]

The gifts must all be used in an attitude of servanthood. Why have the spiritual gifts been given to the church? "Now to each one the manifestation of the Spirit is given for the common good."[7] Christ has apportioned grace to "***each one of us.***"[8]

> . . . to prepare God's people for works of service, so that the body of Christ may be built up until we all reach unity in the faith and in the knowledge of the Son of God and become mature, attaining to the whole measure of the fullness of Christ.[9]

This is what Paul meant when he said he wanted to impart to the Roman Christians some spiritual gift, meaning they would both be "mutually encouraged by each other's faith."[10] Paul admonished the Corinthians to "try to excel in gifts that build up the church."[11] Peter articulated this truth most clearly: "Each one should use whatever gift he has received to serve others, faithfully administering God's grace in its various forms."[12] We cannot be careless in the use of our gifts. Rather we must each use our gift with wholehearted zeal and care.[13]

If gifts are for the administration of God's grace in its various forms, then of course they must be received with an attitude of servanthood as well. As we submit to the gifts of others, we recognize and submit to the authority of Christ, who gave the gift for the common good. Each member's gift is God's grace to the whole body. God's grace is what we all must submit to in order to become more and more like Jesus, becoming mature and attaining to the whole measure of his fullness. And since gifts are given to each member of the body,[14] this means we must all be in submission to each other,[15] so we will not lose out in receiving God's grace. All members have a gift with which to serve. All members must submit to the service and gifts of others. Why is this so? Because "each member belongs to all the others."[16]

The Gifts Administer God's Grace

Of course, everyone has not been given the same gift. Where is the sense in that? All the gifts are needed by the body. "If they were all one part, where would the body be? As it is, there are many parts, but one body."[17]

The following different gifts within the body are specifically mentioned in the Bible:

- Message of wisdom[18]
- Message of knowledge[19]

- Faith[20]
- Healing[21]
- Miraculous powers[22]
- Prophecy[23]
- Speaking in different kinds of tongues[24]
- Interpretation of tongues[25]
- Apostleship[26]
- Teaching[27]
- Those able to help others[28]
- Administration[29]
- Love[30]
- Hope[31]
- Serving[32]
- Encouraging[c33]
- Contributing to the needs of others[34]
- Leadership[35]
- Showing mercy[36]
- Evangelism[37]
- Pastoring[38]

And, of course, there are many other qualities and characteristics that result from our oneness with Christ and his Spirit within us, even though they are not specifically mentioned as gifts such as the "fruit of the Spirit."[39]

About Spiritual Gifts

What is the nature of the various gifts, given for the common good? Are they physical gifts bestowed at birth? No, that cannot be because at birth we are all lost sinners still in need of a savior, let alone gifts from the Spirit. Besides, we must all be "born again"[40] before God enfolds us into the church and we become a true brother. These gifts to individuals for the church are not of a physical nature. Remember? Jesus said, "Flesh gives birth to flesh, but the Spirit gives birth to spirit."[41] In fact, Paul introduces the subject of gifts in 1 Corinthians 12 by saying, "Now about spiritual gifts, brothers . . ."[42]

This is why we can all submit to each other in the church, because we know that all these gifts come from the Spirit.

Yes, we are all different. And some of those differences come from our gender. Now, of course, our flesh and blood bodies belong to God, and all that they are must be devoted to his service. But that does not mean that our physical qualities are the same as our spiritual gifts. On the preceding list of spiritual gifts, none are physical. All are spiritual in nature. Physical traits are used as we exercise spiritual gifts. But without the Spirit's energizing power, a physical trait cannot administer

God's grace to the body of believers. From first to last,[43] it is the work of the Spirit that enables us to administer God's grace to each other. And the Spirit is given to all brothers.

Some of these gifts naturally get more attention than others. Some are more noticeable than others. But this does not mean that one gift is more important than another. It doesn't mean that one gift is less necessary than another. No! Each gift is necessary. Each is important. So it is our duty to see that each gift is recognized as a vehicle of God's grace for the whole body.[44]

The Common Good

Why has God made it this way?

> . . . so that there should be no division in the body, but that its parts should have equal concern for each other. If one part suffers, every part suffers with it: if one part is honored, every part rejoices with it.[45]

Our different gifts should never be a cause for dissension or conflict. Instead, they should help the body work as one unit. And we must always remember that each of our gifts comes from the same God.

> There are different kinds of gifts, but the same Spirit. There are different kinds of service, but the same Lord. There are different kinds of working, but the same God works all of them in all men. Now to each one the manifestation of the Spirit is given for the common good.[46]

> This is how the body, the church is to be ordered, organized, and governed.

Authority Goes with the Gift

It is in this context of the servanthood of the gifts that we must hear Paul's references to leadership and authority within the body. Each gift must be used for servanthood, yet each gift also has authority because it is derived from the member's oneness with Christ himself, and he is the only authority in the church. As we submit to each gift, we recognize Christ's authority as the creator of the gift. This is why we submit to each other as to Christ himself.[47] Each member, each brother is to share in the ministry of reconciliation as we impart God's grace to others through the use of our gift.

This is exactly what Paul is talking about when he told the Corinthians:

> This is why I write these things when I am absent, that when I come I may not have to be harsh in my use of authority—the authority the Lord gave me for building you up, not for tearing you down.[48]

This is the authority of Paul's gift. He is not afraid to use his gift. In fact, he knows it is his commission from God to use his gift.[49] Yet his gift is only one among many. All the gifts have authority. Paul was willing to use the authority of his gift. He was also willing to submit to the authority of other gifts.[50]

This is the authority Paul also encourages in Titus. After summarizing the gospel message, Paul says, "These, then, are the things you should teach. Encourage and rebuke with all authority. Do not let anyone despise you."[51] This is not the authority of Titus's position, but rather the authority of Titus's oneness with the truth, with Christ himself. This authority is available to all believers. Let's remember that we have only one teacher, Christ.[52] That is, he is the only one who can really reveal the truth of God to us.[53] Many are given the gift of passing that truth along to others. But their authority to do so rests only in their unity with the truth Christ taught, with Christ himself,[54] not in some elevated position of teacher, a seminary degree, or even ordination.

The Gift of Leadership

Paul commends[55] those who desire the gift of leadership.[56] Yet it is not an easy task. An overseer must not only be a person of upright character, but also "hold firmly to the trustworthy message as it has been taught, so that he can encourage others by sound doctrine and refute those who oppose it."[57]

Like all the other gifts, leadership must be offered to the body in an attitude of servanthood.

> To the elders among you, I appeal as a fellow elder, a witness of Christ's sufferings and one who also will share in the glory to be revealed: Be shepherds of God's flock that is under your care, serving as overseers—not because you must, but because you are willing, as God wants you to be: not greedy for money, but eager to serve, not lording it over those entrusted to you, but being examples to the flock. And when the Chief Shepherd appears, you will receive the crown of glory that will never fade away.[58]

Submission is the attitude Peter encourages in his fellow overseers. He goes on:

> Young ***men, in the same way be submissive*** to those who are older. All of you. clothe yourselves with humility toward one another, because, "God opposes the proud but gives grace to the humble." Humble yourselves, therefore, under God's mighty hand, that he may lift you up in due time.[59]

Just as Jesus taught,[60] exaltation is God's business. Humility is ours.

This is why the other members of the body are told, "Obey your leaders and submit to their authority. They keep watch over you as men who must give an account. Obey them so that their work will be a joy, not a burden, for that would be of no advantage to you."[61] Yes, leaders will be asked to give an account for the use of their gift. But so will each brother be asked to give an account.[62]

Christ's Authority Administered through Gifts

Remember Jesus' parable of the talents?[63] "After a long time the master of those servants returned and settled accounts with them." Each brother must use his gift to its fullest.[64] Each member must invest his gift wisely for the greatest return.[65] Therefore each member must use his or her gift in service to others as a commission from God[66] and submit to the gifts of others.

When a gift is confirmed by the whole body,[67] its authority to fulfill its function is then recognized by the whole body. Some of us are gifted to teach, and so the rest of us submit to that teaching. Some of us are gifted in administration, so the rest of us submit to that administration, whether it be in organizing a church lunch, getting the announcements into decent order for a newsletter, or setting up the nursery. Some are gifted in helping others, whether it be shoveling the drive, bringing in a meal, or giving a financial gift, so we submit to their aid. Some are gifted in discernment and thus wise in matters of discipline, so we each submit to discipline. Some have the gift of vision and the ability to communicate that to others, so we submit to their vision for the church. All of these gifts are administered, not as individual gifts with personal authority, but as gifts to the whole body, functioning on behalf of the whole church. No gift commands all the others. All have gifts and the authority of Christ to use them. All submit.[68]

Yes, there is valid, biblically taught authority in the church; it is Christ's authority as ministered through the members of the body.[69] But valid authority in the church does not have anything to do with the subordination of women. Men are also subject to valid authority within the church, yet they are all considered as equal in rank before God and among themselves. They are all eligible to be elected to leadership positions, to lead the congregation in worship, to administer the sacraments, to be members in church councils, to hold offices within those councils, and to receive the gifts of leadership, teaching, preaching, discernment in matters of discipline and doctrine, and so on.[70]

The Eye Cannot Say

If it wasn't good for man to be alone[71] in the garden, why is a males-only policy good for the courts of the church?

An old argument from complementarians is that since Jesus chose only males into his inner circle of the twelve disciples, women should also be excluded from all church leadership. But Jesus also chose only Jews into that inner circle. Yet the male/female issue has exactly the same status as the Jew/Gentile issue,[72] that is, no status at all within the family of God, the church.[73] No, "The eye cannot say to the hand, 'I don't need you!'"[74]

Overthrowing Human Authority

Accepting women as equals does not overthrow Christ's authority over the church; it overthrows male authority. It overthrows the innate personal authority of one believer over another. It overthrows all human authority in the church based on anything other than union with ***the*** authority, Christ.

I have heard it said that Paul has set forth a hierarchy of gifts. "And in the church God has appointed first of all apostles, second prophets, third teachers, then workers of miracles."[75] Yet Paul has just said that each gift is necessary and important,[76] and the very next thing he says is that the greatest gift of all is love.[77] Love is "the most excellent way."[78] And love is a gift that each brother has accepted in response to God's love for him. In fact, if you don't have the gift of love, you can't be considered a brother.

The Gift of Love

> Everyone who loves has been born of God and knows God. Whoever does not love does not know God, because God is love. . . . No one has ever seen God; but if we love one another, God lives in us and his love is made complete in us. . . .We love because he first loved us. . . . Whoever loves God must also love his brother.[79]

Even Christ came in servanthood. "Now that I, your Lord and Teacher, have washed your feet, you also should wash one another's feet. I have set you an example that you should do as I have done for you."[80] Yet he taught with authority as our "one Teacher."[81]

Great men of faith, who have been used mightily by God in the administration of grace to his body, have been examples of the truth of Jesus' teaching on greatness:

> The disciples came to Jesus and asked, "Who is the greatest in the kingdom of heaven?" He called a little child and had him stand among them. And he said: "I tell you the truth, unless you change and become like little children, you will never enter the kingdom of heaven. Therefore, whoever humbles himself like this child is the greatest in the kingdom of heaven."[82]

Jesus said of John the Baptist, "Among those born of women there has not risen anyone greater than John the Baptist; yet he who is least in the kingdom of heaven is greater than he."[83] Paul declared himself to be "less than the least of all God's people."[84] James tells us that "Elijah was a man just like us."[85] His prayers were no more influential with God than are ours.

Ministering to Each Other

This is also why we can minister to each other through our worship of God. As we sing and pray and study God's Word, we can all enter in because each member has complete access to God through the righteousness of Christ, each member has the Holy Spirit dwelling within, guiding him or her into all truth, and each member has a gift from the Spirit that enables him or her to administer God's grace to others. "Let the word of Christ dwell in you richly as you teach and admonish one another with all wisdom, and as you sing psalms, hymns and spiritual songs with gratitude in your hearts to God."[86]

Each brother can worship because each comes through Jesus. This is worship in truth since Jesus is the Truth.[87] All the brothers together are the church, the temple, the dwelling of God, the body of Christ.

> As you come to him, the living Stone—rejected by men but chosen by God and precious to him—you also, like living stones, are being built into a spiritual house to be a holy priesthood, offering spiritual sacrifices acceptable to God through Jesus Christ. . . . But you are a chosen people, a royal priesthood, a holy nation, a people belonging to God, that you may declare the praises of him who called you out of darkness into his wonderful light.[88]

The Heart of Worship

And throughout all our worship, the very heart and center is servanthood. "Therefore, I urge you, brothers, in view of God's mercy, to offer your bodies as living sacrifices, holy and pleasing to God—this is your spiritual act of worship."[89] Becoming "living sacrifices" is worshipping in spirit.[90]

As we offer ourselves through servanthood, first to God, which is the first and greatest commandment, and then to each other, which is the second greatest commandment, we are transformed into Christ's likeness. "Do not conform any longer to the pattern of this world, but be transformed by the renewing of your mind. Then you will be able to test and approve what God's will is—his good, pleasing and perfect will."[91] Becoming like Jesus, becoming one with Jesus, is the very essence of worship "in spirit and truth."[92] Jesus is the truth. Self-sacrifice is his nature.[93]

There is a difference between leading in worship because one has a gift from the Holy Spirit that enables one to administer God's grace to others in some special way and leading in worship because one has a special position or attribute that then makes the worship more acceptable to God. The first is the pattern of the New Testament. The second is at best the burden of dead works,[94] and at worst an addition to God's requirements for our access to his presence.[95]

In Spirit and in Truth

We come to God through his grace alone.[96] There is nothing else. Nothing can make us more acceptable to God than the righteousness of Christ.[97] He is the only mediator.[98] All other attempts at mediation, or even improvement or additions to Christ's mediation, are viewed by God as an insult to Christ's sacrifice on our behalf. If anything can be done to make us more acceptable to God than Christ's shed blood has already done, then Christ died for nothing![99]

> What, after all, is Apollos? And what is Paul? Only servants, through whom you came to believe—as the Lord has assigned to each his task. I planted the seed, Apollos watered it, but God made it grow. So neither he who plants nor he who waters is anything, but only God, who makes things grow. The man who plants and the man who waters have one purpose, and each will be rewarded according to his own labor.[100]

> Therefore, brothers, since we have confidence to enter the Most Holy Place by the blood of Jesus, by a new and living way opened for us through the curtain, that is, his body, and since we have a great priest over the house of God, let us draw near to God with a sincere heart in full assurance of faith, having our hearts sprinkled to cleanse us from a guilty conscience and having our bodies washed with pure water. Let us hold unswervingly to the hope we profess, for he who promised is faithful. And let us consider how we may spur one another on toward love and good deeds. Let us not give up meeting together, as some are in the habit of doing, but let us encourage one another—and all the more as you see the Day approaching.[101]

We have perfect access to God through Jesus. We have access to the truth through the Holy Spirit. Therefore we can all worship. And we each have a gift from the Spirit for administering grace to others, so we cannot worship alone. We are a body, and we must worship together because this is how we can teach and admonish one another, spur one another on toward love and good deeds, and encourage one another. In spite of all opposition, it is important that we do not throw away our confidence in this very truth, for it will be richly rewarded.[102]

Oh, the Depth!

Each brother has perfect access to God through the righteousness of Christ. Christ was perfect, without spot or blemish.

Each brother has the word of God because God has written it on our hearts and his own living Word, Jesus, lives within us through his Holy Spirit. The Holy Spirit will guide us into all truth.

Each brother sits with Christ and rules with him through the ministry of reconciliation. Christ sits at the right hand of God in the heavenly realms.

> Oh, the depth of the riches of the wisdom and knowledge of God!
> How unsearchable his judgments, and his paths beyond tracing out!
> "Who has known the mind of the Lord?
> Or who has been his counselor?"
> "Who has ever given to God that God should repay him?"
> For from him and through him and to him are all things.
> To him be the glory forever!
> Amen.[103]

The Authority Question

I have heard the argument that it is improper to challenge the church's traditional position on women because through the ages the church has agreed that Scripture is clear as to their place. Yet I don't think this is true. The women's issue has never been fully discussed and debated across a large spectrum of the church until recent years. Before that it was only assumed. Yet the issue of authority was discussed at great length at the time of the Reformation.

In *The Glorious Body of Christ,* R. B. Kuiper wrote about the attitude of the reformers toward authority in the church. In the chapter on the "Universal Office" of every church member, Kuiper described the stance of the Roman Catholic church at that time.

> Rome draws a sharp line of demarcation between the clergy and the laity. The former are said to be spiritual in a sense in which the latter are not. The former are to rule, the latter are to be ruled. The former are to teach, the latter are to be taught. The latter must accept in implicit faith what the former teach and must bow unreservedly before their authority.[104]

Does this sound familiar?A few paragraphs later Kuiper goes on to say,

> Luther, Calvin and the other Reformers taught that every believer is a priest. But they also stressed the universal prophethood of believers and their universal kingship. Every believer, they insisted, has the right, yes the duty, to apply the touchstone of Holy Scripture to the teaching of the church and, in case these teachings cannot stand that test, to raise his voice in protest. And, instead of merely being governed, the members of the church must, said they, have a voice in its government.[105]

Authority, Women, and the Reformers

The reformers affirmed that all believers have the authority of the truth and that authority is not passed to believers through any hierarchy of human authority or leadership, but rather only though the Holy Spirit and His Word. This is the priesthood of all believers, the prophethood of all believers, the kingship of all believers. This is justification, sanctification, and adoption.

The authority of the church is our oneness with Truth, that is, Jesus Christ, our Lord. And it is not through power or authority that God has chosen to reveal this Truth, but rather through weakness. That is the essence of the life Christ lived on earth and of the life we are also to live.[106]

Even though the reformers saw this clearly concerning authority, they had a blind spot where women were concerned. They just assumed that somehow all this didn't quite apply to women in the same way it did to men. I know of no reformational confession, catechism, or creed that delineates the subordination of women from scriptural evidence. No effort is made to align the doctrine of the exclusion of women from all church government with other great reformational doctrines such as adoption, the communion of the saints, the priesthood of all believers, and church organization chosen, authorized, and maintained by the body as a whole. There is no overall rationale to explain why the rights and privileges granted to all believers are somewhat limited when it comes to women.

These things were never discussed or debated because the position of women was never questioned. There was agreement on the position of women, not through careful study, thought, and discussion, but through assumption. Two or three "proof texts" satisfied the need for a biblical rationale for keeping women in "their place."

And women submitted to those powers instituted among men for the sake of Christ. Being a part of his body, the church, has been much more important to women throughout the ages than has their own position. It is only now, after centuries of growth in the truth, that the church seems ready and able to face this question.

Today many women, myself included, have taken to heart the teaching that they, too, are included in the gospel and can thus be confident in their salvation.[107] It is the redemption Christ paid for us that we defend, not our own rights.[108] It is the freedom Christ died to give us that we no longer are willing to have taken away.[109] It is God's salvation, "such a great salvation,"[110] that we see belittled, not our own persons.[111] We women who are born again by the Spirit, know we are completely sinful, unworthy of any good thing, weak, and completely devoid of life in and of ourselves. We know that it is only through Jesus that we have life.[112] And it is this good news that we are willing to proclaim.[113]

Today many women and men, feel it is time to "hold firmly to the faith we profess."[114] "We have this hope as an anchor for the soul, firm and secure. It enters the inner sanctuary behind the curtain where Jesus, who went before us, has entered on our behalf."[115] With faith and confidence in our Great High Priest, our brother and King, Jesus, and his Holy Spirit that will guide us into all truth, we are now applying the touchstone of Holy Scripture to the teaching of the church. And because we are finding that the traditional teaching on the status of women in the church cannot stand that test, we are raising our voices in protest. It is incongruent to believe that Christ has made women acceptable to sit with him in the heavenly realms with everything beneath our feet, if we are not found acceptable, as a gender, to sit in the councils of the church here on earth?

Is that putting it too strongly? I don't think so. Scripture agrees. "Do you not know that the saints will judge the world? And if you are to judge the world, are you not competent to judge trivial cases? Do you not know that we will judge angels? How much more the things of this life!"[116]

Judging the Things of This Life

Those who believe that the Bible teaches the complete equality of men and women before God and in the church are not leaving the truths of the Reformation. Rather we seek to apply the reformational principles more broadly. Isn't this what the kingship of Christ is all about? Bringing everything into submission to Jesus Christ and the truth of his gospel? To apply the rule of Christ to everything?

All I have said about servanthood/authority, brings us back to two doctrines upon which the church of the Reformation was built: The Kingship of Christ and the priesthood of all believers. These two great truths bring us around full circle, to the words of Jesus, "for you have only one Master and you are all brothers."[117] Jesus is "head over everything"[118] and "head of the body, the church."[119]

Christ Is King

Yes, Christ is our Master. Christ is King. He is the ultimate authority. He is ruler, judge, sovereign. We owe him our full allegiance in every part and parcel of our lives because, of course, he is our life.

Jesus is King, the only King. There is no hierarchy of nobles extending from his throne. Christ has no need of a hierarchy of command beneath him because his subjects all have direct and constant access to him. A chain of command is just that. Its purpose is to pass the command along the chain. But Christ's commands are all directly conveyed to each member through the indwelling, compelling presence of his Holy Spirit.[120]

Yes, Christ rules. But how does he rule? Christ rules by making peace through reconciliation.

Now it is Christ's reconciling work that has made us all brothers, brothers with Jesus and with all other believers. We all are in equal relationship with our brother, the King. Yet we cannot be independent because we all are one together with the King, our head, and with each other, the fellow members of his/our body. We are a kingdom of royal, or kingly, priests.

Christ in Us

The authority of the church comes not from the top down, that is, from a few persons in authority to many persons in submission. Rather the authority in the church comes from the bottom up, that is, many members, each who has Christ living in him, to each unique part that will carry out, in submission, the distinctive tasks designated by the whole, because of gifts recognized by the whole.

- All rule.[121]
- All submit.[122]
- All are interrelated.[123]
- All are interdependent.[124]
- All are one.[125]

The authority of the visible church flows from the King to and through each individual member.[126] The King, as head, holds the whole body together as one through love.[127] So Christ's authority flows from the church as a whole, originating in many members, but with the authority of one body, applied to the church as a whole and to each member individually.[128] Each part of the body, each gift from the Holy Spirit is important, useful, authoritative,[129] because each part is one with the King,[130] the head of the church,[131] and, yes, our brother.[132]

All Rule Because All Submit

This is the law of the kingdom. "Whoever wants to become great among you must be your servant, and whoever wants to be first must be your slave."[133] Even the King is not beyond this law. ". . . just as the Son of Man did not come to be served, but to serve, and to give his life as a ransom for many."[134] In fact, he is King because he is the greatest servant of all. "He . . . became obedient to death—even death on a cross! ***Therefore God exalted him*** to the highest place."[135] It is not just that all rule and all submit. But rather, all rule because all submit.

The Hope of Glory

This is the surprise of the beatitudes, that those who are servants will reign. It is the poor in spirit, the meek, the pure in heart, the peacemakers, the persecuted who reign in the kingdom of heaven.[136]

The rule of Christ is rule through reconciliation. The rule of the church is rule through reconciliation.

These things are true, and we must mold the visible organization and structures of the church to reflect these truths of the organism, the living body of Christ.

The Question

How is the body of brothers to be ordered?
What do we know to be true?

- The church is ordered, organized, and governed by "each other"[137] as follows:
  Through servanthood[138]—
  Each member and the body as a whole demonstrates to the world[139]
  the reconciling power of Jesus Christ.[140]
  Through spiritual gifts[141]—
  Each gift comes from the Spirit.[142]
  The purpose of spiritual gifts is
  for the common good,[143]
  to prepare God's people for works of service,[144]
  and
  to administer God's grace to others.[145]
  Each member receives a gift from the Spirit.[146]
  Spiritual gifts are to be used
  in service to others,[147]
  as a commission from God,[148]
  knowing we will have to give an account.[149]
  Spiritual gifts are to be received
  in servanthood[150]
  as God's grace to us.[151]
  Through worship[152]—
  Each member approaches God in spirit and truth[153]
  through Jesus alone, who is the truth.[154]
  Through self-sacrifice[155]—
  Each member can lead in spiritual worship because
  each has access to God through Christ,[156]
  each has the Holy Spirit within
  to provide oneness with Christ,[157]
  to guide to the truth,[158] and
  to sanctify.[159]
  Each member has a gift for administering God's grace to others.[160]

My sisters Nancy and Esther, me, our mother Winifred, and my sister Meg~1980.

Chapter 12

The Exceptional Women of the Bible: Proof of the Rule

I asked, "But what about Deborah? What about Priscilla?"

The answer came, "They're the exceptions that prove the rule."

Well, it got me thinking!

"The exception that proves the rule." It's an old saying, but a true and wise one. The more I thought about it, the more I realized its validity. The exceptional women of the Bible are the exceptions that prove the rule.

Deborah and Priscilla and Miriam and Phoebe. These women were not silent. They participated in governing. They made decisions. God communicated directly with them. They were inspired to speak words we now consider Scripture. They prophesied. They took leadership in the church. They led in worship. They taught the things of God to men.

Not many women in Scripture did these things. Just a few did. They do seem to be exceptions. Throughout most of Scripture, the story of redemption is told through the words and actions of men.

So these women are exceptions. How do they prove a rule? And more importantly, what rule do they prove?

Proving a Rule

Let's take an example from science to try to understand this. Science also tries to discover the truth from revelation, the revelation of creation. Suppose I have noticed that several things I have set on my windowsill have fallen to the ground when accidentally bumped off their perch. Suppose I begin to formulate a hypothesis that everything I throw out a window will fall to the ground.

Now I decide to do some experimentation to test my hypothesis. Near an open window, I find a book. I throw it out the window. Sure enough, it hits the ground. I see a piece of paper nearby. I throw it out the window. It floats lazily, but, yes, it finally hits the ground too. I notice a tiny paper clip. Out it goes . . . straight to the ground. I pick up my son's basketball, filled with air. Out it goes with the same result.

Should I become worried? I haven't yet found an exception to prove my rule. No, that would be silly. The more things I find to conform to my theory, the more sure I become that indeed I have discovered a truth, a law of nature.

Next I see a helium-filled balloon my daughter has just brought home from a birthday party. In pursuit of scientific enlightenment, I throw it out the window. But alas, it does not hit the ground. It doesn't even go down. It goes up instead.

Now, do I jump up and down and shout for joy because I have found the exception that proves my rule? No. Instead I must take a long, hard look at my theory that everything I throw out the window will fall to the ground.

My experience with the helium balloon makes me realize that my theory cannot possibly be true because I have found something that acts in direct opposition to my hypothesis. Everything I throw out the window will not fall to the ground because I tried it with a helium-filled balloon, and it went up, not down, let alone hit the ground.

Yes. I think we would say that the helium balloon was an exception. Normally, most things you throw out the window will fall to the ground, but not a helium balloon. It is an exception. Consequently, it cannot possibly be proof that the general way things happen, the normal pattern of things falling to the ground, is a rule or law of truth. Something cannot be both an exception to and a proof for the same rule.

But if I think about this exception long enough, if I study hard and do lots of experiments, I may come up with a theory as to why the balloon rises instead of falls as most things do. Actually, all I have to do is remember a little elementary science, and soon enough I will come to Archimedes. I will recall that he discovered the truth of the helium balloon long ago and formulated it into what we now call Archimedes' principle. His principle says that an object will sink if it is heavier than the fluid it displaces but will rise if it is lighter than the fluid it displaces.

No matter how many times I experiment with this principle, I find that it is true. I throw a brick into water. Then I throw a basketball into water. Archimedes holds true.

The trouble is that I cannot find very many things that are lighter than the fluid of air. But every time I do find something—a helium balloon, the hydrogen-filled Hindenburg, a hot air balloon, the principle Archimedes formulated holds true.

How Does an Exception Prove?

The helium-filled balloon was indeed an exception. It was an exception to the way most things generally happen. And yes, it did prove a rule. But not the rule that everything I throw out the window will fall to the ground. The balloon disproved that rule. Rather it prompted me to discover a new truth, a new rule, exemplified by the helium balloon. So the helium balloon turned out to be the exception that proved the rule. It proved the rule of Archimedes' principle by floating upward, even though the normal pattern is that most things I throw out the window go down and eventually hit the ground. In fact, its exceptionality is the very thing that made me look for the new truth. By being an exception, it proved the rule.

"The exception that proves the rule" means:

- An exception is something other than, or different from, the dominant pattern.
- The exception disproves the dominant pattern as an absolute rule. Something can never be both an exception to and a proof for the same rule.
- The rule proved by the exception is some other, more fundamental, less obvious rule.
- The exception ***proves*** because it acts according to the rule even when the prevailing or dominant pattern is otherwise.

Exceptional Women

Now let's go back to the women of the Bible, the exceptional women. Men were usually the leaders. Men usually had the authority. Men were God's agents. Abigail, Anna, Deborah, Esther, Hannah, Huldah, Jael, Junias, Lydia, Mary, Miriam, Phoebe, Priscilla, Rahab, and Ruth—these few women were the exceptions. But when there are exceptions, we then know that what is generally the prevailing pattern cannot be the rule that the exceptions prove.

If Miriam led the congregation in worship, then it cannot be a rule that only men can lead in worship.[1]

If Deborah was a judge in Israel, then it cannot be a rule that women should not make decisions and govern.[2]

If Hannah gave her child to the Lord, then it cannot be a rule that only the man can make decisions for the family.[3]

If Huldah prophesied, then it cannot be a rule that only men can relay God's truth to others.[4]

If Ruth, a Gentile and a woman, was included among the people of God as their equal through a kinsman-redeemer, a shadow of our brother, the Christ, then it cannot be a rule that women should not be included in the church as equals among all other believers.[5]

If Esther, shadowing and picturing Christ, sacrificially gave herself for a people doomed to death,[6] proclaimed God's truth to the world,[7] and ruled with authority as she brought things into submission to God,[8] then it cannot be a rule that God does not intend women to serve, teach, proclaim, or rule.[9]

If Mary spoke inspired words of praise to God that became Scripture, then it cannot be a rule that God speaks only through men.[10]

If Priscilla taught Apollos, then it cannot be a rule that only men can teach other men.[11]

Disproving Prevailing Patterns

These exceptional women disprove the prevailing patterns as rules, even though the patterns express what generally happened in Scripture. Just as the helium-filled balloon disproved my theory, these women in the Bible disprove that only men should lead, teach or exercise authority in the family and church.

If this seems hard to swallow, let's stop a minute to consider God's rules as he has revealed them in Scripture and as we have discovered or formulated them. Do God's rules or laws have exceptions? Jesus is the only way to the Father.[12] Is this an absolute rule? Do all who come to the Father have to come through Jesus? Yes. There is no other way for people to come to God.[13] We cannot find any exceptions to this rule taught in Scripture, so we know that it stands as an absolute law of God.

Here's another rule: "If we confess our sins, he is faithful and just and will forgive us our sins."[14] Are there some sins that God will not forgive when we repent and confess them? No. We cannot find any exceptions to this rule taught in Scripture.[15] Thus we can believe it is an absolute law of God.

Or what about this rule? "All have sinned and come short of the glory of God."[16] Is this a rule that is absolutely true, or do we know of some exceptions? Has God ever told us of a sinless person? Of course, Jesus was the exception. But his exceptionality proved the rule that he is God, not the rule of total depravity. No, we have no record of any other created person being sinless.[17]

So these exceptional women of the Bible should make us wonder what truth is being demonstrated through the revelation of God's Word. These women are the exceptions that prove the rule. The question is, what rule?

Discovering the Rule

Here is another exception about which the Scriptures teach us. You remember the story of David and his friend Jonathan. Jonathan warned David of Saul's plan to kill him, and David immediately ran into hiding. He left in such a hurry that he took no provisions with him. When he arrived in Nob, he went to the priest Ahimelech and asked for provisions. The only thing Ahimelech had was the consecrated bread used in the worship of the God. He gave the consecrated bread to David who ate it, shared it with his men, and went on his way.[18] This event was certainly an exception because eating the consecrated bread was against the laws that God had given through Moses for worship in the tabernacle.[19]

In the New Testament, Jesus refers to this episode when he is also accused of breaking the law, because he and his disciples picked and ate grain on the Sabbath. Jesus responded this way: "Have you never read what David did when he and his companions were hungry? He entered the house of God, and taking the consecrated bread, he ate what is lawful only for the priests to eat. And he also gave some to his companions."[20]

Jesus clearly acknowledged that David did something that was an exception, for it was against the written law of Moses.[21] When Jesus asked the Pharisees if they had read about this action of David's, it was a rhetorical question. Of course the Pharisees were familiar with both David's actions and the Old Testament Law. What Jesus' question really meant was, "Don't you understand the meaning of this exception?"

Jesus knew this exception was not just some inexplicable Old Testament event. Jesus knew that David wasn't allowed to eat this bread because there was no other bread around. God didn't let him act against his law in order to eat rather than starve. God gave manna from heaven. God fed Elijah with bread delivered by ravens. God does not allow his law to be broken just because it seems to be the only way he can provide something. No. God allowed David to break the law, to be an exception, in order to teach a deeper reality than the one the law taught. David's eating the consecrated bread was an exception that proved the rule.

Characteristics of the Rule

But what rule did it prove? Jesus tells us. It proved the rule that God prefers mercy to sacrifice and the acknowledgment of God to burnt offerings.[22] Jesus quoted from the prophet Hosea as he chastised the Pharisees for their lack of understanding. "If you had known what these words mean, 'I desire mercy, not sacrifice,' you would not have condemned the innocent."[23]

Now I must admit that my sympathies are with the Pharisees here. How could they be expected to put these two things together and know that David's actions were right in God's sight? Yet Jesus seems to feel that enough had been revealed to them in the Old Testament Scriptures for them to understand this exception, and Jesus held them accountable for their lack of understanding.

But Jesus went on to say that they should understand the Scriptures even better now that he, the Son of God, was among them. "Or haven't you read in the Law that on the Sabbath the priests in the temple desecrate the day and yet are innocent? I tell you that one greater than the temple is here."[24]

What can we conclude about this exception of David eating the consecrated bread? First we can conclude that God does not allow exceptions to take place; he does not allow his law to be broken; he does not allow things that go against his own nature and character just because he has run out of other ways to get something done. "Surely the arm of the Lord is not too short to save."[25]

> The God who made the world and everything in it is the Lord of heaven and earth and does not live in temples built by hands. And he is not served by human hands, as if he needed anything, because he himself gives all men life and breath and everything else.[26]

> But about the Son he says, "Your throne, O God, will last forever and ever, and righteousness will be the scepter of your kingdom. You have loved righteousness and hated wickedness."[27]

If the act itself of eating this consecrated bread was truly absolute wickedness in God's sight, God would not have used it to provide for David. He could have provided nourishment for David in many other ways, as he did for others in Scripture.[28]

Secondly, we can conclude that when there is an exception to the way things normally happen, it does prove a rule, a deeper reality other than the obvious normal pattern, made even more clear through the revelation of Christ himself.

Jesus said the truth underlying David's act of eating the consecrated bread was that God delights in mercy and acknowledgment more than obedience to rules. This is God's law. There are no exceptions. Jesus had taught this message to his disciples before.[29] God considers the outward signs of our devotion to him meaningless if we "have neglected the more important aspects of the law."[30]

Jesus also made it clear that his presence on earth as both the temple presence of God among his people,[31] and as the bread of life,[32] was the fulfillment not only of the temple worship laws, but also the particular law about the consecrated bread. Christ's presence and incarnated life revealed the deeper reality of God's law, "the more important" aspect of God's law, that of mercy.

And thirdly, we can conclude that God expects ***us*** to understand the meaning of these

exceptions from what he has already revealed to us. Jesus expected the Pharisees to understand the meaning of David's eating of the consecrated bread from the writings of the Old Testament and his own presence among them. He asked them why they didn't understand it. Hadn't they read it! Jesus' rebuke to the Pharisees was so stinging that they began to plot his death that day.[33]

Exceptional Women Prove What Rule?

We can apply these conclusions to the exceptional women of the Bible also. However, we should remember that there is one crucial difference between David's eating of the consecrated bread and the works of these exceptional women I have mentioned. David's eating of the consecrated bread broke a clear law that Moses had written under God's direction, a law that Jesus himself acknowledged.

But the works of these women do not break any written law of God from the Old or the New Testament. These women were exceptions only because their activities were a departure from the prevalent pattern. Most of the people mentioned as a part of God's history of redemption are men. The few women that are mentioned are exceptions to that pattern.

Weak Men?

One explanation I have often heard for these exceptional women is that there were no godly men willing to take leadership, willing to do God's bidding, so God had to use women instead.

Yet if using women to lead were truly against God's righteous will, he surely would not have used them to get his work done.

This is the God who chose Moses, even when Moses was most reluctant, unprepared, unwilling, and without what he deemed the proper qualities to carry out the task God was assigning. But this didn't stop God. He gave Moses what he needed. He made Moses into the man he wanted.[34]

God made Paul into the man he wanted also. It didn't matter that Paul wasn't a believer. It didn't matter that Paul was actively opposing him. It didn't matter that Paul had participated in the stoning of his beloved Stephen. It didn't matter. He wanted Paul. He stopped Saul of Tarsus dead in his tracks, turned him from what he was doing, and made him into the man he needed to do the work he wanted done.[35]

If using women to lead his people, do his work, and carry his message is wickedness to God, certainly the trifling matter of no willing or able men could not make him resort to using a woman rather than a man.

Furthermore, if Jesus expected the Pharisees to understand the real truth demonstrated through David's eating of the consecrated bread when they had so little revelation of God's truth at that time compared to what we now have today, will he not much more expect us to understand the significance of these exceptional women of the Scriptures?

In addition, our understanding should be further enlightened by the presence of Christ himself among us. Through the Scriptures, we are witnesses to his life. Jesus Christ is the Word of God to us. What do we read in his life?

Jesus and Women

God used a woman as the agent for his son's incarnation. The living Word of God came to the world through a woman.[36] It was a woman who first preached to others that Jesus was the Christ.[37] It was women who first proclaimed the resurrection of Jesus.[38]

Jesus was willing to deal directly with women,[39] fulfilling their needs.[40] He raised at least one from the dead.[41] He taught them.[42] He commended their faith.[43]

Jesus allowed women to minister directly to him, serving his needs.[44] Women fed him,[45] washed his feet,[46] prepared his body for burial,[47] wept for him,[48] were faithful to him.[49]

Jesus used women to spread the word of his gospel.[50] Jesus used and continues to use these women of the Bible to teach his truth.[51]

Of all of these examples, I am most struck with the woman who anointed Jesus with perfume from an alabaster jar.[52] Here we have a woman, Mary,[53] who worshiped Jesus. She knew she had lived a sinful life. She recognized that there was nothing good about herself. Yet she brought all that she was and all that she had and yielded it to Jesus. Most of us would say she did it in a most inappropriate way. Yet her worship epitomizes what it means to worship "in spirit and in truth."[54] Her worship was centered completely on Jesus, and her own submission to him. She anointed Jesus with perfume from head to toe. She wiped his feet with her hair. She kissed him. All this she did in the presence of a large company of men, including Jesus' own disciples.

Inappropriate as her worship may seem to us, Jesus accepted her worship, her public worship.[55] Jesus commended her faith,[56] and even instructed the other men present to learn from her.[57] Jesus honored her with inclusion in the gospel history of Scripture so that all believers may learn from her.[58] Through Mary's actions and his reaction, Jesus affirmed the law of servanthood. "Whoever wants to become great among you must be your servant, and whoever wants to be first must be your slave."[59]

Women of the Early Church

The women of the early church continued to reflect these attitudes of Jesus. Women were a part of the decision making process.[60] Women served the church[61] and received recognition and respect for their labors.[62] Women were leaders in the church.[63] Women communicated God's message[64] and were teachers, even of men.[65]

Of all the New Testament writers, Luke in particular is careful to note the inclusion of women in the church on equal terms with men. Women accompanied Jesus, just as the twelve did, as an accepted part of the group.[66] Women heard the gospel and became a recognized and accepted part of the church.[67]

And so we can conclude that these exceptional women prove a rule, just like the exceptional act of David eating consecrated bread proved a rule. This rule is not the obvious, prevalent way things usually occurred; rather it is a rule more subtle, yet truer and more universal and absolute. A rule revealed in the Scriptures of both the Old and New Testaments.

The Rule Discovered

> Then God said, "Let us make man in our image, in our likeness, and let them rule over the fish of the sea and the birds of the air, over the livestock, over all the earth, and over all the creatures that move along the ground."

> So God created man in his own image, in the image of God he created him: male and female he created them. God blessed them and said to them. "Be fruitful and increase in number: fill the earth and subdue it. Rule over the fish of the sea and the birds of the air and over every living creature that moves on the ground."[68]

> Then our sons in their youth will be like well-nurtured plants, and our daughters will be like pillars carved to adorn a palace.[69]

> The Lord gives the command: The women who proclaim the good tidings are a great host.[70]

> Her husband has full confidence in her . . .
>
> Her children arise and call her blessed: her husband also, and he praises her.[71]

> But now, this is what the Lord says—he who created you. O Jacob, he who formed you, O Israel: 'Fear not, for I have redeemed you: I have summoned you by name: you are mine.
>
> Do not be afraid, for I am with you; I will bring your children from the east and gather you from the west. I will say to the north, "Give them up!" and to the south, "Do not hold them back." Bring my sons from afar and my daughters from the ends of the earth—everyone who is called by my name, whom I created for my glory, whom I formed and made.[72]

> This is what the Sovereign Lord says: "See. I will beckon to the Gentiles, I will lift up my banner to the peoples: they will bring your sons in their arms and carry your daughters on their shoulders. . . . They will bow down before you with their faces to the ground: they will lick the dust at your feet.[73]

When the Holy Spirit came upon all the believers, both men and women,[74] Peter said it was in fulfillment of Joel's Old Testament prophesy:

> "'In the last days, God says, I will pour out my Spirit on all people. Your sons and daughters will prophesy, your young men will see visions, your old men will dream dreams. Even on my servants, both men and women. I will pour out my Spirit in those days, and they will prophesy.'[75]

> Jesus replied, "But at the beginning of creation God 'made them male and female.' 'For this reason a man will leave his father and mother and be united to his wife, and the two will become one flesh.' So they are no longer two, hut one. Therefore what God has joined together, let man not separate."[76]

> The wife's body does not belong to her alone but also to her husband. In the same way, the husband's body does not belong to him alone but also to his wife.[77]

> In the Lord, however, woman is not independent of man, nor is man independent of woman. For as woman came from man, so also man is born of woman. But everything comes from God.[78]

> Husbands, in the same way be considerate as you live with your wives, and treat them with respect . . . as heirs with you of the gracious gift of life.[79]

In quoting an Old Testament Scripture from 2 Samuel, Paul wants his readers to be sure to understand that God includes both men and women equally in his family. Paul makes it clear that the reference to "son" in the Old Testament[80] includes both "sons and daughters." "I will be a Father to you, and you will be my sons and daughters, says the Lord Almighty."[81]

Paul clearly enunciates this rule that the exceptional women of the Bible prove:

> You are all Sons of God through faith in Christ Jesus, for all of you who were baptized into Christ have clothed yourselves with Christ. There is neither . . . male nor female, for you are all one in Christ Jesus. If you belong to Christ, then you are Abraham's seed, and heirs according to the promise.[82]

> Now we have read it. Jesus expects us to understand.

The Question

What are we to learn from the exceptional women of the Bible?

What do we know to be true?

- When we find in Scripture a God-directed and commended exception
  to the general pattern of Scripture, Jesus expects us to learn and understand what deeper, more absolute, more important aspect of the law, his truth, is being proclaimed.[83]

- David ate the consecrated bread, which was an exception to the rules of the tabernacle.[84]
  Jesus said this exception proved the rule that God desires mercy not sacrifice,[85]
  expressing a more absolute truth than the rule of the tabernacle laws.[86]
  Jesus expected the Pharisees to understand
  this exception and the rule it proved from their study of Scripture.[87]

- The dominant pattern of behavior throughout the Bible
  is that God has revealed most of his history of redemption
  through the words and actions of men.

- These women are exceptions to this general pattern:
  Miriam[88]
  Deborah[89]
  Jael[90]
  Ruth[91]
  Hannah[92]
  Huldah[93]
  Esther[94]
  Mary[95]
  Anna[96]
  Lydia[97]
  Priscilla[98]
  Phoebe[99]
  Junias[100]
  Mary Magdalene, Mary the mother of James, Salome[101]

- God blessed the world through these exceptional women as they
  received God's Word directly from him,[102]
  led in worship,[103]
  governed,[104]
  proclaimed his message,[105] and
  taught.[106]

- By being exceptions, these women disprove as a rule that God works only through men,
  even though that may be the dominant pattern of the Bible.

- These women prove the rule of a more absolute truth:
  that all believers, including both men and women, are equal,[107]
  through Christ's reconciling work to free us from the curse of sin
  by his death on the cross.[108]

The Question

What should be the role and status of women in the church?

What truth can we apply to make it a slightly simpler question?

- God has chosen and directed women throughout the history of his people, his church,
  to receive his Word directly from him,
  to lead in worship,
  to govern,
  to proclaim his message, and
  to teach.

My sisters, Meg and Esther, with me and my sister Nancy~1995.

CHAPTER 13

Must She Be Silent?
1 Corinthians 14:26–40

Making your way in the dark is very difficult, especially if there is no path, if you are unfamiliar with the lay of the land, if there are obstacles in your way.

In the Dark

I have tried walking through Colorado mountain terrain in the dark. Ron and I are not great at remembering flashlights. It seems like we just don't need one very often. There is usually plenty of light available for what we want to do.

Yet, every year when we go to our church conference in Colorado, we remember why flashlights are helpful. Flashlights are good for getting to the campfire. They're even better for getting back to our cabin after the campfire. We've found that without a flashlight we might stub our toes on big rocks, maybe even trip and fall down. We might run into barbed wire fences or tree branches. We might even lose our way completely, suddenly realizing that we no longer hear another human voice or see a flicker of light in any direction. Ron and I finally learned that if we didn't have a light, the best thing was to go by the road. It was still dark, but at least the way was flat and without obstacles. The trouble was, the road didn't go to the campfire.

Well, I guess others had the same problem because the campfire was finally moved to the middle of the camp near the road. Now the road does go to the campfire. Sometimes the campfire is even held in the lodge, so not only can we find our way, but we can be comfy too.

But something is missing. Now we have a campfire surrounded by noise, lights, distractions. We no longer have the quiet peace of the deep woods or the awesome view of the heavens unhindered by artificial lights. We no longer feel the intense fellowship of sitting together around a fire in a dark wilderness or the majesty of God's creation. Something has been lost.

If we could all just remember to bring flashlights, we could have it all—a clear path and a beautiful campfire.

The Part in Light of the Whole

"Thy Word is a lamp to my feet and a light for my path."[1]

The primary principle for interpreting the Scriptures is that each portion must be interpreted in light of the whole. It is the message of the whole that must light our way. As extensions to this principle, we must use the clear passages to discover the meaning of the less clear passages. Scripture itself teaches us the meaning of Scripture.

Following these hermeneutic rules, we have first considered some of the clear teachings of Scripture that have a bearing on what the status of women in the church should be. Now we come to what is not so clear—the questionable, the difficult.

Of all the passages in Scripture that various people have considered relative to the status and role of women in the church, there are only two passages, really only four verses, which are difficult as they have been traditionally interpreted. "Women should remain silent in the churches,"[2] and "I do not permit a woman to teach or to have authority over a man; she must be silent."[3]

These verses are foundational to the complementarian interpretation. If women are to be silent, certainly they cannot be a part of any church governing structures, make judgments about theological issues, participate in decisions of discipline, lead the congregation in worship, or teach the Scriptures. Complementarians believe these verses are Paul's directive to the church delineating a woman's role within the body of believers.

Why would anyone think otherwise?

The Questionable in Light of the Clear

These passages are difficult to interpret and to understand because their injunctions that women should be silent in the church are in direct conflict with the clear message of Scripture, that women are created in God's image equally with men, the masculine and feminine of man. Women are equally redeemed, along with all other believers, by the blood of Christ. They equally receive the Holy Spirit and the new life his presence gives. Women are equally members of God's family, brothers with all believers and with Christ himself, reigning with him through the ministry of reconciliation.

Therefore, women are one with Jesus and with all other believers in the church. Women are bound, as are all believers, to servanthood, the self-sacrificing love and submission all must give to God and to each other, as the primary directive to Christ's body for the realization of our oneness.

With such clear teaching as this from so many parts of Scripture and so widely agreed upon by believers, anything that would change or limit this status for women must be considered difficult. Any teaching that narrows for some the lofty position granted to all believers by God through Christ's redemption must indeed be very clear, completely authoritative, and without question.

The Clear in Light of the Questionable?

How can women participate as equal members of the church if they must be silent while other members of the body need not be silent? Since our speech, our words, express who we are and what we think and feel, how can we contribute our unique gift to build up the body or fully express our praise to God or edify the body in worship equally with others if we are denied this expression?

This obvious conflict between the clear teachings of Scripture about women's status in Christ's body and these injunctions to silence means that these two passages must be interpreted in light of the clear teachings. We must shine the light of the clear on the unclear to see it properly.

The subordination of women, however, is a doctrine that has been built upon these difficult passages and then used as the light in which all other passages that mention women specifically must be seen. And it seems that the deeper the discussion goes, the greater the number of passages that need to be seen by that light.

The subordination of women has grown up as a parallel doctrine, independent of the clear teachings about the equal status of all believers in Christ and in the church. It is no wonder that conflicts and discrepancies appear when the mind seeks consistency and unity on these two divergent and opposing doctrines. As a result, complementarians use the difficult to modify, change, and limit the clear.

But since the Scriptures are one whole, unified truth, these difficult passages must instead be interpreted in light of the clear truths we have already studied.

What's So Difficult?

The central text of this passage as it deals with the status of women in the church is "women should remain silent in the churches. They are not allowed to speak but must be in submission, as the Law says. If they want to inquire about something, they should ask their own husbands at home; for it is disgraceful for a woman to speak in the church."[4]

These verses of Scripture are difficult because:

- the injunction that "women should remain silent" is in direct conflict with what we have learned from the clear teachings of Scripture;
- this command to silence is in conflict with the context of the verses of 1 Corinthians 14:26–40, which surround verses 34 and 35, as well as the context of the whole of the book of 1 Corinthians; and
- the rhetorical questions that immediately follow this injunction to silence in verse 36 are of controversial significance.

Inclusive Language

One of the things that first strikes me is the all-inclusive nature of the entire book of 1 Corinthians and especially this particular passage of 1 Corinthians 14:26–40.

The book is addressed, "To the church of God in Corinth, to those sanctified in Christ Jesus and called to be holy, together with all those everywhere who call on the name of our Lord Jesus Christ—their Lord and ours."[5] These are the brothers that Paul addresses throughout the whole book. Thus defined, women are brothers.

This particular passage is addressed specifically to these brothers both at the beginning and the end. "What then shall we say, ***brothers***? When you come together, everyone has a hymn, or a word of instruction, a revelation, a tongue, or an interpretation."[6] "Therefore, ***my brothers***, be eager to prophesy, and do not forbid speaking in tongues."[7] Paul is here addressing all the brothers, male and female, of the church in Corinth.

Orderliness in Worship

With this inclusive language, Paul opens his discussion on orderliness in worship by saying that of the brothers, "everyone" should have "a hymn, or a word of instruction, a revelation, a tongue or an interpretation."[8] These things are not a matter of choice or inclination, but rather things that "must be done for the strengthening of the church."[9] These necessary things are not to be done by only a few, not by a special class of Christian or appointed group, but by everyone. And Paul makes no distinction about who is to do what. *Everyone* is eligible to contribute in each area: "a hymn, or a word of instruction, a revelation, a tongue or an interpretation. . . . for the strengthening of the whole church."

The word *everyone* is used many times in the New Testament. Of course. It is a common word with a common meaning: "every person." That includes men and women. "Repent and be baptized, ***every one of you***, in the name of Jesus Christ for the forgiveness of your sins."[10] It is interesting to note that Paul says *everyone* may bring "a word of instruction" and "an interpretation." Women are forbidden participation in these two areas in particular, according to the complementarian interpretation. Yet here Paul says that any "brother" is eligible to bring one of these to worship "for the strengthening of the church."

After Paul opens the discussion by clearly stating that all should take part in the strengthening of the church, he goes on to give some guidelines so that all may truly participate. In my mind's eye, I can see Paul telling the Corinthians the same thing that I might tell a group of children eagerly playing a game.

In my imagination, all the children are clamoring to be it at the same time. I smile and encourage them to calm down, assuring them that everyone will get a turn. I tell them that everyone can play, but they must be patient and wait their turn or else the game will be ruined for everyone and no one will have any fun. Paul is saying the same thing: Calm down. Everyone may contribute in turn, but we must be polite and kind and listen in turn, or no one will be strengthened or encouraged.

If we missed the inclusive nature of Paul's opening statements, he says them again. "For you can ***all*** prophesy in turn so that everyone may be instructed and encouraged."[11] The original Greek uses the word *all* three times. *All* can prophesy so that *all* may learn and *all* be encouraged. Certainly no one would want to exclude women from the latter two instances of *all.* Women need to learn and be encouraged like everyone else. So we can infer that the first *all* includes women as well. Women may prophesy along with everyone else, if it is done in an orderly manner, if they take turns, if they listen to others.

Prophesy That Teaches

Paul says that prophecy is for the purpose of instruction.[12] All are not only to be encouraged by prophesy, but all are also to learn from prophesy. Prophesy can be a form of teaching.

This echoes Paul's previous affirmation from chapter 11 that women may prophesy: "And every woman who prays or prophesies with her head uncovered dishonors her head."[13]

Yet, as everyone participates, there must be peace and order because that is a reflection of God himself. "For God is not a God of disorder but of peace."[14] Peace and order is the way for the church.

"As in All the Churches"?

The King James Version translates verse 33 this way: "For God is not the author of confusion, but of peace, as in all churches of the saints."[15] It treats verse 33 as one complete sentence. The New American Standard Bible also attaches the phrase, "as in all the churches of the saints"[16] to the peace and order that Paul says God's own nature requires of his church.

The New International Version, however, attaches this phrase to the following verses that command the women to be silent. "As in all the congregations of the saints, women should remain silent."[17] This would seem to say that all the churches practiced the silence of women. But since this command to silence is refuted by Paul a few verses later as an ungodly practice, the phrase "as in all the congregations of the saints" must therefore belong with the former sentence where Paul says that peace and order is required of all churches because it comes from God himself.

Women Must Be Silent

Now we come to the very strict declaration that women must be silent.

> Women should remain silent in the churches. They are not allowed to speak, but must be in submission, as the Law says. If they want to inquire about something they should ask their own husbands at home; for it is disgraceful for a woman to speak in the church.[18]

What?
What!
How can Paul say this?

How can Paul possibly tell women they must remain silent after he has just told them they should have "a hymn, or a word of instruction, a revelation, a tongue or an interpretation . . . for the strengthening of the church," as are all the brothers?[19] How can women share their hymn or word of instruction, revelation, tongue, or interpretation if they remain silent?

How can Paul say this to women when he has just told them that everyone can prophesy in turn? How can the women instruct or encourage the others through their prophesy if they must be silent?[20]

How can Paul say this when he has just explained in detail the importance and necessity of every gift, every member in the church? How can women exercise their gift "for the common good" if they must remain silent?[21]

How can Paul say, "it is disgraceful for a woman to speak in the church"? He has just said,

> The eye cannot say to the hand. "I don't need you!" . . . But God has combined the members of the body and has given greater honor to the parts that lacked it, so that there should be no division in the body, but that its parts should have equal concern for each other. . . . Now you are the body of Christ, and each one of you is a part of it.[22]

How can Paul say the women may not even ask a question when he has just told the Corinthians that each one of them has been given a "manifestation of the Spirit . . . for the common good"?[23]

How can Paul say this when he has just upheld the women's new freedom in Christ to pray and prophesy publicly in worship?[24]

How can Paul say this when he has just told us that "in the Lord" men and women are completely interdependent?[25] What does "in the Lord" mean if not "in the church"?[26]

How can Paul say this when his theme in this letter to the Corinthians is that divisions in the church are sinful? How can there be "no divisions" when half of the group is required to be silent and the other half is not? How can the Corinthians "be perfectly united in mind and thought"[27] if none of the women are allowed to voice their thoughts?

How can Paul pass on the greeting of Priscilla to all the Corinthians if it is "disgraceful for a woman to speak in the church"?[28]

How can Paul say it is "disgraceful" for women to speak in the church when they have received grace[29] and been "sanctified in Christ Jesus and called to be holy"?[30]

How dare he?[31]

What? What!

Am I overreacting?

I don't think so.

And furthermore, I don't think Paul did say it.[32]

In fact, I think Paul reacted in just the same way I have reacted when he first heard of this practice. Paul said just what I said, "What? . . . What!"

I do not believe that Paul was the originator of the idea or practice contained in verses 34–35. The reasons I just listed are but some examples of why I don't believe Paul could possibly have promoted such an idea.

Rather, I believe these verses were an idea created by some who wanted to gain power in the church through ruling over the women. Keeping people silent is a classic way of exercising power. This idea must have gained credence within the Corinthian church, causing just one more division that Paul was writing against.

Paul was not willing to let such a departure from the truth stand, so here he first summarized the idea being propagated as a true directive for the church, and then he reacted to it.

I can hear some now saying, "Wait a minute! Where does she get these ideas?"

So the question before you and the church today is, Is this command that the women should be silent a directive from Paul for the church, or is it a custom that Paul is really condemning as improper for the body of Christ? Is Paul commending and promoting this practice, or is he refuting and rejecting it?

This question arises from the two rhetorical questions that follow the injunction to silence. Paul often uses rhetorical questions. It's a familiar teaching technique. The teacher asks questions, and when the students see the answers, the truth becomes more evident.

Paul Rejects False Ideas

Paul often uses this technique to demonstrate the falseness of an idea. The rhetorical question reinforces the rejection of the idea under discussion. The answers to the rhetorical questions are obvious. Sometimes the questions begin, "Do you not know," and then Paul states an obvious truth that refutes the false idea. Sometimes the questions are almost sarcastic as Paul puts down the false thinking.

These rhetorical questions are often used with a small Greek word[33] that expresses disassociation or rejection. Paul introduces both of his questions following the silence injunction with this word. In the following quote of verse 36, I have placed a lightning bolt symbol[34] to illustrate this Greek word and where it occurs. "ϟ Did the word of God originate with you? ϟ are you the only people it has reached?"[35]

Those of us who read our Bibles in English are tipped off to the existence of this tiny word by the exclamation "What?" at the beginning of verse 36 in the King James Version. This type of expression is common in our own language. *What?* is a rhetorical question or expression of disbelief meaning, "You must be joking!" or "Am I hearing you right?" or "You can't mean that!"

Even though the word appears twice in verse 36, the NIV translates it only once as "or" at the beginning of the second question.

After this type of question, Paul often gives a summary statement of the truth so his readers will be clear on exactly what his position is.

Paul's Rhetorical Technique

Below I have given some examples of Paul's use of this technique of rhetorical questions, introduced by the Greek word I illustrate as a lightning bolt symbol and followed by a summary of the truth I have ***emphasized***. All of these examples are from the book of 1 Corinthians.

Paul rejects and refutes the practice of believers idolizing various Christian leaders and thus causing division in the church.

> What I mean is this: One of you says, "I follow Paul"; another, "I follow Apollos"; another, "I follow Cephas"; still another, "I follow Christ." Is Christ divided? Was Paul crucified for you? ϟ Were you baptized into the name of Paul? . . . . ***For Christ did not send me to baptize, but to preach the gospel—not with words of human wisdom, lest the cross of Christ be emptied of its power.***[36]

Paul rejects and refutes the practice of believers solving their quarrels by suing each other in civil courts.

> If any of you has a dispute with another, dare he take it before the ungodly for judgment instead of before the saints? ϟ Do you not know that the saints will judge the world? And if you are to judge the world, are you not competent to judge trivial cases? Do you not know that we

> will judge angels? How much more the things of this life! . . . ϟ Do you not know that the wicked will not inherit the kingdom of God? . . . ***And that is what some of you were. But you were washed, you were sanctified, you were justified in the name of the Lord Jesus Christ and by the Spirit of our God.***[37]

Paul rejects and refutes the idea that sexual sin hurts no one: what you do with your own body is your own business, nobody else's.[38]

> Do you not know that your bodies are members of Christ himself? Shall I then take the members of Christ and unite them with a prostitute? Never! ϟ Do you not know that he who unites himself with a prostitute is one with her in body? For it is said, "The two will become one flesh." But he who unites himself with the Lord is one with him in spirit.
>
> Flee from sexual immorality. All other sins a man commits are outside his body, but he who sins sexually sins against his own body. ϟ Do you not know that your body is a temple of the Holy Spirit, who is in you, whom you have received from God? ***You are not your own; you were bought at a price. Therefore honor God with your body.***[39]

Paul rejects and refutes the idea that it is wrong for him to receive support or money for his work for the gospel.

> This is my defense to those who sit in judgment on me. Don't we have the right to take a believing wife along with us, as do the other apostles and the Lord's brothers and Cephas? ϟ is it only I and Barnabas who must work for a living? Who serves as a soldier at his own expense? Who plants a vineyard and does not eat of its grapes? ϟ Who tends a flock and does not drink of the milk? ***. . . If we have sown spiritual seed among you, is it too much if we reap a material harvest from you? If others have this right of support from you, shouldn't we have it all the more?***[40]

Paul rejects and refutes the practice of eating meat offered to idols or participating in idol feasts.

> The sacrifices of pagans are offered to demons, not to God, and I do not want you to be participants with demons. ***You cannot drink the cup of the Lord and the cup of demons too; you cannot have a part in both the Lord's table and the table of demons.*** ϟ Are we trying to arouse the Lord's jealousy? Are we stronger than he?[41]

Paul rejects and refutes the practice of making the Lord's supper a selfish pleasure feast.

> When you come together, it is not the Lord's Supper you eat, for as you eat, each of you goes ahead without waiting for anybody else. One remains hungry, another gets drunk. Don't you have homes to eat and drink in? ϟ do you despise the church of God and humiliate those who have nothing? What shall I say to you? Shall I praise you for this? Certainly not![42]

The summary statement is quite long, but these are the main points: "***For whenever you eat this bread and drink this cup, you proclaim the Lord's death until he comes. . . . A man ought to examine himself before he eats of the bread and drinks of the cup. . . . So then, brothers, when you come together to eat, wait for each other.***"[43]

Paul rejects and refutes the idea that women must be silent in the church because their participation is disgraceful.

> Women should remain silent in the churches. They are not allowed to speak, but must be in submission, as the Law says. If they want to inquire about something, they should ask their own husbands at home; for it is disgraceful for a woman to speak in the church. ϟ Did the word of God originate with you? ϟ are you the only people it has reached? If anybody thinks he is a prophet or spiritually gifted, let him acknowledge that what I am writing to you is the Lord's command. If he ignores this, he himself will be ignored. ***Therefore, my brothers, be eager to prophesy, and do not forbid speaking in tongues. But everything should be done in a fitting and orderly way.***[44]

Silence Commended or Refuted?

Again, the question: Is Paul commending the practice of silencing the women or refuting it? Given the all inclusive nature of everything he has said so far, it seems strange that he would now contradict himself by excluding the women from any participation.

The two rhetorical questions which follow the idea that women should be silent verge on the sarcastic. "Did the word of God originate with you? Or are you the only people it has reached?" Today we might have said, "Do you have some special revelation from God? Are you the only people God speaks to?"

The obvious answer is "No!" The word of God did not originate with the Corinthians. The Corinthians were not the only people to receive God's Word. Far from it. God's revelation comes to all believers, and it is the same revelation for all believers. The Corinthians had only recently received the gospel. Paul makes it clear in the following verses 37–38 that the Corinthians are the learners here and should humbly accept what Paul is teaching.

Nonsense!

Even in English, in our present-day language structure and usage, when we ask a rhetorical question to which we expect no answer, it often follows a previous idea that we are rejecting. We might even use the word *or* to introduce the questions. Or we might use lightning bolt words such as, *Nonsense! You're joking!* or *The whole idea is crazy!*

Here are a few examples from our own language usage:

- "Dishwashing is women's work. ϟ Don't the rest of you have hands?"
- "Why do I always have to be the one to apologize? ϟ Are you never wrong?"
- "Oh sure. Dad pays for everything. ϟ Don't you know you have to learn to be responsible for yourself. ϟ Does it look like I'm made out of money?"

In the examples I cited from 1 Corinthians, try reading, "Nonsense!" for the lightning bolt symbols that illustrate the small Greek word. Does it make sense?

Common Sense

Which of the numbered alternatives below make more sense following Paul's explanation that all should participate in worship, but in an orderly way, taking turns, for the strengthening, encouraging, and instruction of all?[45]

1. Except for the women. They cannot speak at all. They should be completely silent. This is what the law says. They cannot even ask questions. In fact, it is disgraceful for them to be heard at all.[46]

   We will now add the rhetorical questions and see if the meaning is altered or made more obvious in any way.
2. Women must be silent, excluded completely from all participation! What? Did you write the word of God? Or are you the only one God speaks to?[47]

   Is the meaning further clarified when we add more?
3. Women must be silent! What! Do you have some special revelation from God? If you think you are so spiritual, you had better listen to me,

because what I am saying is straight from God. If you don't listen, no one will listen to you either.[48]

Let's complete the picture.

4. Women must be silent! What! Do you have some special revelation from God? If you think you are so spiritual, you had better listen, because this is God's command. Therefore, all you believers should be eager to prophesy. Don't even forbid the speaking in tongues. Just be sure everything is done in an orderly way.[49]

Silence Rejected!

The nature of the rhetorical questions Paul asks the Corinthians in verse 36, the obvious answer to these questions, Paul's remarks to those who consider themselves to be spiritually gifted, and his summary statement all build to show Paul's rejection of the idea that comes before the questions.

What Law?

The fact that the command for women to be silent is based on the law, but no such law can be found in the Old Testament, is interesting. "They are not allowed to speak, but must be in submission, as the Law says."[50] That would seem to say that those who promoted this practice for women to keep silent were basing it on some special revelation, some revelation not available to all, some revelation not universally accepted as from God.

Earlier in this letter, Paul dealt with a similar subject, again having to do with judging people, putting them in various categories. This time the question deals with which people are to be the most highly esteemed.

> Now, brothers, I have applied these things to myself and Apollos for your benefit, so that you may learn from us the meaning of the saying, "Do not go beyond what is written." Then you will not take pride in one man over against another. For who makes you different from anyone else? What do you have that you did not receive? And if you did receive it, why do you boast as though you did not?[51]

The saying Paul quotes, "Do not go beyond what is written," is not an Old Testament quote. But Paul uses it here to tell the Corinthians that they shouldn't go beyond scriptural standards, standards he has already quoted in 1 Corinthians 1:19, 31, and 3:19, as they judge or rank each other. Why? Because whatever fellow believers are, they are as a result of God's grace to them. So no one can be prideful or infer more from it than God himself does.[52]

The Law and Grace

There were those in the early church who wanted to merge Christianity with Judaism. They wanted to be saved through Jesus, the Messiah, but they also thought they had to continue trying to please God through observance of the law.[53] They were willing to open the doors of the church to the Gentiles, but they had to be circumcised. Yet Paul made it clear that this was the path back to slavery and death. "But now, by dying to what once bound us, we have been released from the law so that we serve in the new way of the Spirit, and not in the old way of the written code."[54] Perhaps some were also willing to allow the women into the church, but they had to be silent, "as the Law says."[55]

In fact Paul told Timothy that the law is no longer the standard for the believer. "We know that the law is good if one uses it properly. We also know that law is made not for the righteous but for lawbreakers and rebels . . . and for whatever else is contrary to the sound doctrine that conforms to the glorious gospel of the blessed God." What is the standard for the believer? "Sound doctrine that conforms to the glorious gospel of the blessed God."

Who said that women must be silent in the church? "The Law says." We don't know what law. We don't know whose law. But now it really doesn't matter anyway, because we are no longer bound by the requirements of the law.[56] We have been freed from its bondage through Christ. Right here in this same letter to the Corinthians, Paul says that he himself is "not under the law."[57] He says that the law is "the power of sin" that has been swallowed up in Christ's victory on the cross, which God gives to us.[58]

The Law and Truth

Paul's inclusion of this information may be our biggest clue that he is refuting this statement. Paul has this to say to those who think the law is the last word on the truth:

> If you rely on the law and brag about your relationship to God: if you know his will and approve of what is superior because you are instructed by the law: if you are convinced that you are a guide for the blind, a light for those who are in the dark, an instructor of the foolish, a teacher of infants, because you have in the law the embodiment of knowledge and truth—you then, who teach others, do you not teach yourself? . . . You who brag about the law, do you dishonor God by breaking the law?[59]

This reprimand by Paul to those who rely on the law also has the same sound as verses 37–38 in this passage: "If anybody thinks he is a prophet or spiritually gifted, let him acknowledge that what I am writing to you is the Lord's command. If he ignores this, he himself will be ignored."[60]

The Lord's Command

Now complementarians might say that what is being rejected and refuted here is the practice of women speaking and participating in the church. Yet Paul's all inclusive language in his admonitions to full participation by everyone[61] would seem to be in conflict with that interpretation.

The correct interpretation is very important because what Paul is "writing to" us concerning whether women may participate in church gatherings or not "is the Lord's command" and can only be ignored at great risk.[62]

Throughout the entire passage, Paul is saying everyone should have opportunity to participate in worship in many different ways. Everyone should participate because this is important for the strengthening, encouragement, and instruction of the whole church. But this participation by all must be done in an orderly way by all taking turns, with only one person at a time speaking, while others listen. This manner of worship is proper because it reflects God's nature of order and peace.

Does this interpretation fit with Paul's final summary statement? "Therefore, my brothers, be eager to prophesy, and do not forbid speaking in tongues. But everything should be done in a fitting and orderly way."[63]

This summary statement is again addressed all inclusively to the brothers to whom this letter of first Corinthians is written. These brothers are told that their desire to share verbally with others in worship is a good thing. These brothers are encouraged to eagerly anticipate and practice full participation in worship. Only one limitation is imposed, that of fitting and proper orderliness. No other limitations are commanded. All participation was to be allowed. Even the speaking in tongues was not to be forbidden, which seems very permissive and open considering that Paul had spoken as if it were not as valuable as some other forms of participation.[64]

The central text of this passage as Paul wrote it is in verses 26 and 39–40.

> What then shall we say, ***brothers***? When you come together, ***everyone*** has a hymn, or a word of instruction, a revelation, a tongue or an interpretation. All of these must be done for the strengthening of the church. . . . Therefore, my ***brothers***, be eager to prophesy, and do not forbid speaking in tongues. But everything should be done in a fitting and orderly way.[65]

Rather than being a passage to limit the participation of women in the church, Paul upholds a woman's full and equal place among the brothers. She may participate with all.[66] She must follow the same design for peace and order that everyone must follow,[67] for this is the nature of God himself.[68] A woman need not be silent. And it is not disgraceful for a woman to speak in the church. Instead, Paul questions those who want to silence the women. "What!"[69]

> Did the word of God originate with you? Or are you the only people it has reached? If anybody thinks he is a prophet or spiritually gifted, let him acknowledge that what I am writing to you is the Lord's command. If he ignores this, he himself will be ignored.[70]

Why? I Don't Know

If full participation for women in church gatherings is the correct interpretation, how could God have allowed this to happen? Why has this truth been hidden for almost two thousand years? Surely if this is true, the church would not have followed the opposite path throughout these centuries!

I don't know why this truth is being rediscovered only now. But I do know that even the heart of the gospel itself, "by grace you have been saved, through faith—and this not from yourselves, it is the gift of God—not of works, so that no one can boast,"[71] was hidden for a thousand years or more. I do know that the church has at other times been deceived by false doctrines for a time. I do know that our struggle to fully attain the truth is just that: a struggle.[72] We can never assume we know all the truth. We can never assume we know all that is to be known.[73]

Perhaps God wanted to reveal his strength through our weakness.[74] Perhaps God wanted to teach us perseverance.[75] Perhaps this is all a part of God's maturing process for his church.[76]

Any straying from the truth brings suffering. Women have not been the only ones to suffer from this false idea. The whole church has suffered.[77] And perhaps God has ordained that the church learn obedience through this suffering, just as Christ did.[78]

I do not know.

What I Do Know

When we don't know, we can do nothing but go back to what we do know.

"***I know*** that my Redeemer lives, and that in the end he will stand upon the earth. And after my skin has been destroyed, yet in my flesh I will see God: I myself will see him with my own eyes—I, and not another. How my heart yearns within me!"[79]

"***For I resolve to know nothing . . . except Jesus Christ*** and him crucified."[80]

> But thanks be to God! He gives us the victory through our Lord Jesus Christ. Therefore, my dear brothers, stand firm. Let nothing move you. Always give yourselves fully to the work of the Lord, because ***you know*** that your labor in the Lord is not in vain.[81]

"And ***we know*** that in all things God works for the good of those who love him, who have been called according to his purpose."[82]

There are many things we don't know, but "***I want to know Christ*** and the power of his resurrection and the fellowship of sharing in his sufferings, becoming like him in his death, and so somehow, to attain to the resurrection from the dead."[83]

"That is why I am suffering as I am. Yet I am not ashamed, because ***I know*** whom I have believed, and am convinced that he is able to guard what I have entrusted to him for that day."[84]

What we know must envelop and transcend what we do not know.

Three Practical Applications

This injunction for women to be silent in the church is usually interpreted in one of three ways:

1. That this is an idea Paul is refuting and rejecting as wrong and out of accord with God's will for the church and how it is to worship him;
2. That women are to be silent at all times in all ways within the structure of the church defined both as a living community and a formal institution; or
3. That women need only remain silent in the government of the church and in the preaching of the word in a formal worship service: that is, the ordained offices of the church institution. Otherwise women are free to fully participate. Except for preaching, that participation might include vocal and individual participation in a formal worship service, such as prayer, singing, Scripture reading, and so on; teaching the Scripture under the oversight of elders or in a nonformal setting; addressing groups and conferences on specialized topics of interest to believers; working with committees or ministries within the structure of the church institution, and so on.

Interpretation 2, though quite logical and consistent with the stringent language of verses 34 and 35 themselves, is held by very few people, probably because it is so difficult to consistently live with when confronted with the real gifts and labors of the women of the church, let alone the rest of the gospel. This interpretation is not really given much credibility among those who have most vocally and aggressively entered into this debate about the status of women in the church. Interpretations 1 and 3 are those held more widely.

Compare these three interpretations carefully after reading again verses 34 and 35.

> Women should remain silent in the churches. They are not allowed to speak, but must be in submission as the Law says. If they want to inquire about something, they should ask their own husbands at home: for it is disgraceful for a woman to speak in the church.[85]

Four Questions

Now, ask four questions about the three interpretations.

Question 1: Which interpretation fits best into

- the immediate context of 1 Corinthians 14:26–40: full participation in worship by all members in an orderly way?
- the broader context of 1 Corinthians 12: the church as one body with many members, each with a spiritual gift that is necessary and important?
- the broader context of 1 Corinthians 13: the nature of love, the "most excellent way"?
- the broader context of 1 Corinthians 11:11–12: a statement of the complete interdependence of men and women "in the Lord" as part of a discussion upholding a woman's new freedom to pray and prophesy in the public worship?
- the broader context of 1 Corinthians 7: a listing of the mutual and equal rights and responsibilities of husbands and wives ?[86]
- the broader context of the whole book of 1 Corinthians: Paul's theme of the refutation and rejection of divisions which mar the oneness of the church? "I appeal to you, brothers, in the name of our Lord Jesus Christ, that all of you agree with one another so that there may be no divisions among you and that you may be perfectly united in mind and thought."[87]

Question 2: Which interpretation best fits with the basic gospel message—the clear teaching of Scripture—that salvation comes only by the grace of God through faith in Jesus Christ to all who believe?[88]

Question 3: Which interpretation can we more easily envision being understood by the first readers of this letter? Whatever Paul's message was to the Corinthian church of the first century, God has the same message for us today.[89]

- Would the Corinthian readers have understood that Paul was commanding the women to be silent only in the preaching of the word in a formal worship service and that this silence also meant that they could not participate in the government of the church, but they could lead Bible studies and speak occasionally under informal circumstances, even though it was not considered proper for them to even ask questions?
- Would the Corinthian readers have understood that Paul was telling them that women could teach men in the informal circumstances of the home under the oversight of their husbands or the elders of the church, but not in the official church structure of services, even though the church may have met in women's homes?[90]
- Would the Corinthians have understood that "in the churches" does not mean the community of brothers as they live, work, and worship together,[91] but just the formal, called worship services of that community, not including prayer meetings, Bible studies or classes, fellowship, or social gatherings, and so on?
- Would the Corinthian women have understood that even though Paul said it was "disgraceful" for them to speak, the work of Christ's grace, which "was not without effect," in their lives was just the same as the work of grace in the lives of the men?[92] Would the Corinthian women have understood that even though it was disgraceful for them to speak, their gifts from the Spirit were still all necessary and important?[93]

Question 4: Which interpretation takes more hermeneutic maneuvering to make everything fit together, within the passage of 1 Corinthians 14:26–40 itself, and with the rest of Scripture as a whole?

Your Word Is a Light

Remember the campfire? Now even if we do take a flashlight, the light of God's Word,[94] and walk the path through the woods, it may seem strange. The path may not be as smooth as the road we have been used to. When we get there, we may not feel as comfortable as we did in the lodge. But we will have reached the real campfire, and the fellowship will be more intense, and the majesty of God's work will be more obvious, as promised.[95]

> The eye cannot say to the hand, "I don't need you!" And the head cannot say to the feet, "I don't need you!" On the contrary, those parts of the body that seem to be weaker are indispensable, and the parts that we think are less honorable we treat with special honor. And the parts that are unpresentable are treated with special modesty, while our presentable parts need no special treatment. But God has combined the members of

the body and has given greater honor to the parts that lacked it, so that there should be no division in the body, but that its parts should have equal concern for each other. If one part suffers, every part suffers with it: if one part is honored, every part rejoices with it. Now you are the body of Christ, and each one of you is a part of it.[96]

The Question

What is the meaning of 1 Corinthians 14:26–40?

What do we know to be true?

- The whole letter and this portion in particular are addressed to brothers.[97]
  Brothers are
  those of "the church of God in Corinth;
  those sanctified in Christ Jesus and called to be holy;
  together with all those everywhere
  who call on the name of our Lord Jesus Christ—their Lord and ours."[98]

- Everyone should have the opportunity to participate when believers come together by contributing something from the following:[99]
  A hymn[100]
  A word of instruction[101]
  A revelation[102]
  A tongue[103]
  An interpretation[104]
  A prophesy[105]

- This must be done
  for the strengthening of the church,[106]
  so that everyone may be instructed and encouraged.[107]

- This must be done in a peaceful and orderly way[108]
  by taking turns,[109]
  by only speaking one at a time,[110]
  by listening when others are speaking,[111]
  because God is a God of peace, not disorder,[112]
  in all the congregations of the saints.[113]

- The context of 1 Corinthians 14:26–40 is
  the "most excellent way" of love;[114]
  the spiritual gifts given to all brothers;[115] and
  the oneness of the body of Christ,[116]
  without divisions.[117]

The Question

What is the meaning of 1 Corinthians 14:34–35?

What do we know to be true?

- If women are silent in the church,[118]
  they cannot speak;[119]
  they cannot ask a question;[120]
  they cannot share a hymn, a word of instruction, a revelation, a tongue, an interpretation, or a prophesy;[121]
  they cannot take turns;[122]
  they should not be eager to prophesy;[123] and
  the church must be divided into two groups using the physical standard of male/female.[124]

- Women cannot be silent
  if they are to have the opportunity to share a hymn, a word of instruction, a revelation, a tongue, an interpretation, or a prophesy;[125]
  if they are to contribute to the strengthening, encouragement, and instruction of all in the church through these means;[126] and
  if they are to be eager to prophesy.[127]

- The injunction for women to be silent originates in the law.[128]
  We have been released from the law.[129]
  We are no longer under the law.[130]
  The law is no longer the standard for believers[131]
  because the law is the power of sin,[132] and
  because the law has been swallowed up in Christ's victory on the cross.[133]
  The standard for the believer is
  "sound doctrine that conforms to the glorious gospel of the blessed God."[134]

- Women are brothers.[135]

- Each brother[136] is
  to have a hymn, a word of instruction, a revelation, a tongue, an interpretation, or a prophesy when the church comes together;[137]
  to contribute strength, encouragement, and instruction to all;[138] and
  to be eager to prophesy.[139]

- Paul often uses rhetorical questions
  introduced by a small Greek word expressing rejection,[140]
  as a part of his refutation of a false idea,[141]
  followed by a summary of the truth of the matter.[142]

- Paul follows the injunction for women to be silent with two rhetorical questions,[143]
  both introduced by the Greek word expressing rejection,[144] and
  followed by a summary of what he is writing.[145]

- What Paul is writing is the Lord's command.[146]

- If we misinterpret what Paul is writing, we will be ignored.[147]

- The context of 1 Corinthians 14:34-35 is
  the call for all to participate in worship for the strengthening of the church;[148]
  the complete interdependence of men and women "in the Lord," created equal by God;[149]
    the new freedom women have through Christ to pray and prophesy;[150]
    the equal and mutual rights and responsibilities of husbands and wives;[151]
    the gospel of Jesus Christ[152]
      that all brothers have received[153]
        through God's grace which is not without effect[154]
      on which all brothers have taken their stand,[155]
      by which all brothers are saved.[156]

- ***The clear teachings of Scripture:***
  oneness[157]
  no difference[158]
  servanthood[159]
  brothers[160]
    Each is redeemed by the blood of Christ.[161]
    Each is sanctified by the Holy Spirit.[162]
    Each will rule with Christ.[163]

"Come, O Lord."[164]

My daughters Christina and Elizabeth and daughter-in-law Ann~1997.

Chapter 14

Must She Be Silent?
1 Timothy 2:8–15

"Shut up!"

My parents taught me this was no decent way to talk. I was never allowed to use these words. Still, I know I did sometimes, especially when a sister was being particularly insulting.

I also remember what it felt like to be on the receiving end of such language. Not good.

Why do we consider this expression such a nasty insult?

Our words express who we are, what we think and feel. Our words also express our need to communicate and share ourselves with others. So when we are told, "Shut up!" we are told that who we are is not important to the listener. Being told "Shut up!" hurts because it is like being told we are nothing.

"Be Quiet!"

This expression is one especially familiar to children. They hear it often. As a teacher, I have used "Be quiet!" more than I care to admit. With these words, I call my students to attention. I want them to be quiet so that they can listen and learn from me. It is very difficult for one to talk and hear at the same time. Students do not usually find "Be quiet!" as insulting as "Shut up!"

"Be silent!"

I have used this expression with my own children. Not often—only when I have become so exasperated with their disrespectful and disobedient mouths that silencing them seemed the only proper response. I have used it as both a reprimand and a punishment. If they were abusing the privilege of speech, it would be denied them for a while, for their own enlightenment and discipline. What I meant by "Be silent!" was that they should not make even the tiniest sound. They shouldn't talk to me. They shouldn't talk to anyone. They should be completely and totally silent.

Is this what Paul is saying to women in 1 Timothy? Is his meaning one of these? Or all of them together?

"I do not permit a woman to teach or to have authority over a man: she must be silent."[1]

Why Difficult?

This verse is difficult for exactly the same reason that we found 1 Corinthians 14:34–35 difficult. The message of this verse, as the church has traditionally interpreted it, is in conflict with the clear teachings of Scripture.

It is also difficult because the Greek word translated in the NIV as "to have authority over"[2] is used only this one time in Scripture. This means we cannot learn from how it was used in other instances. Denied this valuable tool, its meaning is made even more difficult to ascertain.

A Helpful Concept

The traditional interpretation is based on the idea that if a woman is not to have authority over a man, then it must be true that a man is to have authority over a woman.

In mathematics there are three ways that numbers can be related to each other.

x can be greater than y ($x > y$).
x can be less than y ($x < y$).
x can be equal to y ($x = y$).

A math student may be presented with a problem that is a statement of what is ***not*** true. For example, x is not greater than y, ($x \ngtr y$). Before the unknown can be found, the student must first state the problem in terms of what may be true rather than in terms of what is not true.

Here is a concept we can use to help us understand this entire passage. If we first eliminate what we know to be false, we can more easily see what is true.

But here students often make a very common mistake. They assume that since x is not greater than y, then x must be less than y. But if they try to solve the problem based on that statement of truth, the answer will be wrong—wrong because they did not properly state what may be true before going on to solve the problem. If x is not greater than y, that does not necessarily mean that x is less than y. It could also mean that x is equal to y. Both are legitimate possibilities deduced from the true, though negative, statement presented in the original problem.

Who Should Have Authority?

Now Paul has presented us with a true, but negative statement: "I do not permit a woman . . . to have authority over a man."[3] Before we can solve the problem of its true meaning, we must first state the problem in terms of what may be true. The two possibilities are that Paul requires, and consequently, God requires,

1. a man to have authority over a woman, or
2. a man and a woman to be equal in authority.

We know that we must apply the clear teaching of Scripture to those parts that are difficult. Even the briefest shining of the clear on this difficult passage leads us toward the second possibility, that a man and a woman are equal, for "In the Lord, . . . woman is not independent of man, nor is man independent of woman. For as woman came from man, so also man is born of woman. But everything comes from God."[4] The clear teachings of oneness, no difference, servanthood, and brothers demonstrate the complete equality of men and women.

So You Will Know

The book of 1 Timothy was written by Paul to Timothy, his "true son in the faith."[5] It is a personal letter. "Timothy, my son, I give you this instruction in keeping with the prophecies once made about you, so that by following them you may fight the good fight, holding on to faith and a good conscience."[6]

But Paul not only writes personal instructions[7] and encouragement to Timothy, but he also gives him instructions concerning the church in Ephesus of which Timothy is evidently an overseer.[8] "1 am writing you these instructions so that, . . . you will know how people ought to conduct themselves in God's household, which is the church of the living God, the pillar and foundation of the truth."[9]

Paul wants Timothy to administer these instructions[10] in complete fairness, since partiality and favoritism have no place in the church. "I charge you, in the sight of God and Christ Jesus and the elect angels, to keep these instructions without partiality, and to do nothing out of favoritism."[11] Since Paul calls on God to witness this charge to Timothy, we know Paul felt that both the instructions and their impartial administration were from God. In fact, this injunction comes after Paul has given some lengthy examples of how Timothy is to be carefully fair.[12]

False Doctrine

The problem of false teachings is one of the issues Paul addresses throughout this book.[13] Paul originally left Timothy in Ephesus for this very purpose—to stop those who were teaching false doctrines.[14]

These promoters of false doctrine evidently wanted to be thought of as "teachers of the law."[15] Yet Paul contrasts their teachings with "God's work—which is by faith."[16] The goal in stopping the false teaching is "love, which comes from a pure heart and a good conscience and a sincere faith."[17] Paul sees faith as a characteristic of God's work as opposed to the false teachings.

Sound Doctrine

The false teachings are an improper use of the law[18] as contrasted with sound doctrine.[19] Paul gives us a very clear definition of *sound doctrine*: that which "***conforms to the glorious gospel*** of the blessed God."[20] Later he calls it "the sound instruction of our Lord Jesus Christ."[21]

Throughout this letter Paul gives a few specifics of sound doctrine.[22] His purpose here is not to explain the gospel in detail because he knows that Timothy already fully understands and accepts the gospel. But since the gospel is such an integral part of Paul's life, he cannot help but refer to it.

This sound doctrine is God's work which has been entrusted to Paul.[23] Paul not only is a beneficiary of this gospel,[24] but he has also been appointed a "herald and an apostle . . . a teacher of the true faith to the Gentiles."[25]

Conduct in the Church

Chapter 2 is the beginning of Paul's instruction concerning "how people ought to conduct themselves in God's household, which is the church of the living God."[26] He begins by calling upon the church to pray for "kings and all those in authority."[27] In America I am afraid we have grown complacent and have not prayed for our authorities in government as we should, though perhaps we are now waking up. But in other countries, it is common for Christians to pray for the authorities in their governments. Their goal is the same as the one Paul states. These Christians want to be able to live peaceful lives. They want to be able to continue practicing their faith unhindered. They do not want the oppression of government to come to bear on them or their faith. And of course they can pray for this, being assured it is a prayer according to the will of God, "who wants all men to be saved and to come to a knowledge of the truth."[28]

Here Paul interjects a bit of sound doctrine. The truth men need to come to is that "there is one God and one mediator between God and men, the man Christ Jesus, who gave himself as a ransom for all men."[29]

Now we come to the difficult verses that have a direct bearing on the status of women in the church. First Paul addresses the men, and then the women.

To the Men

"I want men everywhere to lift up holy hands in prayer, without anger or disputing."[30]

Suppose we have a guest for dinner. It is the first time this person has been in our home and met my husband, sons, and daughters. After dinner the guest overhears me say to my sons, "Boys, I want you to do a thorough job of the dishes without fighting." What will my guest understand by this direction to my sons?

Will the guest understand that the boys are the only ones who are ever to do the dishes? Or that the boys are the only ones who are supposed to do the dishes thoroughly? No! Our guest will assume, correctly, that the boys are to do the dishes ***without fighting***. She may also correctly assume that this fighting has been a problem in the past when the boys have done the dishes. Now of course, our guest will also assume that I want the boys to do the dishes tonight and that I want them to do a thorough job. But the main thrust of my direction will be understood by all to be "No fighting!"

Paul's instructions to the men are not difficult. They are quite straightforward. The language is very similar to what we would use today, as I have just tried to illustrate. Paul did not mean that women shouldn't pray. He didn't mean that women shouldn't pray with uplifted hands. Nor did he mean that women should pray with anger and disputing.

We can eliminate these ideas as possible meanings for this verse because we know they are not true.

Women are to do all these things. They are to pray[31] because all believers, all brothers, are to pray, as Paul has just said.[32] Women are even to pray with uplifted hands.[33] Lifting up our hands is just a symbol of lifting up our hearts, our souls, ourselves as offerings to God in spiritual worship. "I spread out my hands to you: my soul thirsts for you . . . for to you I lift up my soul."[34]

Women are also to pray without anger or disputing. An attitude of strife and division is completely contrary to worship.[35]

If this is so, why would Paul address only the men with these directions? The only assumption left is that it was the men who were primarily falling into the temptation of quarrelling and disputing. Evidently disputing was a characteristic of the false teachings Paul was so eager to put down.[36]

To the Women

Then Paul goes on to address the women. "I also want women to dress modestly, with decency and propriety, not with braided hair or gold or pearls or expensive clothes, but with good deeds, appropriate for women who profess to worship God."[37]

Let's go back to the illustration of our dinner guest. After talking to the boys about the dishes, I turn to my daughters who are going to a church youth activity after dinner. "Girls, wear something decent tonight. I don't want to have to send you back upstairs to change. And don't worry about what the others will think. Remember to smile and be friendly, and you will be the best dressed girls there."

Dress

What will our dinner guest understand from these instructions? Will she assume that my sons, who are going to the same event, may dress as indecently as they wish? Will she assume that I do not want the boys to smile and be friendly? No! My guest will assume that my daughters have wanted to dress rather immodestly in the past, just to call attention to themselves, to be accepted and admired.

The instructions Paul gives to the women are very similar. Paul is not saying that only women should dress modestly. We know that modesty, decency, and purity are attitudes all Christians should demonstrate through their appearance, through everything they do.[38] So, of course, Paul urges Timothy to treat other young women "with absolute purity."[39]

Nor is Paul saying that men should not array themselves with good deeds. "Good deeds" are appropriate for anyone who professes to worship God, not just women.[40] Hasn't Paul just told Timothy that godliness and holiness please God?[41] Paul also tells Timothy to command "those who are rich . . . to do good, to be rich in good deeds."[42]

Then why did Paul single out the women for this instruction? The only thing we have left to assume is that the women were falling into the temptation of gaining attention through immodest dress and undue attention to their outward appearance, rather than to the good deeds that are the proper adornment for those who worship God.

Talk

Again Paul addresses the women. "A woman should learn in quietness and full submission."[43]

Back to our dinner guest. Suppose that just as our kids are going out the door to youth group, my husband tells them all to have a good time and then singles out the youngest: "Bobby, a boy ought to listen during devotions tonight. Maybe he'd learn something. Understand? No talking!" As the kids hurry through the door to be on their way, my husband calls out, "Remember one thing." A few eyes roll skyward as they slow down a bit. My husband says, "What is it?"

We hear scattered answers, "You love us."

My husband lets them go with, "That's right! We love you each one. Have fun."

And the kids go on their way.

Now, what will our guest understand from these directions to Bobby? Will she think my husband does not want our other children to listen during the youth group devotions? Will she think my husband wants only Bobby to learn, or that only he needs to learn something from devotions? Will our guest assume it's OK with my husband if the other kids talk during devotions and that it's only Bobby he wants to be quiet?

No. I think the guest would find my husband's meaning obvious and assume Bobby has a tendency to talk during the devotions, consequently learning little. Our guest will understand that my husband wants Bobby in particular to guard against this weakness. He wants him to be quiet and listen because he has had a problem with this in the past. My husband wants Bobby to learn, so he requires him to be quiet.

My guest might even assume that since Bobby is the youngest, he has this problem because he is new to the youth group and hasn't really learned the ropes yet. But that would only be conjecture, since no mention was made about why Bobby was yielding to the temptation to talk and was inattentive.

Is Paul saying that only the women should learn "in quietness and full submission"?[44] No. Everyone must learn that way. No one can learn while busy talking. No one can learn while having an attitude of knowing more than the teacher. A learning attitude is one of quiet submission, just as Paul says.

This is the learning attitude for all people, not just for women. All are to learn in quiet submission.[45] Learning means hearing first. Hearing means listening. Listening means being quiet. All in an attitude of submission.[46]

Are women always to be learning? That is, is the learning mode the only mode there is for women? In one sense we are all always learning. We will never have complete knowledge in this life. Yet, in another sense, the purpose of learning is to progress in the attainment of knowledge and its application to our lives. Godly women, and men, are not to be like the "weak-willed women" of Paul's second letter to Timothy, "who are . . . always learning but never able to acknowledge the truth."[47]

The purpose of learning is maturity in the faith. And once we become mature, we are to teach others, just as Paul later instructed Timothy. "And the things you have heard me say in the presence of many witnesses entrust to reliable men who will also be qualified to teach others."[48] The Greek word, here translated "men,"[49] who are to both learn and then teach, actually means "human being." This is the same word which Paul uses in this first letter: "This is good and pleases God our Savior, who wants ***all*** to be saved and to come to a knowledge of the truth."[50] "God . . . whom no ***one*** has seen or can see."[51] This word means both men and women, all human beings. All are to learn,[52] becoming mature,[53] so they can teach others.[54]

So then why is Paul directing this admonition to the women? The only possibility we are left with is that the women were falling into the problem of not listening when they were being taught, and perhaps thinking that either they didn't need to learn from others or that they knew more than others.

All of the Gentiles were newcomers to the Christian religious community, and the women especially may have felt a thrilling sense of empowerment and worth because of their inclusion. The new freedom they had in Christ was heady stuff indeed. Perhaps they went overboard and were using their freedom improperly. Perhaps they fell into the temptation of using their freedom "to indulge the sinful nature" rather than serving "one another in love."[55]

Will Sin Enter In?

And perhaps if women are at some time recognized as equals with all other brothers in the church, this might become a problem again. We have all been in committee meetings where the newest member does all the talking. But if that happens, the church will simply have to face the problem and grow because of it, through it, and out of it.

Even though this is a possible pitfall for some who misunderstand and misuse their freedom in Christ,[56] we cannot allow that to be a reason to curtail the freedom Christ has purchased for us.[57] This is sometimes referred to as the slippery slope of feminism. Many possible dire consequences are predicted if women are allowed to participate fully in the church as equals with the men.

Yet all these possible problems, consequences, and sins are something we have to cope with continually as Christians anyway. Surely if we embrace a gospel that says we no longer need to be bound by the requirements of the law,[58] sin will be the result! Paul responded to this very objection as he laid out the basic elements of the gospel message.

> What shall we say, then? Shall we go on sinning so that grace may increase? By no means! . . . if we died with Christ, we believe that we will also live with him."[59]

> What then? Shall we sin because we are not under law but under grace? By no means! . . . You have been set free from sin and have become slaves to righteousness.[60]

By Faith

The summary of Paul's answer is simply, "For in the gospel a righteousness from God is revealed, ***a righteousness that is by faith*** from first to last, just as it is written: 'The righteous will live by faith.'"[61] All of Scripture is an enlargement on this truth. Rather than becoming more sinful when we submit to the gospel in true faith, we become more righteous. Scripture is the history of those who have been set free from rules yet somehow become more holy! "But now that you have been set free from sin and have become slaves to God, the benefit you reap leads to holiness, and the result is eternal life. For the wages of sin is death, but the gift of God is eternal life in Christ Jesus our Lord."[62]

Just as Paul says to Timothy in this letter, "Beyond all question, the mystery of godliness is great," but he doesn't explain how it all works. He simply recites the facts of Christ's life. "He appeared in a body, was vindicated by the Spirit, was seen by angels, was preached among the nations, was believed on in the world, was taken up in glory."[63]

Mystery Realized

It is a mystery how all this makes us righteous both before God in heaven, and more and more so in our lives here on earth as well. Yet through faith this mystery is made real. "Now faith is being sure of what we hope for and certain of what we do not see."[64]

> For those God foreknew he also predestined to be conformed to the likeness of his Son, that he might be the firstborn among many brothers. For those he predestined, he also called; those he called, he also justified; those he justified, he also glorified.
>
> What, then, shall we say in response to this? If God is for us, who can be against us? He who did not spare his own Son, but gave him up for us all—how will he not also along with him, graciously give us all things? Who will bring any charge against those whom God has chosen? It is God who justifies. Who is he that condemns? Christ Jesus, who died—more than that, who was raised to life—is at the right hand of God and is also interceding for us. Who shall separate us from the love of Christ? Shall trouble or hardship or persecution or famine or nakedness or danger or sword? . . . No, in all these things we are more than conquerors through him who loved us. For I am convinced that neither death nor life, neither angels nor demons, neither the present nor the future, nor any powers, neither height nor depth, nor anything else in all creation, will be able to separate us from the love of God that is in Christ Jesus our Lord.[65]
>
> Amen.

This is "the glorious gospel of the blessed God," which Paul says defines *sound doctrine*.[66] It is "by faith from first to last."[67] Faith is the essence of "God's work,"[68] which had been entrusted into Timothy's care.[69] This is "the new way of the Spirit."[70] And we have the promise, "So I say, live by the Spirit, and you will not gratify the desires of the sinful nature."[71]

So if the church ever recognizes women as full and equal brothers in the family and the church, it will not be because we foresee no problems. No. It will be because we have exercised our faith to believe that these things are true.

Adam Was First

In verses 12 through 14, we come to Paul's strict injunctions to women and his reasons for them. The first reason Paul gives for not permitting "a woman to teach or to have authority over a man" is "For Adam was formed first, then Eve."[72]

Is Paul saying that Adam was somehow more deserving of privilege, or better equipped to handle responsibility, or just plain better because God created him first? Is Paul saying that since Adam was made first, a man should have authority over a woman?

Primogeniture is the favored position of the firstborn. Is Paul commending primogeniture as from God, meaning Adam received special blessing, privilege, and empowerment from God because he was first?

Here is God's view of this principle and tradition of primogeniture.

- Jacob and Esau: Even though through primogeniture Esau should have received the blessing, God gave the blessing to Jacob[73] and used him to father a chosen people and the Messiah.[74] The New Testament adds,

> Just as it is written, "Jacob I loved but Esau I hated." What then shall we say? Is God unjust? Not at all! For He says to Moses, "I will have mercy on whom I will have mercy, and I will have compassion on whom I have compassion."[75]

- David: God's choice of David to be king was a surprise to both Jesse and Samuel. Jesse thought his eldest should be chosen. But God chose David, the last and youngest. Samuel understood God's standard for that choice: "The LORD does not look at the things man looks at. Man looks at the outward appearance, but the LORD looks at the heart."[76]
- Jesus: Summarizing a law of his kingdom, Jesus said, "But many who are first will be last: and the last, first."[77]

Jesus restates this law: "And whoever wishes to be first among you shall be your slave."[78] When the Jews made special claim to be God's children because they were direct descendants of Abraham, Jesus quickly set them straight about who were true descendants of Abraham and thus children of God and his rightful inheritors. "If God were your Father, you would love Me."[79] "And do not think you can say to yourselves, 'We have Abraham as our father.' I tell you that out of these stones God can raise up children for Abraham."[80]

God's standard for choosing people for special blessing or position is very different from man's standard. His standard may not make sense to the world.

> Brothers, think of what you were when you were called. Not many of you were wise by human standards; not many were influential: not many were of noble birth. But God chose the foolish things of the world to shame the wise; God chose the weak things of the world to shame the strong. He chose the lowly things of this world and the despised things—and the things that are not—to nullify the things that are, so that no one may boast before him. It is because of him that you are in Christ Jesus, who has become for us wisdom from God—that is, our righteousness, holiness and redemption. Therefore, as it is written: "Let him who boasts boast in the Lord."[81]

The one we now boast in, our Lord Jesus Christ who lives in us and we in him, the second Adam, is "the firstborn over all creation"[82] and he has redeemed us "that we might be a kind of firstfruits of all he created."[83]

God does not choose by the world's standards. He chooses according to his will as his nature dictates. This is the clear teaching of *no difference*. God invites all who believe to receive his blessings in equal abundance.[84]

In this very letter, Paul reminds Timothy "to do nothing out of favoritism" or partiality.[85] Favoritism is our judging by any standard other than God's cleansing work of redemption and regeneration[86] and the consequent fruit. God "wants all men to be saved and to come to a knowledge of the truth."[87] This is the gospel to which sound doctrine must conform.[88]

So Paul cannot mean that a man should have authority over a woman because Adam was made first. Being made first is not a reason for one believer to be ranked above and put in authority over another believer. Besides, the clear teaching of brothers tells us that all believers are in equal relationship not only to Jesus Christ, but to each other as well.

Then why did Paul say this?

The only possible meaning left is that Paul gives Adam's firstness as a reason to say that a man should be equal to a woman. We must consider Paul's reference to the order of creation as a call to equality, a rebuke to the women that levels, not to the men building a hierarchy of authority. All come to God through Christ alone. No other circumstance of life affects our salvation or our standing in God's eyes. Paul did not permit a woman to have authority over a man, and Paul thought it important to remind the women of the fact that Adam was "formed first," a good fact to help the women realize they are not to be prideful, are not above a man, or should not assume any position of authority, privilege, or status over him.

What Paul is calling for is for the women not to consider themselves as above the men in any sense, but rather as equal with the men, as their brothers in the Lord, their fellow heirs.

Eve Was Deceived

There is one more reason Paul gives for not permitting "a woman to teach or to have authority over a man": "And Adam was not the one deceived; it was the woman who was deceived and became a sinner."[89]

Is Paul saying that since Eve ate the forbidden fruit before Adam did that Adam was in some sense less guilty or superior to Eve? Does Paul mean that since Eve sinned first, she must have a man in authority over her as a punishment, or a necessity because of her greater sin? Or does the fact that Eve was deceived mean that a woman is too stupid or ignorant or even foolish to manage her own life? Does a woman lack the proper faculties for being responsible for herself?

No! This cannot be the meaning because Scripture clearly teaches exactly the opposite. All have sinned.[90] All are equally guilty.[91] Regardless of the nature of the sin, any sin at all, no matter how innocent, or without harm it may seem to us,[92] it is enough to condemn one to death forever.[93]

All sin is totally heinous in God's sight. The only way anyone can stand before God is through the shed blood of Christ.[94] Paul has just reminded Timothy of this: "For there is one God and one mediator between God and men, the man Christ Jesus, who gave himself as a ransom for all men."[95] Any sin that could possibly be imputed to us has been forgiven, cleansed, and forgotten upon our confession and repentance.[96]

Deceivability, or gullibility as some have said, is not a reason for a man to be over a woman either. All of us are vulnerable to Satan's deceits. Paul was concerned about this very possibility in the Corinthian church. "But I am afraid that just as Eve was deceived by the serpent's cunning, your minds may somehow be led astray from your sincere and pure devotion to Christ. . . . And no wonder, for Satan himself masquerades as an angel of light."[97]

Without Christ, all of us are totally foolish, without hope, susceptible to the simplest lies with which Satan might tempt us.[98] Faith is our only protection against Satan's lies. Even those who are wise by the world's standards still can only come to God through faith. Their wisdom is worthless to them for learning about God, or becoming godly. "Has not God made foolish the wisdom of the world?"[99] Instead, God has purposely chosen the "foolish things . . . the lowly things . . . the despised things."

If Paul does not mean that women are inferior, less able, less deserving, or more guilty because Eve was deceived and sinned first, then what does he mean? The only possibility we have left is that Paul is reminding the women again that they are not superior to the men in any way. Paul is once more giving a reason for the women to realize that the men are equal to them before God and in the church too.

Good News, But . . .

The complementarian view interprets these two reasons, Adam was created first and Eve sinned first, to mean that men are to be in authority over women. This makes Eve's creation status and guilt seem to be beyond the cover of Christ's reconciling and purifying blood.

For women, this "good news, ***but*** . . ." leads to false feelings of inferiority and guilt because these reasons force them to look at who they are, in and of themselves, and at what they have done, rather than at who Jesus is and what he has done. This point of view can only lead to deep humiliation and depression.

For men, these two arguments lead to false feelings of superiority and self-righteousness because they are based on who the men are and what they have done, rather than on who Jesus is and what he has done. This leads to pride and arrogance.

These two arguments, when interpreted as reasons for a man's authority over a woman, are like two small toes left sticking out from under the covers, the cover of the gospel, on a dark and bitterly cold night. The whole body is affected.

The idea that these two arguments are reasons for men to be in authority over women is in exact opposition to the gospel.[100] We are justified, we are sanctified, we are adopted by faith—nothing else matters in God's eyes. Nothing we are or do has any influence on God as to how he will treat us, what status he will assign us, or what gifts he will give us.

A Call to Equality

If x is not greater than y	**($x \ngtr y$)**
and x is not less than y	**($x \nless y$)**
then x is equal to y	**($x = y$)**

If a woman is not to have authority over a man,
and a man is not to have authority over a woman,
then a man and a woman are equal in authority.

This conforms to the gospel.[101]

Paul summarizes this very same gospel message to the Ephesian church of which Timothy was a minister.

> For he himself is our peace, who has made the two one and has destroyed the barrier, the dividing wall of hostility, . . . His purpose was

> to create in himself one new man out of the two, thus making peace, and in this one body to reconcile both of them to God through the cross, by which he put to death their hostility.[102]

> This mystery is ***that through the gospel the Gentiles are heirs together with Israel, members together of one body***, and ***sharers together in the promise of Christ Jesus.***
>
> I became a servant of this gospel . . . to make plain to everyone the administration of this mystery, . . . that now, ***through the church, the manifold wisdom of God should be made known*** to the rulers and authorities in heavenly realms, according to his eternal purpose which he accomplished in Christ Jesus our Lord. In him and through faith in him we may approach God with freedom and confidence.[103]

> I urge you to live a life worthy of the calling you have received. Be completely humble and gentle; be patient, bearing with one another in love. Make every effort to keep the unity of the Spirit through the bond of peace. There is one body and one Spirit—just as you were called to one hope when you were called—one Lord, one faith, one baptism: ***one God and Father of all, who is over all and through all and in all.***[104]

> Pray . . . that I will fearlessly make known the mystery of the gospel.[105]

Perhaps the women had mistakenly attached too much importance to Paul's teaching that Adam was responsible for plunging all mankind into sin,[106] thus making women in some way less guilty than men. The women may have also felt that their ability to bear children, making them the agents for continuing the human race, somehow made them superior to men in general. Women have often made this false assumption, even to this present day. But this is conjecture. We don't really know since Paul makes no mention as to the reasons behind his reprimand.

Women are not at a loss for reasons to declare themselves superior to men any more than the men are. Both men and women can fall into the temptation of thinking more highly of themselves than they ought.[107] Both men and women can fail to "consider others better than" themselves.[108] Both men and women can fall into the sin of looking down on their brother, forgetting that we will all stand before God's judgment seat someday and be judged according to his standards, not ours.[109]

Perhaps as a result of these erroneous ideas, the women were lording it over the men, taking undue authority to themselves, setting themselves up as teachers who knew more than the men, possibly even teaching the false doctrine of female superiority and preeminence. Maybe the women had begun to misidentify freedom for power and were becoming authorities unto themselves, apart from God, his

Scripture, and the plain truth of the gospel message, that we "are all brothers" and have "only one Master . . . one Teacher, the Christ."[110]

This interpretation is also in line with other possible meanings of the word translated in the NIV as "have authority." Other translators have determined that this word means "usurp authority" (KJV) or "exercise authority" (NASB) or "domineer over" (NEB).[111] These translations carry the idea that the authority the women are not permitted is a lording over, superior type of attitude which may have caused the women to take teaching and authority to themselves. This attitude would have been completely wrong in the church, where all members are brothers, "each one" having "the manifestation of the Spirit . . . for the common good."[112]

Through Childbirth by Faith

"But women will be saved through childbearing—if they continue in faith, love, and holiness with propriety."[113] This verse is difficult because the idea that childbearing somehow has any effect on our salvation is completely contrary to the clear teaching of the gospel. But perhaps we can make some progress in determining its meaning if we once again eliminate what we know is not true.

We know that childbearing has no effect on our salvation. We know that our salvation comes only through faith,[114] through our belief in Jesus Christ and his work of redemption on our behalf.[115] So we can eliminate the possibility that Paul is meaning in any sense that women can help gain their salvation through giving birth to children.

Childbearing has through the ages been the greatest threat to the physical life of a woman. Women had to continually contend with a fear of death.[116] In this modern age when so many of the perils of pregnancy and childbirth have been eliminated, it is difficult for us women to really feel the life threat that was so obvious to all our female ancestors. Yet dangers still exist. At the very least, the pain is still there and must be dealt with. The curse pronounced to Eve in the garden has certainly been realized. "I will greatly increase your pains in childbearing; with pain you will give birth to children."[117]

Could Paul have meant that women could be assured that they would physically survive the life threatening ordeal of childbirth if they continued "in faith, love and holiness with propriety?" No. We can't assume this since history speaks so loudly against it. Uncountable numbers of women throughout the centuries since Paul wrote these words have died in childbirth with the prayer of true faith on their lips. Besides, our eternal salvation is no guarantee that we will be without problems here on earth. And all of us must still undergo physical death before we can fully realize our salvation, unless Christ should return first.[118]

Well, what else is left? What else can we think?

The only possibility left is that women could be saved, even through childbearing, whether they lived or not. They would be saved even through death, if they continued "in faith, love and holiness." This is the simple gospel message. If we believe, we will be saved. We are saved through faith, which is God's gift to us. Love and holiness are the beautiful result of this gift of faith.[119] Love and holiness come to us through the work of the Holy Spirit[120] as he conforms us to the likeness of Jesus.[121]

Paul gave this exact same message to the Colossians. "But now ***he has reconciled you*** by Christ's physical body ***through death to present you holy*** in his sight, without blemish and free from accusation—***if you continue in your faith***, established and firm, ***not moved from the hope held out in the gospel.***"[122]

Why did Paul bring up childbearing anyway? Perhaps because the women had found it a reason for looking down on the men. Yet, I find this verse has a more comforting tone.

Paul has been quite sharp with the women. He has recognized their sin, called it to everyone's attention, and rebuked them soundly, just as he advised Timothy to deal with all sin in the church.[123] But now he comes back to the grace and loving-kindness of the gospel.

Paul has brought up Eve's sin as a reminder to the women that they are no different from the men, for all have sinned.[124] Now he brings up childbearing to reassure the women that even though they still must suffer with the consequences of Eve's sin, difficult childbirth,[125] he wants to make it very clear that they are under no condemnation because of it.[126] Salvation will still belong to the women if they simply exercise the gift of faith.

And why does he add "with propriety"? Just as a reminder that propriety in dressing modestly, learning in quiet submission, and not thinking themselves better than the men would be an evidence of true faith.[127]

Universally True

Are the attitudes Paul confronts in these verses universal? Do all men always pray with quarrels and disputing? Do all women everywhere always dress immodestly and have a superior, domineering, unteachable attitude?

No. This is not the attitude or behavior of all brothers. True Christian behavior was modeled by the Philippians whom Paul commends.

> I thank God every time I remember you . . . because of your partnership in the gospel . . . being confident of this, that he who began a good work in you will carry it on to completion until the day of Christ Jesus. . . . so that you may be able to discern what is best and may be pure and blameless until the day of Christ, filled with the fruit of righteousness that comes through Jesus Christ—to the glory and praise of God.[128]

Are these injunctions that Paul directs to the men first and then to the women for all men and women, in all places, at all times?

Yes, of course. Neither men nor women are ever to pray with anger and disputing. Both women and men should dress modestly, with the good deeds of sanctification as their most beautiful garment. Both women and men should learn with a quiet and submissive attitude. Neither women nor men should ever take authority over each other, but rather they should each learn from the example of how God mercifully saved Paul with "unlimited patience."[129] We must each realize that "Christ Jesus came into the world to save sinners" of whom we, each one of us, are the worst.[130] Neither women nor men may exercise authority over each other, but rather "serve one another in love"[131] in imitation of Jesus.[132] Neither men nor women are permitted to teach or have authority, based on anything other than union with the teacher and the authority who is the Christ, over other believers.[133] All men and women are to act in these ways all the time and in every place.

Are these injunctions culturally bound? Since Paul was writing to people in another culture, does this mean that what he has written does not apply to our culture?

Not at all. What Paul had to say to Timothy and the church in Ephesus certainly does apply to us today, in our culture also, for the reasons I have just stated.

God neither justifies, sanctifies, nor adopts anyone on the basis of intelligence/gullibility, righteousness/sinfulness, being first/second/last, or any special ability or gender characteristic such as being able to bear children. God blesses only on the basis of his own love.[134]

All come to God's love by faith in God's grace alone, just as Paul reminds Timothy.[135]

Culturally Bound?

The complementarian's traditional interpretation of the specific injunctions to women in 1 Timothy 2:11–12 is not comprehensive and absolute because it is understood apart from the clear message of the whole Scripture, applies only part of these verses, and applies these parts to women only. This traditional interpretation may sound comprehensive when explained that all women everywhere must be silent at all times, must never teach, and must always be under the authority of men. But when viewed from a truly comprehensive stand, its limitations are clearly seen:

- All women everywhere—rather than all people
- Must be silent at all times—rather than just when learning
- Must never teach—rather than not being permitted to teach only when their teaching is based on anything other than ***union with the teacher***, the Christ, who is the Truth.

- Must be under the authority of men:
  —rather than not having authority over another because all believers are brothers.
  —rather than not having authority over another because all brothers are called to servanthood.
  —rather than not having authority over another based on anything other than ***union with the authority***, Jesus Christ, through a spiritual gift.

Thus this traditional interpretation limits the universal applicability of all of God's Word to all people.[136]

Our Dinner Guest—An Illustration

It's late and the kids have finally gotten back from their youth group meeting. They all trail into the kitchen for yet one more snack. We have enjoyed a quiet evening visit with our guest. But hearing loud voices in the kitchen, I go to see what is happening.

Our guest follows a few minutes later and finds me saying to my daughter, "I will not allow you to talk to your brother that way. Just watch your mouth and show a little respect. Remember he is older than you are. Besides, it was you who broke the dishwasher last week."

Now what will our guest understand from hearing those words? After making a hasty retreat from the tension of the kitchen, she might assume that my daughter had been talking quite disparagingly and disrespectfully to her older brother. Would our guest assume I had meant by my words that I wanted my eldest son to talk "that way" to my daughter? Would she have assumed that I wanted my son not to show respect for my daughter? Would she have assumed that since I mentioned my son being the older of the two that I meant he was the one who should be talking "that way"? Or would our guest understand that since it was my daughter who broke the dishwasher, therefore, I expected my son to be disrespectful to her?

No. Our guest would know that I love my children equally and want them to have mutual respect and love for each other. She would understand that my words to my daughter were a call to equality. Our guest and my children would both see from my speech that even though I recognized that wrongs had been done, I didn't think being judgmental and acting superior were in order. Our guest would have recognized my references to my son being older and my daughter breaking the dishwasher as reprimands to my daughter, not reasons for my son to take on a superior attitude. They would have all recognized that I expected my children to all treat each other with kindness and respect.

Our guest might wonder what all the fuss was about. From what she overheard, she might have assumed that my daughter was yelling at my son about how he did or didn't do the dishes, especially since the dishwasher was mentioned. But she wouldn't really know.

Conduct According to Sound Doctrine

The illustration of "Our Guest" is from my own imagination. But Paul gives us other examples from the real life of Timothy and the church in Ephesus. Read 1 Timothy 1:3–4, 3:2–3, 8–9, 11, 5:4–5,14,16, 6:1–2,11–12, and 17–19. How do we interpret these verses? Are the exhortations given to these specific people meant only for them exclusively?[137] Is the opposite behavior therefore required of all other people?

Summary

Let's review. What is the meaning of 1 Timothy 2?

Paul begins by emphasizing the necessity of prayer, especially for those who had authority over the lives of the Christians. They were to pray for peace, so the gospel would be not be hindered in any way.

Then Paul goes on to address some things that were hindering the prayer, the worship of the Ephesian church. The men were having lots of quarrels and arguments. Paul tells the men to stop these arguments.

The women were being immodest in their desire for attention. They were so consumed with voicing their own thoughts and ideas that they weren't listening and learning from others. The women were developing a superior attitude and were placing themselves above the men, telling them what to believe and what to do.

Paul tells the women to stop being so self-centered. They should stop flaunting their appearance and instead dress in good deeds, the proper attire for Christians. They must stop acting superior and start listening and learning. Paul tells the women to treat the men with the respect and love which they themselves expect. The women are not to set themselves above the men because, after all, Adam was created before Eve and it was Eve who was deceived.

But after this harsh reproach, Paul reminds the women that he is not unsympathetic to the ever-present suffering and fear of death through childbearing that is their unique burden. He encourages them to remember that the truth of the gospel triumphs over all their suffering, even death. He closes with the reminder that true evidence of their faith will be found in a life conforming to Jesus through the work of the Spirit. This is the basis for their inclusion in the church as equal brothers, just as Paul has already written to them.

> And ***you also were included*** in Christ when you heard the word of truth, the gospel of your salvation. Having believed, you were marked in

> him with a seal, the promised Holy Spirit, who is a deposit guaranteeing our inheritance until the redemption of those who are God's possession—to the praise of his glory.[138]

Paul's rebukes and instructions to both the men and the women can be summarized this way:

> You, my brothers, were called to be free. But do not use your freedom to indulge the sinful nature; rather, serve one another in love. The entire law is summed up in a single command: "Love your neighbor as yourself." If you keep on biting and devouring each other, watch out or you will be destroyed by each other. So I say, live by the Spirit, and you will not gratify the desires of the sinful nature.[139]

Context

Does this interpretation fit with the context of the book of 1 Timothy? Apart from the personal advice Paul gives to Timothy, the main themes of this letter are:

- False teaching is to be stopped, and "sound doctrine that conforms to the glorious gospel of the blessed God" is to be taught.[140]
- In the church people must conduct themselves according to the sound doctrine of the gospel because the church is "the pillar and foundation of the truth." [141]
- Favoritism or partiality has no place in the church.[142]

Yes. It fits.

The Question

What is the meaning of 1 Timothy 2:8–15?

What do we know to be true?

- All are to pray[143]
  with uplifted hands[144]
  and without anger or disputing.[145]

- All are to dress modestly[146]
  with good deeds[147]
  in demonstration of their profession of faith.[148]

- All are to learn[149]
  with a quiet and submissive attitude,[150]
  becoming mature, [151]
  so they can teach others.[152]

- No brother is to place himself over or above another,[153]
  thinking more highly of himself than he ought to think,[154]
  considering himself better than others,[155] or
  looking down on his brother,[156]
  for we are all brothers[157] and
  we are called to serve one another in love:[158]
  the clear teachings of brothers and servanthood.

- No brother is to teach or have authority
  based on anything other than union with the teacher, the authority, the Christ.[159]
  For we have only one Master.[160]

- In Christ's body, being first is of no value, meaning, or consequence
  toward the ranking of brothers.[161]

- All have sinned,[162]
  being equally guilty in God's eyes,[163]
  deserving only death.[164]

- Salvation comes to ***all*** who believe through faith alone[165]
  in the shed blood of Christ,[166]
  resulting in love and holiness[167]
  as the Holy Spirit conforms us to the image of Jesus:[168]
  the clear teaching of oneness.[169]

- The context of 1 Timothy 2:8–15 is
  the refutation of false doctrine,[170]
  which pertains to the improper use of the law,[171]
  the encouragement of sound doctrine, [172]
  which conforms to the gospel,[173]
  which is how people ought to conduct themselves in the church,[174]
  because the church is the pillar and foundation of truth,[175]
  without partiality:[176]
  the clear teaching of no difference.

My mother Winifred with her daughters Nancy, me, and Meg~2004.

Chapter 15

The Middle of the Road: How Safe Is It?

Moody Bible Science Films—how I loved seeing those as a kid. There was one about bees, one about blood, one about water. One I remember particularly well was about the five senses. A scientist carried out an experiment by wearing huge glasses, sort of like binoculars strapped to his head, that made everything appear upside down. Supposedly he never peeked, but only looked at the world through his upside-down glasses. He wore them for weeks. When he looked down at his feet, they were at the top of his view. After a while he was tempted to look up when he wanted to see his feet. But that was wrong because his feet were still down, even though his eyes seemed to tell him otherwise. The glasses kept leading him to look in the wrong direction. Besides that, he was always bumping into stuff.

Looking at the world through upside-down glasses just didn't seem to be working out very well. Then one day as he was wearing his glasses, suddenly everything turned right-side-up again. He checked to be sure the glasses were still working properly, that is, turning everything upside down. Sure enough, they were. But because his brain had gotten tired of the mess it was having to cope with, it turned everything right-side-up again.

He continued to wear his glasses for a while longer. Then at last he laid the experiment aside, wondering what he would see when he again looked at the world through his natural eyes. Once again, everything was upside-down. But soon his brain put it all back in order, right-side-up. It seems the human brain seeks to make things consistent with what it perceives to be true.

Perceptions—Reality—Consistency

I am reminded of this experiment as I think about the issue of the status of women in the church. When I look at things from the complementarian point of view as I did for most of my life, there are things I bump into because they don't seem consistent with what I know to be true.

Of course, my perceptions and understanding are not perfect. I am a sinner. And so, as a Christian committed to God's Word as the only infallible rule for faith and life, I have tried to take my understanding of truth from the Bible. This is our starting point.

Let's begin with the matter of words and how we understand their meaning. The Bible is written in words, so we must understand them correctly. We cannot simply make assumptions without allowing the Bible itself to define their meaning.

We have already talked about the words *submit, head*, and *weaker*. How does Scripture use the word? This is how we must use the word also.

Helper

Here is a word we have not mentioned yet—*helper*. This word is given great significance by the complementarian viewpoint. It is used to describe Eve at the time of her creation. "The Lord God said, 'It is not good for the man to be alone. I will make a helper suitable for him.'"[1]

The complementarian position assumes this word means "assistant," with a connotation ranging from mommy's little helper to vice president, because they are forced to look in this direction by their perspective that God created woman to be subordinate to man.

This definition points toward an authority structure. The helper is not the one in charge. The helper is there only to aid the one in charge with the accomplishment of his own goals.

Consequently, it is easy to see why one would interpret this verse from Genesis to mean that God intended Eve to be only an assistant to Adam, to do his bidding, to serve his needs and ends. Adam is seen to be in charge. And Eve is seen to be his helper.

But how does the Bible use, and thus define, *helper*? The Hebrew word translated "helper"[2] with reference to Eve is used many times throughout the Old Testament.

"After Moses had sent away his wife Zipporah, his father-in-law Jethro, received her and her two sons. One son was named . . . and the other was named Eliezer, for he said, 'My father's God was my ***helper***: he saved me from the sword of Pharaoh.'"[3]

> Hear, O Lord, the cry of Judah: bring him to his people. . . . Oh, be his ***help*** against his foes! . . . There is no one like the God of Jeshurun, who rides on the heavens to ***help*** you and on the clouds in his majesty. . . . Blessed are you, O Israel! Who is like you, a people saved by the Lord? He is your shield and ***helper*** and your glorious sword.[4]

"May the Lord answer you when you are in distress . . . May he send you ***help*** from the sanctuary."[5]

"Come quickly to help me, O Lord my Savior."[6]

"But I am the Lord your God . . . You are destroyed, O Israel, because you are against me, against your ***helper***."[7]

These verses certainly give a different meaning to the word *helper*. At the very least, they eliminate all possibility of it meaning one who is under the authority of the one helped.

Of the twenty-one times this word is used in the Old Testament, it refers to God as helper sixteen times.[8] As the Old Testament uses this word, the helper is the one in the stronger position of power and ability. The helper is a rescuer, deliverer, one who saves. The one being helped is in a position of need.

Adam was in extreme need. "It is not good for the man to be alone."[9] God solved his problem. Eve did not solve Adam's problem. God did. But God created Eve to be the agent of his help for Adam. God made "a helper suitable for him."[10] Adam and Eve became "one flesh."[11] Now mankind was complete. "So God created man in his own image, in the image of God he created him: male and female he created them."[12] Now man, mankind, was "very good."[13] The creation of Eve rescued Adam from aloneness.

The Curse

A simple question: If "and he shall rule over you"[14] is a part of the curse of sin as God related it to Eve, how can it also be the way God created things to be in the beginning when there was no sin?

The curse is a statement of how things are in a sinful, fallen world, the conditions of death. "I will greatly increase your pains in childbearing . . . Your desire will be for your husband, and he will rule over you. . . . Cursed is the ground because of you . . . It will produce thorns and thistles for you. . . . for dust you are and to dust you will return."[15] Death was the consequence of Adam's and Eve's disobedience.[16]

In the beginning "one flesh" was the creation norm.[17] "One flesh" was life, "and he shall rule over you" was death. "One flesh" was very good,[18] but "And he shall rule over you" culminates in "for dust you are and to dust you will return."[19]

But Christ has become the victor over death.[20] Jesus became a curse for us.[21] Jesus suffered all the characteristics and conditions of death,[22] so that we might be recreated to a new life.[23] Through Christ's redemption, the characteristics and conditions of the curse, of death, are reversed and reconciled.[24]

Of course, until Christ comes again, we can no more completely overturn the curse of "he shall rule over you" than we can stop ourselves from dying. But as the agents of Christ's rule, we must bring his reconciling power to bear where possible. We can practice the Lamaze method of natural childbirth and use medical help when necessary. We can pull the weeds from our gardens. We can inoculate our children against fatal diseases.

In the same way, we must eradicate the subordination of women where possible, in the church and in the Christian family. This will not overturn the curse. But it will, as far as God's grace permits, recognize and submit to the reconciling reign of him who is "head over everything"[25] yet came "to serve and give his life as a ransom for many,"[26] thus "making peace through his blood."[27]

In the beginning God did not create man to be in authority over the woman. *Helper* has nothing to do with authority structures. It has to do with going from "not good" to "very good," from being "alone" to being "one flesh," from being "the man"[28] to being "man," the human race.[29]

Perfection Negates Authority

Another simple question: What would be the purpose or use of a hierarchy of authority in a perfect world? A world in which all human beings are in perfect communication with and submission to their creator? A world in which all human beings would seek to serve one another in love and submission according to their creator's law?[30]

The same question can also be applied to a hierarchy of authority within the Godhead. Why? What for?

The answer is as simple as the question. There would be no need for an authority structure where all seek to "serve one another in love."[31] A hierarchy of authority would never be used. It would serve no purpose. It would not exist.

Where sin does not exist, God's law functions in perfection. And where there is perfection, there is oneness. The words translated "perfect" in the Bible mean "complete, finished, whole."[32] "And above all these things put on charity, which is the bond of perfectness."[33] "And over all these virtues put on love, which binds them all together in perfect unity."[34] This perfection is seen in our triune creator God. "God is love."[35] "The Lord our God, the Lord is one."[36]

"I in them, and thou in me, that they may be made perfect in one."[37] "I in them and you in me. May they be brought to complete unity."[38]

The Question

What does the word *helper* mean?

What do we know to be true?

- Sixteen of the twenty-one times *helper* is used in the Old Testament it refers to God helping those in need.[39]
- According to Old Testament usage, a helper is usually one who rescues, delivers, or saves one who is in need.[40]
- The Hebrew word for "helper" is not related to authority, nor does it have any bearing on any particular position in a hierarchy of authority.

Have I Misunderstood?

When I read the Scripture from the complementarian point of view, I am continually bumping into something. If I accept the traditional interpretations of the silence injunctions, I trip over other verses that tell me to pray, sing, teach, admonish, encourage, and, yes, even preach. All of these things are very difficult to do if one is silent.

Let's take the Great Commission, for example. We have all heard inspiring and challenging sermons from this text. "Go you therefore and make disciples of all nations, baptizing them in the name of the Father, the Son, and the Holy Spirit, teaching them to observe all things whatsoever I have commanded you. And surely I am with you always, to the very end of the age."[41]

Was I mistaken to be moved by this last commanding challenge of our Lord? Was the preacher wrong to include me in his audience? Were these verses not meant to include me? Yet these words have been sharp and powerful in my life. Have I misunderstood? Do these verses really only apply to the church in general, but not to me specifically? Does this then mean that the last phrase of comfort, the assurance of Christ's constant presence, is not for me specifically either?

Even though Scripture is addressed to all people everywhere,[42] I understand this does not mean that each person who reads Matthew 28:19–20 will become a teacher of the Scriptures. Teaching is a gift of the Holy Spirit.[43] But the Holy Spirit may use the Scriptures as a means to give hearts the desire and conviction to teach.[44] There is a difference between the Holy Spirit not specifically applying a scripture to my life because it speaks of and to a different spiritual gift than the one I have been empowered with and a scripture not applying to me because I have been found unacceptable by God to receive this word as a part of God's message to me. If we don't all believe that all Scripture is God's message to all of us, the Holy Spirit will be deprived of a means of grace.[45]

Here is another example. "Don't let anyone look down on you because you are young, but set an example for the believers in speech, in life, in love, in faith, and in purity."[46] God used this verse as a great challenge to me when I was young. I didn't come to it on my own. It was my church that challenged me to internalize and actively live this admonition.

But the context here is crucial. The preceding verse says, "Command and teach these things."[47] The following verse says, "Devote yourself to the public reading of Scripture, to preaching and to teaching."[48] Is it improper of me to think these verses can be applied to myself? If it is improper, on what grounds? If it is improper, then was that middle verse also incorrectly applied to me?

You see, if I say that the injunction for women to be silent is not directed to all women, but rather only to those women, and men, who are using their speech to domineer or teach what is false, and I cite these commands to teach, preach, and baptize as part of my discussion, complementarians may answer by saying that the first of these verses, the Great Commission, was spoken to the apostles only, and the second to Timothy, a man, a pastor.

So what am I to conclude? Are these passages only for men, or more specifically, pastors and overseers? Is this an accepted rule of interpretation? If it is, my Bible study will indeed be thrown into disarray. I can immediately eliminate Proverbs, Luke, Acts, 1 and 2 Timothy, Titus, Philemon, and 3 John from my Bible since these were all written specifically to men. If this is not a proper rule for interpreting the Scriptures, then what do these verses that command us to teach, preach, pray, and baptize say about the universal application of the command for women to be silent?

Some complementarians may respond by saying that these scriptural injunctions to teach, preach, and baptize do not apply to women, not because these Scriptures were first addressed to men, but because we understand from other Scriptures that women are to be silent.

Wait a minute. Isn't this argument going in circles?

Round and Round

I ask, "How do we know that 'women should remain silent'[49] is a universal command applicable to all women? What about those scriptures that command us to teach, preach, baptize?"

. . . Lots of back and forth discussion . . .

The final answer comes back. "Those scriptures don't apply to women because women are to be silent."

Can you answer a question by restating the question?

But the discussions don't always seem that simple. The dots in the conversation above represent many complex arguments. But all that discussing usually ends in a restatement of the complementarian position and the "silence" Bible passages. The seeming Bible commands for women's silence are always their bottom line, their ultimate answer. It is circular reasoning. The premise is used to prove the premise. Here are two examples:

Egalitarian Interpretation: Why are women not to be overseers in the church?

Complementarian Interpretation: Women are not to be overseers in the church because women are not to have authority over men.[50]

Egalitarian: Why, then, does Paul commend "anyone" who desires to be an overseer?[51] The same word used for "anyone" here is also used in John 3:3 to describe those who must be born again in order to see the kingdom of God. Certainly that includes women!

Complementarian: We know that "anyone" in 1 Timothy 3:1 means males only because Paul goes on to say that the overseer must be "the husband of but one wife."[52]

Egalitarian: This same phrase is used to describe deacons,[53] and we know that Phoebe was a deacon.[54] Most churches interpret this phrase to mean, "having not more than one spouse." Many single men are accepted as overseers. Besides, the word translated "wives" in 1 Timothy 3:11 NIV can also be translated "deaconesses."[55]

Complementarian: We know overseers must only be males because of 1 Timothy 2:12, which limits the eldership to males since women are not to "have authority over a man."

Egalitarian: How do we know that *head* means "authority over"?

Complementarian: *Head* means "authority over." This is how it is usually used in other ancient Greek writings. This is further supported by the fact that a wife is told to "submit" to her husband, her "head." [56]

Egalitarian: But "submit" is a voluntary, self-motivated action resulting from the Spirit writing the law of servanthood on our hearts, not because of authority.

Complementarian: We know *submit* means "submitting to an authority" because a wife is to submit to her husband, her head. And *head* means "authority over."[57]

Round and round we go.

Here is another specific passage that seems to command me to do what the complementarian position forbids me to do.

Are You Talking to Me?

> Let the word of Christ dwell in you richly as you teach and admonish one another with all wisdom, and as you sing psalms, hymns and spiritual songs with gratitude in your hearts to God. And whatever you do, whether in word or deed, do it all in the name of the Lord Jesus, giving thanks to God the Father through him.[58]

If I am not supposed to teach, why does Paul tell me to do it here? Why does he tell me to both "teach and admonish"? Why does he tell me to teach and admonish, not just other women, but "one another"? Surely there were women among the "holy and faithful brothers in Christ at Colosse."[59] Yes, of course! He greets Nympha by name, and the church that meets in her house.[60]

If Paul is not addressing me or any other woman in these verses, does this also mean that the "word of Christ" should not dwell in me richly? That I should not "sing psalms, hymns and spiritual songs"? Or that I should not sing them "with gratitude" in my heart to God?

Where does Paul start and stop talking to me? How can I tell when and where to draw the line? Are 1 Corinthians 14:34–35 and 1 Timothy 2:12 my guide for where to draw the line? Do these verses interpret all of Scripture for me, a woman?

We have red letter editions of the Bible to highlight the words of Christ. Perhaps we need green letter editions so women will know what to skip, what really wasn't written to them. Certainly these words would have to be in green: "Speak to one another with psalms, hymns and spiritual songs."[61] I cannot speak and be silent at the same time. But would the preceding verses be in green too? "Be very careful, then, how you live" or "be filled with the Spirit."[62] Or what about those that follow, "always giving thanks to God" or "submit to one another"?[63]

What about all those verses that describe people of God speaking throughout history? Should they be in green too? Just in case I might make application to my life by following their example?

"Wait a minute!" I hear some saying. "You've gone overboard here. You have completely misunderstood."

You're right. I have misunderstood. I don't get it. It's too complicated for me. When I look at Scripture from the complementarian point of view, I just don't know when God is talking to me, and when he isn't.

Who Am I?

The question is, Who am I as a woman believer?

Am I a "brother,"[64] or not?[65]
Am I a "saint,"[66] or not?[67]
Am I one of "anyone,"[68] or not?[69]
Am I one of "every/each one,"[70] or not?[71]
Am I included in "all,"[72] or not?[73]
Am I a part of mankind, "man,"[74] or something apart, only a woman?[75]
Is the Bible written to me,[76] or not?[77]

The Question

Is the injunction for women to be silent
a universal command applicable to all women in the church?

What do we know to be true?

- All believers are commanded to
  - teach,[78]
  - preach,[79]
  - admonish,[80]
  - baptize,[81]
  - prophesy,[82] and
  - pray.[83]

Daily Life in the Real World

Not only does the complementarian perspective lead me to bump into things within the Scriptures, but it also trips me up as I look at our daily lives lived out in the Spirit. The essence of this conflict is how the complementarians deal with the spiritual giftedness and fruitfulness of women. And I am certainly not alone in feeling this conflict. Others, even complementarians feel this too.

John Piper and Wayne Grudem have edited the book, *Recovering Biblical Manhood and Womanhood: A Response to Evangelical Feminism.* I am going to cite several examples from this book because it has been widely read and recognized as a summary of the position that Scripture teaches and demands the subordination of women to men in the home and church.

Piper and Grudem have found a wonderful quote to illustrate this conflict, which we all feel between the complementarian position and real women of God. In 1868 Hudson Taylor wrote a letter from England to his fellow missionary on the field in China, Miss Faulding.

> I do not know when I may be able to return, and it will not do for Church affairs to wait for me. You cannot take a pastor's place in name, but you must help (Wang) Lae-djun to act in matters of receiving and excluding as far as you can. You can speak privately to candidates, and can be present at Church meetings, and might even, through others, suggest questions to be asked of those desiring baptism. Then after the meeting you can talk privately with Lae-djun about them, and suggest who you think he might receive next time they meet. Thus he may have the help he needs, and there will be nothing that anyone could regard as unseemly.[84, 85]

Or let's take a more up to date example, again from *Recovering Biblical Manhood and Womanhood.*

> #43. Q: Why is it acceptable to sing hymns written by women and recommend books written by women but not to permit them to say the same things audibly?
>
> A: . . . we (do not) say that what a woman writes in books and articles cannot be spoken audibly. The issue for us is whether she should function as part of the primary teaching leadership (=eldership) in a fellowship of women and men. We have not, of course, ruled out either small or worldwide ministries of teaching other women. Neither have we ruled out occasional lectureships and periodic addresses

> (as distinct from recognized Bible teaching in the church) in which women address men as well as women, for example, at the Urbana Missions Conference or any number of local and national conferences and convocations.
>
> We use the qualifiers occasional and periodic because the regularity of teaching one group of people is part of what constitutes the difference between official teaching leadership, which is withheld from women in 1 Timothy 2:12, and the unofficial[86] guidance given by Priscilla and Aquila in Acts 18:26. We recognize that these lectures and addresses could be delivered in a spirit and demeanor that would assault the principle of male leadership. But it is not necessary that they do so.[87]

Divided Thinking

How do complementarians deal with these conflicts? Through the invention of terms, principles, and distinctions, such as formal/informal, primary/secondary, regular/occasional, official/unofficial, public/private, written/verbal, emerging church/established church. Supposedly these qualifiers help us define when women "must remain silent" and when that isn't necessary, when women may teach and when they cannot.

Let me quote Piper and Grudem again:

> We admit there are ambiguities in applying Paul's instructions about an established church to an emerging church. We admit that there are ambiguities in separating the Priscilla-type counsel from the official teaching role of 1 Timothy 2:12.[88]
>
> If Paul did not have every conceivable form of teaching and learning in mind, what did he mean? . . . We would say that teaching inappropriate for a woman is the teaching of men in settings or ways that dishonor the calling of men to bear the primary responsibility for teaching and leadership.[89]

This conflict felt so keenly by both sides of this issue is further characterized by the use of the word *leadership*.

Piper and Grudem say they "prefer to use the term leadership for the man's special responsibility rather than authority."[90]

"Why?" I ask. If the whole issue is based on authority, why shy away from the word?

I am sure the word *leadership* is preferred because *authority* is not something we have been able to live with very comfortably in our real lives together in the church. *Leadership* is preferred because it is a recognized spiritual gift, one that is necessary to the church on every level. But leadership is not what this issue is about.

The biblical support for the complementarian position is not concerned with leadership, but with authority. Leadership is a legitimate spiritual gift,[91] among many. Authority is not. Those with this gift of leadership will be held accountable for how they use it, as will all brothers concerning the gifts they each have been given.[92] Leadership is one aspect of the grace God gives for the "common good"[93] to "serve others."[94] Authority is not. Leadership and authority are not the same. The words are not interchangeable.

Hermeneutical Oddities

Now all these qualifying words and adjustments may help resolve the conflict between the complementarian view and our daily experiences in the church, yet it is a far cry from the very scriptures complementarians are seeking to uphold.

> Women should remain silent in the churches. They are not allowed to speak, but must be in submission, as the Law says. If they want to inquire about something, they should ask their own husbands at home: for it is disgraceful for a woman to speak in the church.[95]

Piper and Grudem state their concern that the case for the complete equality of men and women in the church and home is built upon

> . . . the increasing prevalence and acceptance of hermeneutical oddities devised to reinterpret apparently plain meanings of Biblical texts; . . . and the consequent threat to Biblical authority as the clarity of Scripture is jeopardized and the accessibility of its meaning to ordinary people is withdrawn into the restricted realm of technical ingenuity.[96]

In the same book Paige Patterson quotes Clark Pinnock as viewing the egalitarian position as one based on "hermeneutical ventriloquism."[97]

But it seems to me that it takes a great deal of exegetical maneuvering to support distinctions such as primary/secondary, audible/verbal, formal/informal, official/unofficial, public/private, emerging church/established church, and occasional/periodic as biblical principles. Are these words ever used in Scripture? Are these ideas ever taught?

Divided Living

It is as if we have made some very comfortable furniture. To us it seems beautiful and well crafted. The only problem is it doesn't fit in our house. What shall we do? Well, we build another house.

Or consider it this way. There are seemingly conflicting scriptures. How can we obey them all? Our motivations are good. We want to be true to God's Word in every regard. So we solve this problem by dividing life into various little cubicles, or boxes. In this box we will obey this scripture. In this other box over here, we will obey this scripture. That way we can obey everything, and everyone will be happy. Certainly this is how many churches today are solving this issue of the status of women. Yes, it is comfortable because no matter what our idea on this issue, we can probably find some little cubicle within the church in which to act it out.

But is this an accurate portrayal of the Christian life? Is this a biblical picture of our new life in Christ? Is this how Scripture describes our life together as his body? Should our lives be filled with all these little divisions and distinctions with one precept to be applied here and another over there? Is this freedom? Or is this the endless tyranny of the law?

To me it sounds like a lot of little legalistic maneuvering. Don't heal a man on the Sabbath, but if your sheep falls in a hole on the Sabbath, you can pull him out.[98] Honor your parents, but if you say your goods are "corban," then you don't have to worry about providing for them.[99] Or, if you swear by the temple, it doesn't mean anything, but if you swear by the gold of the temple, you are bound by your oath.[100]

New Life—One Integrated Whole

What I see taught in Scripture is that the life of the Christian is one consistent and integrated whole,[101] the same all the time, everywhere, and in all circumstances. I believe the Bible teaches the uniformity, consistency, and integrity of the Christian life. The new life in the Spirit is one unified whole. What is true in one instance will be true throughout. If this were not the case, how could all the law and the prophets be summarized in just two commands: Love God and love your neighbor?[102] Or through the complete mutuality and reciprocity of the Golden Rule?[103]

How did Jesus view these boxes, these innumerable stipulations for determining what is in line with the law and what is not? Could the words Jesus applied to the pharisaical rules quoted above also apply to the complementarian viewpoint that maintains the subordination of women? "You have let go of the commands of God and are holding on to the traditions of men. . . . You have a fine way of setting aside the commands of God in order to observe your own traditions!"[104]

The Question

Can the commands for women to be silent, not to teach, or to have authority be reconciled with the gifts and fruitfulness of real Christian women?

What do we know to be true?

- The distinctions of formal/informal, primary/secondary, audible/verbal, official/unofficial, public/private, emerging church/established church, and occasional/periodic are not taught in Scripture.

- The Christian life is one integral whole.[105]
  The two great commandments sum up all the law and the prophets.[106]
  The Golden Rule of complete mutuality and reciprocity
  is the heart of the law and the prophets.[107]

- Jesus viewed rules that detail all the various possibilities of how we are to fulfill the law as "setting aside the commands of God in order to observe your own traditions."[108]

Will Homosexuality Follow?

If women are recognized as equal members of the church beside men, will homosexuality follow next?

This is a question being asked loudly by those who are committed to the complementarian view.

> #26. Q: Doesn't Paul's statement that "There is . . . neither male nor female . . . for you are all one in Christ Jesus"[109] take away gender as a basis for distinction of roles in the church?
>
> A: No. Most evangelicals still agree that this text is not a warrant for homosexuality.[110]

Did you have to go back and reread that once or twice? I certainly did. A very abrupt turn in thinking was taken and I got lost.

This answer[111] equates homosexuality with a role in the church.

Role Distinctions

Much confusion has arisen from complementarians' undefined use of the phrase *role distinctions.*

What does *role* mean? Any dictionary will do. It means "the part one plays."

Distinctions mean differences.

From this I assume that *role distinctions* means the different parts we play, the different work we do, the different responsibilities we have.

This is simple division of labor. It makes sense to divide up the work. Some are given one task and some another.

I believe in role distinctions. I believe they are biblical. The gifts of the Spirit are one example of role distinctions.[112] Role distinctions in the church should emerge through mutual decision and consent on the basis of spiritual and physical gifts, temperament, education, skills, and interests.

Those who are stronger should lift the heavier loads. Those who know should teach those who don't. Those with patience should care for the children. Those with strong voices should lead the singing. Those with a head for numbers and a sense of proportion should handle the money. Those with a love for growing things should do the gardening.

But this is not how complementarians use the phrase. What they usually mean is rank distinctions.

Rank Distinctions

Rank has several different meanings, but when referring to people, it usually means placing them in order in a hierarchical structure, such as rank in the military. A rank distinction may be one specific role distinction among many.

According to Romans 12:6–8, we have different roles. But that does not mean different ranks.[113] The difference between role and rank is easily seen in any group where all members are of equal rank. Yet still the members will all be different from one another, carrying out different roles. And no one will thus assume that the members must be different in rank also. Their equality is innate to being a member of the group, transcending their differences, and roles.

The Danvers Statement[114] uses the term *roles* a number of times. For example, "Distinctions in masculine and feminine roles are ordained by God as part of the created order, and should find an echo in every human heart."[115]

I could agree if they really meant "role distinctions." But they don't. It is clear that what is meant by these "role distinctions" is really the subordination of women to men, that women are under the authority of men. The Statement goes on to say that "sin . . . inclines women to resist limitations on their ***roles,***" but through Christ's redemption "wives should forsake resistance to their husbands' ***authority.***"[116], (emphasis mine).

Sometimes complementarians use *role distinctions* to mean "rank, subordinate/authority," but sometimes they revert to the commonly understood meaning of "task, work, or responsibility differences," as they have in the question and answer #26, which I have quoted above. Egalitarians do not claim that Galatians 3:28 takes away gender as a basis for distinction of roles in the church. In some of the different roles we play, our sex will be a determining factor. For example, those who have wombs should have the babies. Those who have sperm should impregnate the wombs. Those with breasts should nurse the infants.

However, the egalitarian perspective does argue that Galatians 3:28 takes away gender as a basis for distinction of rank in the church.

This confusion of language only serves to muddle our thinking and blur the true intent of those who use this phrase in such a manner.

Confusion

The confusion is very evident. Many are saying that equality for women with men and the acceptance of homosexuality are similar issues, based on the same scriptural ideas. Once during a discussion of the status of women in the church, a pastor said he felt the hermeneutic that builds a case for female equality also leads to the acceptance of homosexuality.

Is this true? If we believe that Scripture teaches the equality of women with men, must we also accept homosexuality? Do the passages that apply to one apply to the other?

Women and Homosexuality

What is the clear message of the Scriptures concerning women? That they are made in the image of God, redeemed by Christ, filled with the Spirit, and participate in Christ's rule through the ministry of reconciliation, equally with men.

The clear message of the Bible concerning homosexual behavior is that it is a characteristic of the total depravity and wickedness of mankind apart from God.[117] Women are not a characteristic of separation from God. Women were created by God in his own image. This creation of "man, . . . male and female," was "very good."[118]

Homosexual conduct is one aspect of sexual immorality, which includes all sexual activity outside the marriage commitment between one man and one woman, the creation ordinance.[119] Just as marriage pictures the oneness of Christ and his church, so sexual immorality pictures the broken and depraved state of mankind apart from his creator.

All sexually immoral conduct is the fruit of an unredeemed life. Homosexual activity is an act of the sinful nature.[120] Women are not.

No sexually immoral person will inherit the kingdom of God.[121] Women who have been "born of . . . the Spirit" will "see the kingdom of God."[122]

Homosexual behavior is sin. People who practice sexual immorality are not to be tolerated within the church.[123] Godly women are "brothers,"[124] "fellow citizens with God's people and members of God's household,"[125] "which is the church of the living God."[126]

Homosexual Behavior Is Sin

There need be no confusion here. Homosexual behavior is condemned in the New Testament, not because it is a sin that cannot be covered by the blood of Christ's redemption. All sin, no matter how depraved or perverted, is forgiven when confession and repentance is made.[127] Instead it is condemned because it is an evidence of a life separated from God, in darkness and death. Therefore it must not exist among those who have been born of the Spirit.

Paul told the Ephesians that they used to be full of wicked and evil actions. But now that they had been redeemed, their lives should reflect union with Christ and the fruit of his Spirit.

> But among you there must not be even a hint of sexual immorality, or of any kind of impurity, or of greed, because these are improper for

> God's holy people. Nor should there be obscenity, foolish talk or coarse joking, which are out of place, but rather thanksgiving. For of this you can be sure: No immoral, impure or greedy person—such a man is an idolater—has any inheritance in the kingdom of Christ and of God. Let no one deceive you with empty words, for because of such things God's wrath comes on those who are disobedient. Therefore do not be partners with them.
>
> For you were once darkness, but now you are light in the Lord. Live as children of light (for the fruit of the light consists in all goodness, righteousness and truth) and find out what pleases the Lord. Have nothing to do with the fruitless deeds of darkness, but rather expose them. For it is shameful even to mention what the disobedient do in secret. But everything exposed by the light becomes visible, for it is light that makes everything visible. This is why it is said: "Wake up, O sleeper, rise from the dead, and Christ will shine on you."[128]

"Those who belong to Christ Jesus have crucified the sinful nature with its passions and desires. Since we live by the Spirit, let us keep in step with the Spirit."[129]

The confusion that identifies the acceptance of homosexual behavior with the acceptance of women as equals may stem from a misunderstanding of the clear Scripture teaching that I have called "No Difference."

If women are recognized as equals with men in the church, does this mean that all distinctions between persons, sexual and otherwise, are obliterated? Not at all! Please go back and read the chapter on "No Difference." Reread the section on spiritual gifts in the chapter entitled "Rule Through Reconciliation."

Likenesses and Differences

Oneness in Christ's body is not achieved through sameness. It is demonstrated through servanthood. We do not all become the same when we are made fellow citizens[130] and co-heirs.[131] God has made us all different. Our gender is one of our differences. Our spiritual gifts are another.[132] These differences, however, do not make a difference.[133] These differences are role distinctions, not rank distinctions.[134]

Let me try to be more precise. In what ways may believers be different?

- Date of birth
- Date of rebirth
- Specific sins
- Specific good deeds
- Specific gift of grace from the Spirit
- Natural abilities

- Looks
- Health
- Social status
- Political power
- Material wealth
- Language
- Culture
- Nationality
- Race
- Gender

There are many more we could list. Our differences are numerous.
In what ways are all believers the same?

- All have been predestined to be conformed to the likeness of Jesus.[135]
- All have been called by God.[136]
- All have believed that Jesus is the Son of God.[137]
- All have confessed their sin and repented of it.[138]
- All are justified through the shed blood of Jesus Christ on their behalf.[139]
- All may approach God in freedom and confidence.[140]
- All have denied themselves and are following Jesus.[141]
- All receive the Holy Spirit, who sanctifies their lives, making them one with Christ.[142]
- All receive a gift of grace from the Spirit.[143]
- All are children of God.[144]
- All are brothers with Jesus.[145]
- All rule with Christ through the ministry of reconciliation.[146]
- All will someday judge the world with Christ.[147]
- All, consequently, are also able to make judgments within the church.[148]
- All are brothers with each other.[149]
- All must serve each other in love.[150]

There are many more we could list. The ways in which we are the same are numerous.

Differences Make No Difference

When I say our differences do not make a difference, I mean that the ways in which we are different have no effect whatsoever on the ways in which we are the same.

Our differences have meaning and influence in every area of our lives. Our differences mean that we all lead different lives. Our gender makes a difference; it matters in sexual relationships. Our gender affects with whom we are to have moral sexual relations, who we are to marry. Sex is what sex is all about.

In the church our differences also have meaning and influence. Our differences are reconciled through Christ.[151] Our differences give us an opportunity to "serve one another in love."[152] In the church our differences allow us to uniquely administer God's grace to others,[153] "to prepare God's people for works of service, so that the body of Christ may be built up until we all reach unity in the faith and in the knowledge of the Son of God and become mature, attaining to the whole measure of the fullness of Christ."[154] So we can become "a perfect man,"[155] "a complete man."[156]

The ways in which we are the same, our likenesses, mean that we must "do to others what [we] would have them do to [us], for this sums up the Law and the Prophets."[157] No longer can one be above another. The ways in which we are the same mean that we are equal in rank in God's family, before the Father, and among the brothers, because we are one.[158]

Likenesses Yield Equality

The perfect equality of all believers is not based on our differences, nor does it obliterate our differences. Our perfect equality is based on our sameness.

Homosexual conduct, however, makes a difference because it is an evidence that there is no sameness. It is not merely a difference among believers, as is our gender, age, IQ, and so on: it is a sin. One who engages in homosexual activity may not be the same in the ways all believers are the same, as listed above. Why? Because homosexual relations, along with all sexual immorality, is a characteristic of the old life, and is thus excluded from our life in Christ, our sameness, our oneness. Homosexual behavior is not a difference that can minister anything to the church. Homosexual behavior is a sin, one of the "fruitless deeds of darkness." No partnership can exist between sexual immorality and those "light in the Lord."[159]

The Ultimate Double Standard

Let's go back to the original question. Does the acceptance of male/female equality as a scriptural principle lead to the acceptance of homosexual behavior?[160]

Absolutely not!

The acceptance of homosexual conduct does not grow out of a belief in the perfect equality between men and women. A homosexual relationship is the ultimate rejection of the way God created male and female to relate. Male and female were created to be one.[161] Male and female are completely interdependent upon each other,[162] both in the family and in the church.

Instead, its acceptance may be an outgrowth of traditional double standard thinking. When we begin to separate by sex into enclaves that rule and enclaves that serve, when segregation seems easier than reconciliation, when one sex can get along just fine without the other, when one sex alone can do the job, whether that job be deciding doctrinal matters or managing the nursery, we may eventually come to accept homosexual relationships as a natural consequence to such thinking. When the interdependence between men and women erodes so badly that the only thing men want or need women for is sex, or the only thing women want or need men for is sex, it is only a short step to the acceptance of homosexual behavior as a sensible option for those who prefer it.

The Question

Is the acceptance of homosexual conduct
based on the same scriptural teachings as the equality of women?

What do we know to be true?

- Sexual immorality is any sexual relationship outside of the life-long marriage commitment of
  one man and one woman.[163]
  Homosexual conduct is sexual immorality, which is sin.[164]
  It is a characteristic of separation from God, which is death.[165]

- Those who practice sexual immorality will not inherit the kingdom of God.[166]
  Believing women will.[167]

- People who practice sexual immorality are not to be tolerated within the church.[168]
  Believing women are "brothers."[169]
  Believing women are "fellow citizens" in "God's household," the church.[170]

- Homosexual conduct is evidence of an unredeemed life.[171]
  Believing women "keep in step with the Spirit."[172]

- The equal rank of all believers is based on our likenesses,
  not on our differences, or role distinctions.[173]
  The ways in which we "brothers" are different, or our role distinctions, have no effect on the ways in which we are the same.[174]

Where Is the Safest Place?

How safe is the middle of the road?

When two opposing ideas both seem true, we often try to walk between, to stay in the middle. We try to go in this direction here and that direction there.

Actually, the middle of the road is a notoriously dangerous place. Cars come at us from two different directions. It takes careful attention, a lot of dexterity, and good judgment to stand in the middle of the road and not get hit. It certainly is not a place of freedom. Nor is it safe.

Most of those committed to the complementarian position consider their stand rather middle of the road. At least I do not personally know anyone who says it is a disgrace for a woman to be heard within the community of God's people.

Most of those I hear in support of the subordination of women say women are only excluded from church government and the teaching of men. Women are free to participate in everything else. Of course the specific applications of this may be quite different from person to person and church to church. (Some might say a woman should never pray aloud in public. Others might feel it is quite permissible for a woman to explain God's Word to both men and women under the oversight of the male church governing authorities.)

I think many take the middle-of-the-road position because they feel safe there. They cannot feel comfortable with the complete domination of women by men or the complete silencing of women. But, there are those verses that say "women should remain silent"[175] and that Paul didn't permit a woman "to have authority over a man."[176] So they take the position that women can do some things, but not everything. Women can serve in some ways, but not in every way. And above all, the men must maintain control. Men must be in authority.

The rationale is that if you can't quite be sure of exactly what the Bible teaches about every aspect of this issue, this middle-of-the-road approach is best.

Articulation of Truth

Sometimes it takes a long time for the church as a whole to enunciate clearly what is true.

Salvation by faith alone. This was not always an obvious truth. There are so many scriptures telling us that inclusion in God's kingdom requires us to be good, to obey God's law. Throughout the history of the church, there have been many who felt confused by these two seemingly opposing truths. They thought the middle of the road was the safest and best approach. So they believed in faith, but they also believed in certain required good works. They believed in faith, but they also believed in circumcision. The believed in faith, but they also believed in penance.

They believed in faith, but they also believed in purgatory. It was the middle of the road, but how safe was it?

The truth was there, but it was obscured by contradicting ideas, teaching, actions, and church policies. The truth was so obscured that most people didn't really get it.

If something is true, the church must radiate that truth to the world in every way possible. If something is true, the church must live it completely, for its own maturing.

If something is true, but we hedge it around with contradicting ideas, teachings, actions, and church policies, we may be guilty of obscuring the gospel. How safe is that?

If

If it is true that women are to be silent and we let them speak, how safe is that?

Or if it is true that women are truly equal brothers and we choose to keep them under human authority, how safe is that?

If our physical differences make no difference in our salvation and we choose to allow it to make a difference in the church, the brotherhood of the redeemed, how safe is that?

If we have only one master and we choose to appoint masters among ourselves, how safe is that?

The Way to Safety

Where can we be safe on this issue? Only in the center of God's will. We know the way.

> Therefore, I urge you brothers, in view of God's mercy, to offer your bodies as living sacrifices, holy and pleasing to God—this is your spiritual act of worship. Do not conform any longer to the pattern of this world, but be transformed by the renewing of your mind. ***Then you will be able to test and approve what God's will is—his good, pleasing and perfect will.***[177]

Safety is not found in authority or in compromise, but in self-sacrifice. "If anyone would come after me, he must deny himself and take up his cross daily and follow me. For whoever wants to save his life will lose it, but whoever loses his life for me will save it."[178]

Once we know God's will, we must do it.[179]

In the Desert

A man is lost in the desert. He has been three days without food or water under the scorching sun. He has come to the end of his strength. Miraculously he comes upon a pool of water. But he has heard tales of such pools in the desert where the water is poisoned. A quick death comes to all who drink such water. On the other hand, he knows he cannot live much longer without water. He doesn't know what to believe. He doesn't know what to do. If he drinks, he may die. If he doesn't drink, he may die. What should he do to be safe?

In order to be safe, the man decides to drink only as much water as will fit into the palm of his hand. He decides to drink water only from the middle of the pool away from the scum covered edges. He decides to drink only at noon when the sun is at its hottest.

Is this a safe solution? A palmful of water will not get him to the next oasis. But if the water is poisoned, even a drop will kill him. He is certainly not free either. He is bound by his lack of knowledge of the truth. He doesn't know what to believe.

Safety in the Gospel

This is the way many seem to feel about the status of women in the church. But we need not be hampered by a lack of knowledge of the truth. The Bible tells us what to believe. "Believe in the Lord Jesus Christ and you will be saved."[180] We must believe the gospel, the good news of Jesus.

One hermeneutic rule derived from the principle of *sola scriptura*, the "Scriptures Only," is that no church doctrine or conduct should be established that is contrary to Scripture or in addition to Scripture, where Scripture is silent or even ambiguous.[181] The gospel is not ambiguous. We will be safest in the gospel.

The Burden of Proof

Therefore, it follows that any doctrine or practice that limits the application of the gospel must carry the burden of proof. And indeed it is a great burden, proving that the work Christ accomplished on the cross doesn't fully apply in some instances in this life.

All are one—but not equal. Or all may be equal before God—but not equal in the church.

Servanthood is the law of Christ's kingdom—but some submission is nonreciprocal. All are brothers—but some must be in authority over others. All have been given a spiritual gift—but some spiritual gifts are limited by physical qualifications. All are to teach and admonish one another—but not women—at least not in some circumstances.

It is a burden. It is not freedom.[182]

The Highest Standard of Proof

Another principle of interpretation derived from *sola scriptura* is that since the Bible, along with its illumination by the Holy Spirit,[183] has been complete and available for almost two thousand years, the more widely established a biblical interpretation is, the higher the standard of proof that is required to establish an alternative interpretation. It is true that the Christian church has practiced the subordination of women for the majority of its history. But the complete equality of men and women in the family and the church has the highest standard of proof in Christendom. It conforms to the gospel of Jesus Christ.[184]

Just as Jesus said, "You will know the truth, and the truth will set you free."[185]

But the real burden of proof is with the Holy Spirit. I believe that God has already written the law of the equality of men and women on the ***hearts*** of many multitudes of believers. If the time has come for this mystery to be fully revealed, the Spirit will now put it into the ***minds*** of believers also.[186]

I have asked some friends to read over what I have written. They have suggested that I not use phrases like "I think," "I believe," and "it seems to me," because they are weak words, a weak way to introduce an idea.

Yet I still find myself wanting to use them. Not because I do not believe that what I am saying is true, but because at this point it is largely only what ***I*** believe is true. I am asking God to open other hearts and minds[187] as confirmation to me that what I am saying is true. This is the burden of proof I seek.[188]

Christ Crucified

But aside from that, the Holy Spirit does not convince with words, but with his power. This is what our wisdom must rest on, not the wisdom of this world. I do not mind being weak, because "then I am strong."[189]

Following Paul's example,

> I resolve to know nothing . . . except Jesus Christ and him crucified. I came to you in weakness and fear, and with much trembling. My message and my preaching were not with wise and persuasive words, but with a demonstration of the Spirit's power, so that your faith might not rest on men's wisdom, but on God's power.[190]

This is my prayer for what I have written, and for you as you read it.

The Question

Who has the burden of proof
on this controversial issue of the status of women in the church?
The complementarian interpretation? Or the egalitarian interpretation?

What do we know to be true?

- The egalitarian interpretation seeks to apply the truth of the gospel to women in the family and in the life of the church.[191]

- The egalitarian interpretation seeks to reconcile all Scripture teachings to the gospel message that all believers are equal before God, while treating each scripture portion with integrity and respect.

- The complementarian interpretation seeks to limit the application of the gospel to women in the family and the church.

The Question

How can we know God's will on this issue?

What do we know to be true?

- God's will is revealed to and confirmed in us through self-sacrificing, spiritual worship.[192]

I Am

...who was and is and is to come...

ο κυριος ο ων και ο ην και ο ερχομενος ο παντοκρατωρ

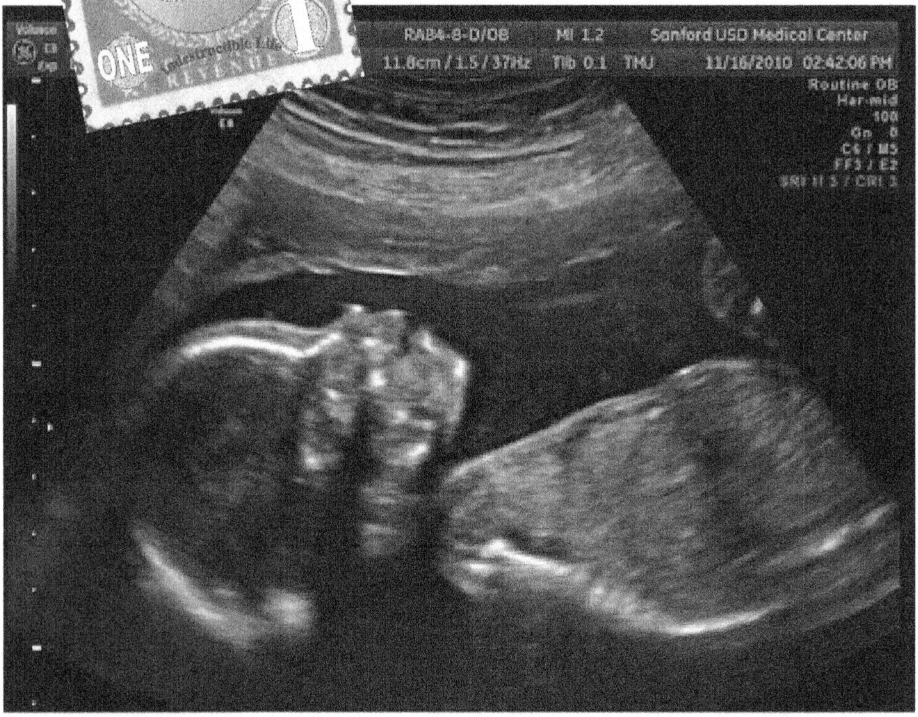

FULL RIGHTS

My granddaughter Eden~2010.

Chapter 16

Sons: You Are All Sons

Galatians 3:26

The other day I was watching an interview on TV. The interviewee was introduced as a progressive nun. In the course of the discussion, she referred to "our mother, God." The interviewer stopped her and asked, "Doesn't that make you feel just a little uneasy? I'm sure that is not what you were taught." The nun answered, "Yes, you're right. But I think it's important for women to feel respected and included when they worship."

I thought to myself, "Oh great! Another woman making us women look bad by trying to make God over in her own image." I know we cannot rearrange God to suit ourselves with language that is completely unbiblical.

Then it struck me with great joy. I don't have to make God over in my own image. He is making me over in his image. I don't have to call God "mother" to feel valued. God has called me a "son." And what could be more biblical? "Those who are led by the Spirit of God are sons of God. . . . For those God foreknew he also predestined to be conformed to the likeness of his Son, that he might be the firstborn among many brothers."[1]

Father and Son

God describes himself as "Father." We cannot pass that off as insignificant. Some would like to paraphrase the Bible to read that God is our "parent." But this would be quite inappropriate for those who believe in the inspiration of the Scriptures. The concept of *sola scriptura* demands that we make faithful translations of the Bible and not paraphrase to suit ourselves.

But God's Fatherhood cannot be considered apart from the sonship he confers on every believer.

Some would also like to change the translation "sons"[2] to "children." They feel that "children" would be more inclusive, telling the reader that everyone, regardless of sex, can be included in God's family.

But I think God's message to us is even greater than mere inclusion into his family. Of course, it is wonderful that we are all included. But it is even more wonderful that we are all included as sons. If the reader feels that the position of son is in any way, regardless of how remote or subtle, better, more privileged, or more honorable than the position of just a child, then God is communicating something very important to that reader by his use of the word *son*.

Whatever value is attached to God being our Father, rather than just our parent, that same value in equal proportions must be attached to each believer being a son, not just a child.

God has chosen to make us his sons. God uses the same word to describe a believer's relationship to him[3] that he uses to describe his relationship with his only begotten son, Jesus.[4] We would be no more content to read in our Bibles, "God sent his ***Child***, born of a woman"[5] than we would be to read, "by Jesus Christ and God the ***Parent***, who raised him from the dead."[6] If those translations seem to be diminishing in any way, then so is this one: "Because you are ***children***, God sent the Spirit of his ***Child*** into our hearts, the Spirit who calls out, 'Abba, ***Parent.***'"[7]

But God knows mankind. God speaks his reconciling word to a human race still affected by the curse.[8] Consequently, he has chosen instead to communicate to us in these words, "Because you are sons, God sent the Spirit of his Son—into our hearts, the Spirit who calls out, 'Abba, ***Father.***'"[9] This is the truth of the incredible value of God's redemption of each believer. Each believer is brought to the absolute pinnacle of status in God's family. Each believer has been brought to an absolutely equal status with every other believer in God's family.[10]

God's Fatherhood is not physical gender, and neither is my sonship. Fatherhood and sonship in God's family transcend these physical limitations. "Yet to all who received him, to those who believed in his name, he gave the right to become ***children of God***—children born not of natural descent, nor of human decision or a husband's will, but born of God."[11]

Children Are Sons

We need not fear that God looks upon our standing in his family[12] as in any way diminished because of our physical gender. God calls all believers his children. And just so that we will fully understand his meaning, he defines *children* as "sons."

> Those who are led by the Spirit of God are ***sons of God***. For you did not receive a spirit that makes you a slave again to fear, but you received the Spirit of ***sonship***. And by him we cry, "Abba, Father." The Spirit himself testifies with our spirit that we are ***God's children***. Now if we are ***children***, then we are heirs—heirs of God and co-heirs with Christ.[13]

> You are all ***sons*** of God through faith in Christ Jesus, for all of you who were baptized into Christ have clothed yourselves with Christ, ***There is neither . . . male nor female***, for you are all one in Christ Jesus. If you belong to Christ, then you are Abraham's seed, and heirs according to the promise. . . . that we might receive the full rights of sons.[14]

I Am a Son

This is what the book of Galatians is all about. I am a son.

In the spirit of saving the best till last, I close my presentation of *The Full Rights of Sons* with Galatians 3:26–4:7. I have saved this till last because I have heard the accusation that the egalitarian position is built on only one verse: "There is neither Jew nor Greek, slave nor free, male nor female, for you are all one in Christ Jesus."[15] This is a beautiful line from Scripture, but the equality of women before God and among the brothers is very clear even apart from this plain and simple statement of truth.

These words are icing on the cake. They express what I read in every word of Scripture. Let me emphasize the ***I*** in that last sentence. Every word of Scripture speaks of Jesus. Jesus died to save me. Let me emphasize the ***me*** of that last sentence. Every word of Scripture is about my redemption. Let me emphasize the ***my***. Thus, for me, a female, every word of Scripture radiates the truth encapsulated in this verse.

Paul Slandered

Some have said that Paul was a male chauvinist. But that is a false slander.

By explaining the freedom[16] I have in Christ so carefully to me, Paul has been an agent for the administration of God's grace in my life.[17] He has been one of the preachers through whom I heard the gospel. I heard and I believed. Since I believed, I called on the name of the Lord, and he saved me. Paul's feet are indeed beautiful. He brought "good news" to me.[18]

I am used to reading Scripture with the understanding that it has been written to me, for me, and about me. The verses with the word "woman" in them speak to me, of course! They speak specifically to my gender. In fact, when Paul does speak specifically about women, he treats them as equals. Paul always upholds women's status as equals among all the believers, before God, and within the church. But if it were only these specific references to women that spoke to me, I would not know much of the gospel.

No Chauvinistic Gospel

The gospel is not chauvinistic or exclusive. It includes all. And nowhere is that more clearly enunciated than in Paul's letter to the Galatians.

Not long on introductions in this letter, Paul gets right to the point. "I am astonished that you are so quickly deserting the one who called you by the grace of Christ and are turning to a different gospel."[19]

This different gospel was that some were forcing the Galatians "to follow Jewish customs."[20] Paul called it "no gospel at all." These teachings threw people "into confusion" and were a perversion of "the gospel of Christ."[21] These ideas were so perverted that Paul said those teaching such things should go to hell, "be eternally condemned!"[22]

Why did Paul consider these teachings "no gospel at all?" Because a salvation that depends to any degree on anything human is not good news. Whether these human things be our innate heritage of characteristics and abilities or our effort—how hard we try—they can never measure up to what God requires. God will accept only complete and perfect righteousness.

The Galatians were being confused and led away by this false teaching. Paul calls them "foolish"[23] for allowing such teaching to take hold in their midst.

The Good News

The sinful human will and desire to fulfill God's requirements by ourselves, either by being someone in particular or by doing specified things, is the false gospel Paul is refuting. Faith and belief in Jesus Christ is the needed good news. Only through Jesus can we become who we need to be because ***he*** is who we need to be.[24] Through Jesus we do what we need to do because ***he*** has already done it.[25]

Paul goes so far as to say that a return to trying to fulfill God's requirements, or living by the law,[26] is no life at all; it is death.[27] Living by the law is being "prisoners" of sin,[28] returning to "slavery,"[29] and falling "away from grace."[30]

Paul did not consider it safe to compromise on this issue. He didn't think the Gentiles should be circumcised as even a token fulfillment of God's requirements, or as a compromise with their Jewish brothers who thought circumcision was necessary, along with faith in Jesus.

Paul thought the only safe place on this issue was to completely renounce observing the law or God's requirements. "Mark my words! . . . if you let yourselves be circumcised, Christ will be of no value to you at all."[31] Anything else is opposed to the gospel of Christ.[32] "It is for freedom that Christ has set us free. Stand firm, then."[33] Anything else would be hiding the truth of the gospel.[34]

"What, then, was the purpose of the law?"[35]

Law and Righteousness

Yesterday I went bowling. For me, at least, bowling is a very graphic illustration of trying to gain righteousness through obedience to God's requirements as set out in the law. When I threw the first ball, it went into the gutter. Then I started to work on my technique. I tried to make my approach smoother. I tried not to twist my wrist. Some other members of my group gave me a few pointers. Stand on the dots. Give a good swing to your arm. Point your thumb where you want the ball to go. Don't drop the ball; let it slide onto the floor.

Sometimes I knocked down a few pins, and sometimes the ball went into the gutter. No matter how hard I tried to do all the proper things perfectly, it did not seem to have much effect on the pins. Even if I practiced daily and improved, I don't think I could ever bowl a perfect game. And even if I bowled one perfect game, I doubt that I could always bowl a perfect game. Somewhere along the line, I would miss a pin, and then it wouldn't be a perfect game.

Law and Faith

Standing on the dots, swinging my arm, pointing my thumb, sliding the ball are not the same as knocking down the pins. Trying to keep the law, keeping it to the best of our ability, is not the same as righteousness. We may slap each other on the back and say, "Good try. You'll get it next time." But that is not the same as righteousness. Lots of practice is not the same as righteousness. There is only one thing that is righteousness—knocking down all the pins, every one of them, all the time.

The law shows us what sin is, our inability to be righteous. Consequently, it shows us our need for a redeemer. "So the law was put in charge to lead us to Christ that we might be justified by faith. Now that faith has come, we are no longer under the supervision of the law."[36]

Once we come to faith, we are "released from the law."[37] Why? Because the gospel is the fulfillment of the law.

> Therefore, there is now no condemnation for those who are in Christ Jesus. because through Christ Jesus the law of the Spirit of life set me free from the law of sin and death. For what the law was powerless to do in that it was weakened by the sinful nature, God did by sending his own Son in the likeness of sinful man to be a sin offering. And so he condemned sin in sinful man, in order that the righteous requirements of the law might be fully met in us, who do not live according to the sinful nature but according to the Spirit.[38]

This is the gospel. This is what our "sound doctrine" must conform to.[39]

Law→Faith→Righteousness

Through faith in Christ, every requirement of the law is met.[40] We cannot obey the law. We are sinners. But Christ Jesus lived a perfect life.[41] He obeyed the law perfectly. He has satisfied the requirements of the law for us.

This is freedom. "Through Christ Jesus the law of the Spirit of life ***set me free*** from the law of sin and death."[42]

This is perfection.

> The law is only a shadow of the good things that are coming—not the reality themselves. For this reason it can never . . . make perfect those who draw near to worship. . . . Therefore when Christ came into the world, he said: "Here I am. I have come to do your will" . . . by that will we have been made holy through the sacrifice of the body of Jesus Christ once for all, . . . because by one sacrifice he has ***made perfect forever*** those who are being made holy.[43]

> Jesus Christ is "***the perfect law that gives freedom.***"[44]

In the midst of this glorious gospel are the verses which particularly apply to the issue of the status of women in the church.

All

Paul begins, "You are all ***sons*** of God through faith in Christ Jesus."[45] Jesus is the Son of God.[46] Consequently, through him we are also made "sons."

"You are all sons of God through faith in Christ Jesus." Who are sons? ***All*** who have been baptized into Christ and *all* who have clothed themselves with Christ.[47]

Paul must have been emphasizing *all*, because next he defines it. "There is neither Jew nor Greek, slave nor free, male nor female, for you are ***all*** one in Christ Jesus."[48] *All* means everyone. No matter what categories of people you can think of, they are sons if through faith in Christ Jesus, they have been baptized into Christ and have clothed themselves with Christ. There is no other requirement for sonship. The necessity of any other characteristic or action is "no gospel at all."

Circumcision

The controversy over observing the law in the life of the church centered on the rite of circumcision, the removal of the foreskin of a male's penis. Circumcision was instituted by God as a sign of the covenant between himself and Abraham. "I will establish my covenant as an everlasting covenant between me and you and your descendants after you for generations to come, to be your God."[49] This all-inclusive covenant was God's announcement of the gospel, in advance, to Abraham.[50]

I don't know why God chose circumcision as a sign of his covenant with Abraham. I don't know why he chose something from which women, by the very nature of the act of circumcision, were completely excluded. Nor do I know why God chose to begin to reveal his redemption through only one man, Abraham.

The Sign of the Covenant

But I do know the intent of God's choosing Abraham and the intent of the covenant God made with Abraham, of which circumcision was a sign. The intent, or goal, of God's covenant with Abraham was all-inclusive, not exclusive. Through this covenant, God intended to make a nation for himself from the descendants of Abraham.[51] And even though Ishmael was circumcised,[52] God was going to establish the covenant through the promised son, Isaac.[53]

Peter told the good news at Pentecost. "Repent and be baptized, ***every one of you***, in the name of Jesus Christ for the forgiveness of your sins. And you will receive the gift of the Holy Spirit. ***The promise is for you and your children and for all who are far off—for all whom the Lord our God will call.***"[54] "Every one" of us is invited to be a part of this covenant through a "promise."[55]

Since Christ's coming, circumcision is no longer necessary because he has circumcised the hearts of all who believe.[56] Circumcision is a shadow. Christ is the reality.[57] He is the promised one.[58] Through this promise we receive freedom.[59] This promise is realized through faith,[60] and "you, brothers, like Isaac, are children of promise."[61]

The All-Inclusive Covenant

We know that no one had a problem accepting that free Jewish males were sons. But now Paul even includes those who formerly had been excluded, the Greek or Gentile, the slave, the female. Even though the covenant had always been all-inclusive, before Christ came the sons had been under the "guardians and trustees" of the law, "in slavery under the basic principles of the world."[62]

With Christ's appearing, the full intent of the covenant is made manifest. Through faith no one is excluded from sonship.[63]

> You are all sons of God through faith in Christ Jesus, for all of you who were baptized into Christ have clothed yourselves with Christ. There is neither Jew nor Greek, slave nor free, male nor female, for you are all one in Christ Jesus. If you belong to Christ, then you are Abraham's seed, and heirs according to the promise. . . .
>
> . . . when the time had fully come, God sent his Son, born of a woman, born under law, to redeem those under law, that we might receive the full rights of sons. Because you are sons, God sent the Spirit who calls out, "Abba. Father." So you are no longer a slave, but a son: and since you are a son, God has made you also an heir.[64]

This is the gospel.

Those who are committed to the subordination of women agree. This is the gospel. They agree that it is wonderful. They agree that all are included in the gospel. But . . .

Good News, But . . .

Yes. For complementarians, there is a "but." The *but* is that the gospel Paul has so clearly enunciated here for the Galatians only speaks of women's spiritual standing before God. The *but* is that this good news does not apply to our standing in the church. "You are all sons" does not mean that we are all of equal rank in the church. It does not mean that God intends our sonship and equality to be practiced in this life . . . only in the next.

The *but* is that there is a limitation on the gospel. The gospel doesn't fully apply in the family or in the church. Even though we are "all sons," some of us are still to be under the authority of others in this life. Even though we are all sons, some us are to be over some of the rest of us. Even though we are all sons spiritually speaking, we who are "all sons . . . through faith" remain in a hierarchy of authority here on earth.

I cannot accept this.

Contrary to Faith

This interpretation is completely contrary to the entire business of living by faith. The Christian life is the struggle to make real here on earth the hope we have in heaven. "Christ in you, the hope of glory."[65] Hebrews 11 is a long list of those who acted according to what God said was true instead of what the world said was true.[66]

Where was this circumcision controversy taking place? In the churches of Galatia. In real churches, here on earth, in this life, differentiation was being made between believers. Not all were considered in the same light. Equality as sons and equal status in the church were being based on some characteristic other than faith. But our standing before God is not based on human anything. "To all who received him, to those who believed in his name, he gave the right to become children of God—children born ***not of natural descent, nor of human decision or a husband's will***, but born of God."[67]

Galatians 3:28 is Paul's statement to real physical people in a real physical situation. Was Paul telling the believers of the churches of Galatia that even though Jew and Greek, slave and free, male and female were all spiritually sons of God, he didn't expect that to make a difference in the way the Galatians related to each other in their earthly churches?

Act in Line with the Truth

If this were Paul's meaning, why did he confront Peter when he began to "separate himself from the Gentiles"?[68] If this were Paul's meaning, why did he tell the Gentile Galatians not to "let yourselves be circumcised"?[69]

Paul spoke this way because our spiritual standing before God does make a difference here on earth, to our life in the church. Paul is addressing a very down-to-earth problem, but a spiritual truth is the solution. Why? Because spiritual truth must be acted out in our physical lives. We must act "***in line with the truth of the gospel.***"[70]

This is what living the Christian life is all about, as Paul reaffirms. "So I say, live by the Spirit, . . . Since we live by the Spirit, let us keep in step with the Spirit."[71] Paul's final words to the Galatians were, "Neither circumcision nor uncircumcision means anything; what counts is a new creation. Peace and mercy on all who ***follow this rule.***"[72] Paul isn't just being theoretical. He expected these truths to be applied to the everyday lives of the Galatians. Our new life in Christ is not just for the next life.[73] The "new creation" which we have become through faith in Jesus is a rule we must follow in this life.[74]

The New Self

This principle[75] is found throughout the Scriptures. What is true before God in heaven, we must by faith endeavor to make true here on earth. Even though sin will still have its effect, even though we cannot perfectly demonstrate the truth, nevertheless, we must live according to the new way.

> So I tell you this, and insist on it in the Lord, that you must no longer live as the Gentiles do, in the futility of their thinking. . . . You, however, did not come to know Christ that way. Surely you heard of him and were taught in him in accordance with the truth that is in Jesus. You were taught, with regard to your former way of life, to put off your old self, which is being corrupted by its deceitful desires; to be made new in the attitude of your minds; and to put on the new self, created to be like God in true righteousness and holiness.[76]
>
> "Now you are light in the Lord. Live as children of light."[77]
>
> "To live is Christ."[78]

"Whatever happens, conduct yourselves in a manner worthy of the gospel of Christ."[79]

"So then, just as you received Christ Jesus as Lord, continue to live in him."[80]

"See to it that no one takes you captive through hollow and deceptive philosophy, which depends on human tradition and the basic principles of this world rather than on Christ."[81]

> Since, then, you have been raised with Christ, set your hearts on things above, where Christ is seated at the right hand of God. Set your minds on things above, not on earthly things. For you died, and your life is now hidden with Christ in God.[82]

> If we claim to have fellowship with him yet walk in the darkness, we lie and do not live by the truth. But if we walk in the light, as he is in the light, we have fellowship with one another, and the blood of Jesus, his Son, purifies us from all sin.[83]

"This is how we know we are in him: Whoever claims to live in him must walk as Jesus did."[84]

"And now, dear children, continue in him."[85]

If . . . Then

"***You are all sons of God through faith in Christ Jesus***, for all of you who were baptized into Christ have clothed yourselves with Christ. There is neither Jew nor Greek, slave nor free, male nor female, for you are all one in Christ Jesus."[86]

If this is the gospel, then sound doctrine is also the standard for how we are to conduct ourselves "in God's household, which is the church of the living God, the pillar and foundation of the truth."[87]

If this is the truth, then this is how we must love each other. "Let us not love with words or tongue but with actions and in truth."[88]

If this is the truth, then we must obey it. "You were running a good race. Who cut in on you and kept you from obeying the truth?"[89]

If this is our standing in the Spirit, then this is how we must live. "So I say, live by the Spirit."[90]

If this is the way of the Spirit, then this is how we must serve. "But now, by dying to what once bound us, we have been released from the law so that we serve in the new way of the Spirit, and not in the old way of the written code."[91i]

If this is God's will for us in heaven, then this is how we should act on earth. "Your will be done on earth as it is in heaven."[92]

If this is perfection, then we must aim for it. "Aim for perfection."[93]

If this is what is true by faith, then we must live it out. "For in the gospel a righteousness from God is revealed, a righteousness that is by faith from first to last, just as it is written: 'The righteous will live by faith.'"[94]

If we are "all sons of God" through justification by faith rather than justification by law, then that is how we must also live.[95] "For through the law I died to the law so that I might live for God."[96]

If this is the grace of God, then we dare not set it aside here on earth. "I am crucified with Christ and I no longer live, but Christ lives in me. ***The life I live in the body, I live by faith*** in the Son of God, who loved me and gave himself for me. ***I do not set aside the grace of God***, for if righteousness could be gained through the law, Christ died for nothing!"[97]

If this is how Jesus Christ has loved us, then this is how we must love one another. "My command is this: Love each other as I have loved you."[98]

If this is how Christ accepts us, then this is how we must accept each other. "Accept one another, then, just as Christ accepted you."[99]

Not only does Jesus want us to accept each other as he accepts us, but he also wants us to treat each other in the same way we would treat him. Paul instructed the Romans to accept Phoebe "in a way worthy of the saints."[100] The saints are all sons of God, all brothers and co-heirs with Jesus. Paul asked Philemon to welcome Onesimus, a slave, "as you would welcome me."[101] And how was Paul himself welcomed by the Galatians? As if he were "Jesus Christ himself."[102] "The King will reply, 'I tell you the truth, whatever you did for one of the least of these brothers of mine, you did for me.'"[103]

If it is true . . .

If it is the gospel . . .

If it is the grace of God . . .

If it is by faith . . .

that "there is neither Jew nor Greek, slave nor free, male nor female, for you are all one in Christ Jesus"[104] . . . we must live it out.[105]

We Must Live It

This is the clear teaching of Scripture. Christ died to make the truth real in our lives. It will never be fully or perfectly realized in this life because we still struggle with sin. But, nevertheless, it is really true. The truth of the gospel is true here on earth. The truth of the gospel is true now. The truth of the gospel is true in me. The truth of the gospel is true in the church, the household of God, "the pillar and foundation of truth."[106]

This is the mystery of the oneness of the church. Through the gospel we are all "heirs together with Israel, members together of one body (*the church*), and sharers together in the promise (*the gospel*) in Christ Jesus."[107] If we share together in the promise of Christ Jesus, then we must live that out as members together of one body.

Being a Gentile makes no difference because we are all "children of Abraham," God's chosen people through faith.[108] Therefore, there can be no special positions of rank, privilege, or status among brothers.

Being a slave makes no difference because we have all been "set free" by faith.[109] Therefore, there can be no hierarchy of authority among brothers.

Being a female makes no difference because we "are all sons of God through faith."[110] Therefore, women cannot be subordinate to men among brothers.

There can be no differentiation among brothers, among sons, with regard to rank, privilege, freedom, or authority because we "are all one in Christ Jesus."[111]

Since we have now been set free from these "basic principles of the world,"[112] we "receive the full rights of sons."[113]

Adoption

The Greek word translated "full rights"[114] in the 1984 NIV is more commonly translated "adoption," as in the KJV or NASB. Full rights are assumed in the concept of adoption. Adoption clearly emphasizes that the full rights do not come out of nowhere but are based on the underlying relationship of being adopted, being made a son. The relationship comes first, then the rights.

This is further clarified by Paul in Romans when he speaks of his brothers, the people of Israel: "Theirs is the ***adoption as sons***; theirs the divine glory, the covenants, the receiving of the law, the temple worship and the promises. Theirs are the patriarchs, and from them is traced the human ancestry of Christ, who is God over all."[115] Here adoption is defined by the privileges and rights the adoptees receive. And what could be greater than divine glory, the covenants, the law, temple worship, and ***the promises***! Yes, the rights and privileges are full!

These rights and privileges are further explained when Paul tells the Ephesians,

> In love he predestined ***us to be adopted as his sons*** through Jesus Christ, . . . In him we have redemption through his blood, the forgiveness of sins, . . . And he made known to us the mystery of his will . . . In him we were also chosen, . . . And ***you also*** were included in Christ when you heard the word of truth, the gospel of your salvation. Having believed, you were marked in him with a seal, the promised Holy Spirit, who is a deposit guaranteeing our inheritance until the redemption of those who are God's possession—to the praise of his glory."[116]

I love the phrase "you also" that Paul used above. He wanted to be sure that the Gentile Ephesian brothers,[117] men and women,[118] understood they were no longer outsiders. Yes, even we women, we females, are included in Christ. And being included means we are adopted sons through faith and consequently have the Holy Spirit, who ***guarantees*** our inheritance, our full rights!

Full Rights

What are the "full rights of sons"?

- God's love: "How great is the love the Father has lavished on us, that we should be called children of God!"[119]
- God's promises: "Theirs is the ***adoption as sons***; theirs . . . the promises."[120]
- Inclusion in God's family: "If you belong to Christ, then you are Abraham's seed."[121]
- Indwelling of the Holy Spirit: "Because you are sons, God sent the Spirit of his Son into our hearts, the Spirit who calls out, 'Abba, Father.'"[122]
- Life: "But if by the Spirit you put to death the misdeeds of the body, you will live, because those who are led by the Spirit of God are sons of God."[123]
- Freedom: "So you are no longer a slave, but a son."[124]
- Being heirs of God: "Since you are a son, God has made you also an heir."[125]
- Being co-heirs with Christ: "Now if we are children, then we are heirs—heirs of God and co-heirs with Christ."[126]
- A share in Christ's sufferings: "Now if we are children, then we are heirs . . . if indeed we share in his sufferings."[127]
- Discipline: "Endure hardship as discipline; God is treating you as Sons."[128]
- A share in God's holiness: "God disciplines us for our good, that we may share in his holiness."[129]
- Righteousness: "For he chose us in him . . . to be holy and blameless in his sight. In love he predestined us to be adopted as his sons through Jesus Christ."[130]
- Christ likeness: "Now we are children of God . . . when he appears, we shall be like him, for we shall see him as he is."[131]
- A share in Christ's glory: "Now if we are children, then we are heirs—heirs of God and co-heirs with Christ, . . . in order that we may also share in his glory."[132]
- Oneness in Christ: "You are all sons of God . . . For you are all one in Christ Jesus."[133]

This is "an inheritance that can never perish, spoil or fade." This is the inheritance that heaven guards for us.[134]

"I pray also that the eyes of your heart may be enlightened in order that you may know the hope to which he has called you, the riches of his glorious inheritance in the saints."[135]

Rich Indeed

We are rich indeed!

These are the "rights of sons." This is what Christ died to give us.[136] This is what "all . . . through faith in Christ Jesus"[137] receive, because we are no longer slaves,[138] no longer under the law of sin and death,[139] no longer foreigners and aliens,[140] but "sons."[141]

Yet this list cannot really be considered "the ***full*** rights of sons." These are merely a few of the rights, benefits, and privileges directly linked to sonship in Scripture. The fact is if we are one with Jesus and his co-heirs, then our inheritance is "all things" just as his inheritance is.[142] We really have no idea of the scope of the glory God has planned for us since before time began. "No eye has seen, no ear has heard, no mind has conceived what God has prepared for those who love him."[143]

What Counts?

In summary, What is the meaning of Galatians 3:26–4:7?

The letter to the Galatians is primarily about how sonship, full and equal membership in the church, is acquired. The question was, Is sonship acquired through reliance on who we are and what we do or by faith in Christ alone?

Paul's answer? The churches of Galatia, which included Jews and Gentiles, free and slave, men and women, were to consider all brothers as full and equal members of the church with no regard whatsoever to their personal characteristics or effort.

In fact, the Gentiles were not to compromise on this issue by allowing themselves to be circumcised. This would only promote the false notion that the promise could be realized through self-reliance, rather than through faith alone. Circumcision would only perpetuate exclusion, rather than the inclusion which was the original intent and scope of the promise. Circumcision would only further concentrate on a shadow rather than on the reality in Christ. Circumcision was for children under guardians, not sons receiving the full rights of sons. Perpetuating these things was stepping outside of the grace God has freely offered us in Jesus Christ.[144]

Now that faith has been revealed,[145] circumcision has no value. "The only thing that counts is faith expressing itself through love."[146] Circumcision doesn't mean anything anymore. "What counts is a new creation."[147]

There is only one criteria for inclusion in God's household, the church. We are included on the basis of our faith in the grace of God, nothing else.[148] Through our faith God makes us righteous,[149] fulfilling all the requirements of the law.[150] It is through faith alone that we become sons of God and receive the full rights of sons.

Paul has summarized it so much better than I can.

> But now a righteousness from God, apart from law, has been made known, to which the Law and the Prophets testify. This righteousness from God comes through faith in Jesus Christ to all who believe. There is no difference, for all have sinned and fall short of the glory of God, and are justified freely by his grace through the redemption that came by Christ Jesus. God presented him as a sacrifice of atonement, through faith in his blood. . . . he did it to demonstrate his justice at the present time, so as to be just and the one who justified those who have faith in Jesus."[151]

> Therefore, since we have been justified through faith, we have peace with God through our Lord Jesus Christ, through whom we have gained access by faith into this grace in which we now stand. And we rejoice in the hope of the glory of God.[152]

Being a Jew or a Greek made no difference. Both were to be considered of equal status in the church. This truth was meant to have its effect in real, concrete ways in the daily life of the specific churches of Galatia. For it is the life we "live in the body" that we must "live by faith in the Son of God."[153]

The differences of slave/free and male/female are in exact parallel with Jew/Greek.[154] These differences are to have exactly the same significance in the church as the Jew/Greek difference, which is no significance at all as to rank, position, status, or spiritual gifts.

Paul saw this issue as a very broad discussion. The gospel nullifies any human effort[155] to gain our own salvation or contribute to our own righteousness or to be justified through obedience to the requirements of the law.[156] It nullifies all the human characteristics and distinctions of who we are.[157] These human things are contrary to grace. When we rely on the human, we fall away from grace through faith.[158]

Our status in God's family "depends on a promise."[159] And thus, we, who have been made righteous through that promise[160] are to "live by faith"[161] in God who made the promise and in Jesus Christ his Son, the promised one.[162]

For Abraham, living by faith meant believing the promise, the truth of God, in spite of all human evidence to the contrary.[163]

For us living by faith means believing the promise. "You are all sons of God," in spite of all physical evidence to the contrary. "This is the victory that has overcome the world, even our faith. Who is it that overcomes the world? Only he who believes that Jesus is the Son of God."[164]

Through faith we are all Jews, spiritually Jews, a chosen people.[165] Through faith we are all free, spiritually free, no longer slaves "under the basic principles of the world," no longer "under law," but "set free."[166] Through faith in Jesus Christ we are all male, spiritually male, circumcised by Christ,[167] "sons of God," and his "heirs."[168] This is what matters in the church, a spiritual temple in which God dwells by his Spirit.[169]

"For ***you are all one in Christ Jesus.***"[170]

"In him we live and move and have our being."[171]

"For we were all baptized by one Spirit into one body."[172]

"Here there is no Greek or Jew, circumcised or uncircumcised, barbarian, Scythian, slave or free, but Christ is all, and is in all."[173]

"For us there is but one God, the Father, from whom all things came and for whom we live; and there is but one Lord, Jesus Christ, through whom all things came and through whom we live."[174]

"There is one body and one Spirit—just as you were called in one hope when you were called—one Lord, one faith, one baptism: one God and Father of all, who is over all and through all and in all."[175]

"Oh, the depth of the riches of the wisdom and knowledge of God. . . . ***For from him and through him and to him are all things***. To him be the glory forever! Amen."[176]

The Question

What does Galatians 3:28 mean?

What do we know to be true?

- Through faith all are "children of Abraham."[177]
  All are "children of promise," . . . "born by the power of the Spirit."[178]
  All receive the blessing given to Abraham by faith in Christ Jesus,
  so we might receive the promise of the Spirit.[179]
  This is why we have been redeemed.[180]

- Through faith all are "sons of God."[181]
  All are "heirs."[182]
  As heirs of God[183] all receive
  A share in God's holiness[184]
  Righteousness[185]
  Christ-likeness.[186]
  As co-heirs with Christ[187] all receive
  A share in Christ's sufferings[188]
  discipline[189]
  A share in Christ's glory[190]
  All things[191]
  All receive the "adoption" and the "full rights of sons:"[192]
  God's love[193]
  God's election[194]
  Indwelling of the Holy Spirit[195]
  Life[196]
  Freedom[197]

- "All" includes all those who believe
  regardless of their race, nationality, political or social status, or gender.[198]

- Faith is:
  Belief in Jesus Christ.[199]
  The standard for sonship.[200]
  The means by which we are made righteous.[201]
  Not the basis for the law.[202]
  Not human effort.[203]
  Not reliance on observing the law.[204]
  The only thing that counts.[205]
  How the righteous live.[206]
  The means by which we live "in the body."[207]

The Question

Does Galatians 3:28 express only a spiritual truth
that has no effect on the physical, earthly life of the church?

What do we know to be true?

- We must act in line with the truth of the gospel.[208]
- We have an obligation to live according to the Spirit.[209]
- We must follow the rule that the new creation is the only thing that counts.[210]
- We must conduct ourselves according to sound doctrine that conforms to the gospel.[211]
- We must love according to the truth.[212]
- We must aim for perfection.[213]
- We must live by faith.[214]
- We must love each other as Christ loves us.[215]
- We must accept others as Christ accepts us.[216]
- We must be members together in the church, just as we are sharers together in the promise.[217]

The Question

What is the status of women in the church?

What truth can we apply
to make it a slightly simpler question?

"You are all sons of God
through faith in Christ Jesus,
for all of you who were baptized into Christ
have clothed yourselves with Christ.

There is neither
Jew nor Greek, slave nor free, male nor female,
for you are all one in Christ Jesus.

If you belong to Christ,
then you are Abraham's seed,
and heirs according to the promise.

. . . when we were children.
we were in slavery
under the basic principles of the world.

But when the time had fully come,
God sent his Son,
born of a woman,
born under the law,
to redeem those under the law,
that we might receive the *adoption*[218] and full rights of sons.

Because you are sons,
God sent the Spirit who calls out, 'Abba, Father.'

So you are no longer a slave, but a son:
and since you are a son,
God has made you also an heir."[219]

". . . what counts is a new creation.
Peace and mercy to all who follow this rule."[220]

My granddaughters Eden, Katy, Charis, and Faith~2011.

CHAPTER 17

Simply Put: By Faith

Romans 1:17

By faith in God's grace
(Romans 3:22–26)
we are made brothers,
(Hebrews 2:11)
Redeemed into the body of Christ.
(1 Corinthians 12:27)
We are made sons,
(Galatians 3:26)
Recreated into God's household,
(Ephesians 2:19–22)
which is the church.
(1 Timothy 3:15)

The ways in which we are different
have no effect on our relationship to God since we are all children of God,
or on our relationship to each other since we are all brothers in Christ.
(1 Corinthians 12:4–6)

Thus we live out the mystery
(Ephesians 3:6)
that men and women, all brothers, are equal
as to worth, privilege, service, status, rank, freedom, and authority,
(Matthew 23:8–12)
before God, our one Master,
(Matthew 22:37–38)
and among each other, the brothers.
(Matthew 22:39–40)

We are one,
(1 Corinthians 12:12)
created one in the family,
(Matthew 19:4–6)
and recreated one in the church.
(Ephesians 2:14–22)

We are equal,
(1 Corinthians 11:11–12)
created equal in the family,
(Genesis 1:27–28)
and recreated equal in the church.
(Galatians 3:28)

Our oneness is realized and demonstrated through servanthood,
(Ephesians 4:1–6)
as is our equality,
(Matthew 7:12)
in the image of our God,
(Matthew 20:25–28)
who is one God.
(John 17:20–23)

This is the gospel.
(Galatians 2:20)
This is how we must live,
(Romans 15:7)
by faith.
(Romans 1:17)

Examine the Scriptures,
which are able to make you wise for salvation
through faith in Christ Jesus,
to see if these things are true.
(Acts 17:11; 2 Timothy 3:15)

My daughter Christina and daughter-in-law Christie with their daughters Eden and Faith~2012.

Works Cited

Bilezikian, Gilbert. *Beyond Sex Roles*. Grand Rapids, MI: Baker Book House, 1985.

Fenton, Edward. "'The Baptism for the Dead' in 1 Corinthians 15 and Numbers 19." *Semper Reformanda* 4, no. 1 (Spring 1995): 3–9.

Hebrew/English Interlinear, Greek/English Interlinear, and Lexicon: Interlinear Bible. Accessed November 1, 2012, http://interlinearbible.org.

Johnson, Alan F. Johnson, ed. *How I Changed My Mind About Women in Leadership*. Grand Rapids, MI: Zondervan, 2010.

Kuiper, R. B. *The Glorious Body of Christ*. Grand Rapids, MI: Wm. B. Eerdmans, 1967.

Marshall, Alfred. *The Nestle Greek Text with a Literal English Translation*. Grand Rapids, MI: Zondervan, 1975.

Martin, Faith. *Call Me Blessed*. Grand Rapids, MI: Eerdman's, 1988.

McIlhenny, Charles. "Letter From the left Coast: Feminism and Gayism." *The Christian Statesman* (July–August, 1992): 38.

Dictionary and Thesaurus: Merriam-Webster Online. Accessed January 4–24, 2013, http://www.merriam-webster.com/dictionary.

Piper, John and Wayne Grudem, eds. *Recovering Biblical Manhood and Womanhood*. Wheaton, IL: Crossway Books, 1991.

Reformed Presbyterian Church of North America. *The Report of the Committee on the Role and Service of Women*. Reformed Presbyterian Church of North America, 1990.

Schaff, Philip. Vol. 3 of *The History of the Christian Church*. Grand Rapids, MI: Eerdmans, 1910.

"The Westminster Confession of Faith" and "The Westminster Larger Catechism." *The Constitution of the Reformed Presbyterian Church of North America.* Pittsburgh, PA: Crown and Covenant Publications, 1989.

Young, Robert. *Analytical Concordance to the Bible.* Grand Rapids, MI: Wm. B. Eerdmans , 1970.

Key:
11:45 = Bible Book Chapter 11: Verse 45.
37 = Page Number 37.
10.63 = Chapter 10. Endnote Number 63.

Old Testament

New Testament

Mark:

Ephesians:

Philippians:

Colossians:

2 Timothy:

Titus:

Index of Topics

Key:

37 = page number 37.
10.63 = Chapter 10, Endnote number 63.

"You are ***all*** sons of God through faith in Christ Jesus,
for ***all*** of you who were baptized into Christ have clothed yourselves with Christ.
There is neither Jew nor Greek, slave nor free, male nor female,
for you are ***all*** one in Christ Jesus.
If you belong to Christ, then you are Abraham's seed,
and heirs according to the promise. . . .
that we might ***receive the adoption and full rights of sons.***"
(Galatians 3:26–4:5)

My family~2006.

[1] 2 Tim. 3:14–17.
[2] 2 Tim. 1:7 KJV.
[3] Rom. 8:14–17; Gal. 4:4–7.
[4] 1 Tim. 1:10–11.
[5] 1 Tim. 3:15.
[6] Rom. 11:36 NIV 2011 (*Holy Bible, New International Version*®, NIV® Copyright © 1973, 1978, 1984, 2011 by Biblica, Inc.® Used by permission. All rights reserved worldwide.)
[7] Acts 17:11.

Chapter 1 – The Interpretation of Scripture: Finding Our Way

[1] 1 Tim. 1:10–11; Gal. 2:14; Phil. 1:27.
[2] John 14:26, 16:13.
[3] Luke 24:45; John 16:13.
[4] John 1:1–5, 9, 14, 18.
[5] John 5:39–40.
[6] 1 Cor. 14:34.
[7] Col. 1:15.
[8] 1 Cor. 15:29.
[9] James 2:22.
[10] Rom. 13:1.
[11] Eph. 6:5.
[12] 1 Pet. 2:18.
[13] Acts 5:29.
[14] Since I first wrote those words, I have read an excellent article which explains that the baptism "for the dead" that Paul speaks of in 1 Cor. 15:29 refers to the Old Testament ceremonial washing required for those who had touched a dead body in Num. 19. This ceremonial washing was itself a picture of Christ as he cleanses us from our sin and sin's consequent death through Christ's own death and resurrection as in Rom. 6:3–4. Edward Fenton, "'The Baptism for the Dead' in 1 Corinthians 15 and Numbers 19," *Semper Reformanda*, 4, no. 1 (Spring 1995), 3–9.
[15] "The Westminster Confession of Faith," 1.9, *The Constitution of the Reformed Presbyterian Church of North America.* (Pittsburgh, PA: Crown and Covenant Publications, 1989), A-11.
[16] John 17:17.
[17] John 16:13.
[18] John 14:6.
[19] John 1:17.
[20] John 8:32.
[21] John 5:39, 14:6, 16:13.
[22] Luke 11:9–13, 24:45; Eph. 1:17–18; James 1:5.
[23] John 17:17; 2 Tim. 3:16–17.
[24] Matt. 22:37–40; Rom. 15:4–6; 2 Pet. 1:20–21.
[25] Heb. 4:12.
[26] 1 Tim. 3:15.
[27] 1 Tim. 1:10–11; Gal. 2:14; Phil. 1:27.
[28] John 14:6, 15:26, 16:13–14.
[29] Gen. 24:27; 2 Sam. 2:6, 15:20; Ps. 25:10, 40:11, 57:3, 61:7, 85:10, 86:15, 89:14, 138:2; Prov. 3:3, 14:22, 16:6, 20:28 (the KJV translation of these Old Testament references is especially clear); John 1:14, 17; Col. 1:6; 2 John 3.
[30] John 8:32; 2 Cor. 3:17; James 1:25.
[31] John 3:21; 1 John 3:19-24.

Chapter 2 – Oneness: You Are All One

[1] Matt. 19:4–6.
[2] Eph. 5:31–32.
[3] Matt. 22:30.
[4] 1 Cor. 15:44–49.
[5] John 17:11, 21.
[6] Gen. 1:26–27.
[7] Gen. 1:31.
[8] Gen. 2:18.
[9] Gen. 1:27.
[10] Gen. 2:25.
[11] Gen. 3:7–12.
[12] Matt. 19:3–6.
[13] Rom. 5:17–18.
[14] Eph. 2:12–22.
[15] 1 Cor. 3:16–17, 12:24–25.
[16] Matt. 19:6.
[17] Eph. 4:1–16.
[18] Gen. 1 and 2.
[19] 1 Cor. 12:12, 27; Eph. 4:l–16.
[20] 1 Cor. 7:25–35.
[21] Col. 3:3–4; Rom. 8:29.
[22] Deut. 6:4.
[23] John 1:1, 14:6; 1 John 5:6, 20.
[24] 2 Cor. 13:14.
[25] John 17:11.
[26] Gal. 3:26–28.
[27] 1 Cor. 12:4–6.
[28] 1 Cor. 12:25.
[29] 1 Cor. 12:7.
[30] Eph. 4:4–5.
[31] John 17:23.
[32] Gen. 1:26; Matt. 28:19; John 14:26; 2 Cor. 13:14; 1 Pet. 1:2.
[33] Deut. 6:4; John 17:11.
[34] Gen. 1:26–27.
[35] John 17:26; 1 John 4:16–17; 1 Cor. 10:16–17; Eph. 4:11–13, 24; Phil. 2:1–2.
[36] Gen. 1:27.
[37] Gen. 2:23.
[38] 1 Cor. 11:11–12.
[39] Gen. 1:27.
[40] 1 Cor. 12:14, 27.
[41] Rom. 3:22–24; Col. 3:3–4.
[42] Col. 3:10–11.
[43] 1 Cor. 12:4–5.
[44] 1 Cor. 12:7; Eph. 4:12.
[45] 1 Cor. 12:21–24.
[46] 1 Cor. 12:4–6.
[47] 1 Cor. 12:25; Eph. 4:13.
[48] 1 Cor. 12:25.
[49] Gen. 2:23–24; Matt. 22:30.
[50] Gal. 3:28; Eph. 4:4–6, 5:31–32.
[51] Deut. 6:4; John 17:11.
[52] Matt. 19:3–6.
[53] Eph. 2:15–16.
[54] John 14:7–11, 26.
[55] Matt. 19:4–6.
[56] 1 Cor. 12:12, 15, 24, 25; Eph. 2:14–16.

Chapter 3 – No Difference: God Does Not Show Favoritism

[1] Rom. 9:16–18; Exod. 33:19.
[2] Titus 3:5.
[3] Isa. 55:1–3; Matt. 11:28; Luke 9:23; John 7:37; Rom. 10:11, 13; 1 Tim. 2:3–4; Rev. 22:17.
[4] Acts 10:34.
[5] Job 34:18–19.
[6] Rom. 3:22–24.
[7] Rom. 9:16.
[8] Rom. 9:13–16; Titus 3:5.
[9] Rom. 9:10–29.
[10] Rom. 9:16.
[11] Ibid.
[12] Titus 3:5.
[13] Job 34:18–19.
[14] Ibid.
[15] 1 Sam. 16:7; John 7:24; Gal. 2:6.
[16] Job 34:19.
[17] Rom. 3:23.
[18] Acts 10:11–15.
[19] Matt. 7:15–20.
[20] Gal. 5:22–26; Eph. 5:8–10; Acts 10:15.
[21] Deut. 1:17; Eph. 6:9.
[22]. 19:15; James 2:1–12.
[23] Lev. 19:15; Deut. 1:17.
[24] 1 Sam. 16:7; Gal. 2:6.
[25] Eph. 6:9.
[26] Gen. 12:2–3, 15:6.
[27] John 8:31–47.
[28] John 8:39.

[29] John 8:39–41, 44.
[30] Acts 10:34; Rom. 2:11.
[31] Acts 10:15.
[32] Gen. 25:23.
[33] Rom. 9:8.
[34] John 3:3–6.
[35] Gal. 4:21–31.
[36] Rom. 9:10–29.
[37] 1 Cor. 15:50; John 6:63; 1 Pet. 1:23.
[38] The Hebrew word for "Gentile," הַגּוֹיִם *(hag·gō·w·yim)*, is also translated "nations," and "heathen." Robert Young, *Young's Analytical Concordance to the Bible* (Grand Rapids, MI: Wm. B. Eerdmans, 1964, 1969, 1970), 17 of Index–Lexicon to the Old Testament.
[39] 2 Kings 21:2.
[40] Ps. 9:5.
[41] Isa. 42:1 KJV.
[42] Jer. 4:3, 7 KJV.
[43] Jer. 46:1 KJV.
[44] Ezek. 4:13 KJV.
[45] Matt. 10:5–6.
[46] Matt. 6:31–32 KJV.
[47] Matt. 20:18–19.
[48] Acts 10:34–35.
[49] Acts 10:47, 11:17.
[50] Rom. 10:12–13.
[51] Rom. 10:9–11.
[52] Rom. 15:7.
[53] Col. 3:11.
[54] Rom. 15:14.
[55] Acts 10:11–15.
[56] Lev. 19:15; Matt. 7:15–20.
[57] Gal. 5:22–26.
[58] Matt. 7:1–5.
[59] Deut. 1:17; Rom. 14:4, 10, 12; Eph. 6:9.
[60] John 8:15.
[61] Lev. 19:15; James 2:1–12.
[62] Lev. 19:15; Deut. 1:17; Col. 3:11.
[63] Col. 3:11.
[64] Gen. 12:2–3, 25:23; Zech. 9:10; Mal. 1:11; John 3:3–6, 8:31–47; Acts 10:34; Rom. 9; 1 Cor. 1:50.
[65] 1 Sam. 16:7; John 7:24; Gal. 2:6; Col. 3:11.
[66] Rom. 10:12; 1 Cor. 12:13; Col. 3:11.
[67] Gal. 3:28.
[68] Eph. 4:4–5; Col. 3:11.
[69] Gal. 3:28.
[70] Acts 10:9–23, 15:9.
[71] Acts 10:34–35.
[72] Acts 10:47, 11:17, 15:8.
[73] Rom. 10:10.
[74] Ibid.
[75] Rom. 10:12–13; Acts 15:11.
[76] Rom. 15:7.
[77] Gal. 2:11–13.
[78] Gal. 2:14.
[79] Gal. 3:26–29.
[80] Interestingly, throughout history, as God slowly unfolded his plan to include the Gentiles in the gospel, the Gentiles he chose to reveal this truth through were often women. Rahab (Josh. 6:17, 25; Matt. 1:5; Heb. 11:3) and Ruth (Ruth 4:10–14; Matt. 1:5) were Gentiles and women brought into the house of Israel, into the ancestry of the Messiah. There was also the widow who provided for Elijah (1 Kings 17:9–24; Luke 4:24–27) and the woman of Syrian Phoenicia whom Jesus commended for her great faith even though she was not a Jew (Mark 7:24–30).
[81] Gal. 5:6, 6:15.
[82] *The Report of the Committee on the Role and Service of Women*, Reformed Presbyterian Church of North America (1990), 1.41.
[83] Sometime in the years between writing this study and its publication, those who hold the traditional interpretation of the Bible that women are subordinate to men in the family and church began calling themselves "complementarians." From this point forward, I will do the same as a nod of respect to them, many of whom are my dear personal acquaintances, brothers and sisters in the Lord from whom I have learned much about the Bible and the Christian life. However, the term *complementarian* is a euphemism and not a real description of their position. That man and woman, men and women are complementary to each other is universally agreed upon. The real essence or point of difference between the two biblical interpretations is about equality. Complementarians believe the Bible teaches that men do and must have

authority over women; biblical egalitarians believe that men and women are equal as to worth, privilege, service, status, rank, freedom, and authority. I also fully realize that there are many variations of belief within each term and know that neither complementarians nor egalitarians are all of one mind.

[84] Acts 17:28.
[85] Gal. 2:20–21; 2 Cor. 5:16–18.
[86] Col. 3:1–11.
[87] 1 Cor. 12:13.
[88] See also Rom. 2:17–29, 10:4, 9–13.
[89] See also 1 Cor. 13:1–3.
[90] See also Rom. 2:28–29; 2 Cor. 5:15–18.
[91] 2 Cor. 5:17.
[92] 2 Cor. 5:16.
[93] Col. 3:11.
[94] Gal. 3:28.
[95] Rom. 10:12.
[96] Acts 10:9–23, 15:9.
[97] Rom. 3:22–24.
[98] Gal. 3:26–29.
[99] Col. 3:11; Eph. 4:4–5.
[100] Gal. 3:28.
[101] Acts 10:9–23, 15:9.
[102] Acts 10:34–35.
[103] Acts 10:47, 15:8.
[104] Rom. 10:10.
[105] Ibid.
[106] Rom. 10:12–13; Acts 15:11.
[107] Rom. 15:17.
[108] Gal. 2:14.
[109] Gal. 5:1; Rom. 2:17–29, 10:4, 9–13.
[110] Gal. 5:6; 1 Cor. 13:1–3.
[111] Gal. 6:15; Rom. 2:28–29; 2 Cor. 5:16–17.
[112] *Report of the Committee on the Role and Service of Women*, 1.41.
[113] 1 Cor. 12:13; 2 Cor. 5:16–18; Gal. 2:20–21; Col. 3:1–11.

Chapter 4 – Servanthood: Serve One Another in Love

[1] Rom. 12:1.
[2] Matt. 20:20–28.
[3] Matt. 20:26–27; Mark 10:42–44.
[4] Matt. 16:24; Luke 9:23.
[5] Matt. 7:12.
[6] Matt. 22:39–40.
[7] Matt. 11:29.
[8] Eph. 4:22–24, 5:1–2.
[9] Matt. 20:25–28.
[10] Matt. 20:25; Luke 22:25–26; Gen. 3:16; Rom. 1:29–30.
[11] Matt. 20:26; Rom. 12:16; 1 Cor. 13:4–5; Phil. 2:3; 1 Pet. 5:2–3.
[12] Matt. 20:26; Isa. 55:8–9; Rom. 12:2; 1 Cor. 4:19; Eph. 4:22–24; 1 John 2:15–17.
[13] Matt. 20:26–27, 22:38–40, 7:12, 18:1–5; Rom. 12:9–10, 13:8–10; Gal. 5:13; Phil. 2:1–5; Eph. 5:1, 2, 21; Col. 3:12–14.
[14] Matt. 20:28, 11:29; Eph. 5:1–2; Phil. 2:5–7; 1 Pet. 2:21–24; 1 John 3:16.
[15] Matt. 20:28; Eph. 4:22–24, 5:1–2; Phil. 2:2–5.
[16] Dictionary and Thesaurus: Merriam-Webster Online, Accessed January 4, 2013, http://www.merriam-webster.com/dictionary/subordinate.
[17] 1 Pet. 5:5 KJV.
[18] John 10:17–18; Luke 2:51; Phil. 2:6–7.
[19] Eph. 5:22–33.
[20] Eph. 5:1–2.
[21] Eph. 5:21.
[22] James 4:6–12.
[23] Mark 8:34.
[24] Eph. 5:22–25.
[25] John 15:13.
[26] Phil. 2:1–11.
[27] Phil. 2:6–8.
[28] Matt. 28:16–20.
[29] John 13:3–5.
[30] Matt. 23:8–12.
[31] Mark 9:35; Phil. 2:7, 9; Rev. 1:8, 17, 18.
[32] Phil. 2:5.
[33] Phil. 2:2–4.
[34] Eph. 5:2; Heb. 9:14.
[35] Rom. 6:11, 13, 12:1–2;1 Pet. 2:24.
[36] Rom. 6:5; 1 John 4:19.
[37] Mark 8:34–35; John 12:23–26; Rom. 6:1–14, 12:1–2; Col. 3:3–4.
[38] 1 Pet. 3:1, 7.
[39] 1 Pet. 2:23–24.
[40] 1 Pet. 2:21.
[41] Matt. 22:37–39.
[42] Matt. 7:12.
[43] 1 Cor. 7:2, 3, 4, 5, 10, 11, 12, 13, 14.
[44] 1 Cor. 12:25; 2 Cor. 8:13–15.
[45] Luke 22:25–26.
[46] Matt. 22:38–40.

[47] 1 Cor. 7:4; Eph. 5:28.
[48] Eph. 5:1, 2, 21.
[49] Eph. 5:1, 2, 25; John 15:12–13; Phil. 2:1–11.
[50] Phil. 2:6; Matt. 23:8–12, 28:16–20; John 13:3.
[51] John 10:17–18.
[52] Phil. 2:6–8; John 13:1–5.
[53] Mark 8:34–35; Rom. 6:1–14, 12:1–2; James 4:6–12.
[54] 1 John 4:19; Mark 8:34–35; John 12:23–24, 13:14; Rom. 6:1–14; Col. 3:3.
[55] Eph. 5:1–2, 21; Phil. 2:1–5; Matt. 7:12, 22:39; 1 Cor. 4:7; 1 Pet. 3:8, 4:8, 5:5.
[56] Matt. 7:12.
[57] Matt. 22:39.
[58] l Pet. 2:13.
[59] Matt. 5:38–48.
[60] 1 Pet. 2:13, 21, 23.
[61] Heb. 13:12–13.
[62] 1 Pet. 3:7.
[63] See 1 Pet. 3:6 for God's pattern for our response to oppression that may be generated by man–made institutions, as contrasted to Hosea 2:16 for God's pattern for reconciliation. We must not confuse the two. However, they are related since both come from the law of servanthood. Peter speaks of the first in the context of the second (1 Pet. 3:8, 4:8, 5:5 KJV).
[64] 1 Cor. 12:21–22.
[65] 2 Cor. 11:30, 12:9–10, 13:4.
[66] 2 Cor. 12:10.
[67] 1 Pet. 3:7.
[68] Rom. 8:17.
[69] 1 Pet. 1:6–7, 2:20; 3:14; 4:12–14.
[70] 1 Pet. 2:13, 3:1, 5–6.
[71] 1 Pet. 2:18–19.
[72] 1 Pet. 3:6, 14.
[73] 1 Pet. 2:23, 4:19.
[74] 1 Pet. 3:5, 4:19.
[75] Eph. 6:9.
[76] 1 Cor. 4:3–7.
[77] 1 Pet. 3:7.
[78] Rom. 8:17.
[79] Pet. 2:23, 4:19.
[80] 1 Cor. 4:5.
[81] God honored and commended the arguments of both Sarah (Gen. 21:8–12) and the daughters of Zelophehad (Num. 27:1–7) when they appealed to the authorities over them for justice.
[82] 1 Pet. 2:16.
[83] Gen. 12:10–20, 20:1–17.
[84] Philem. 8–9, 14–17; Eph. 6:9.
[85] 1 Pet. 3:7.
[86] 1 Pet. 3:8–9.
[87] 1 Pet. 4:8–11.
[88] 1 Pet. 5:5 KJV.
[89] 1 Pet. 1:6–7, 2:20, 3:14, 4:12–14.
[90] 1 Pet. 2:16.
[91] Ibid.
[92] Acts 15:8–11, 19.
[93] John 17:23.
[94] 1 Cor. 3:17.
[95] 1 Pet. 2:13; Matt. 5:38–48.
[96] 1 Pet. 2:13, 14; Mark 12:17.
[97] 1 Pet. 2:18.
[98] 1 Pet. 3:6.
[99] Rom. 13:1–7; Gen. 12:5.
[100] Matt. 5:39–41; Gen. 12:10–20.
[101] 1 Pet. 2:18.
[102] 1 Pet. 2:13, 21; Heb. 13:12–13.
[103] 1 Pet. 2:18, 22–23.
[104] 1 Pet. 2:24.
[105] 1 Pet. 2:23, 3:6.
[106] 1 Pet. 2:18–19, 23, 3:5, 4:19; 1 Cor. 4:3–7.

Chapter 5 – The Head of the Body: What Does It Mean?

[1] 1 Cor. 11:3.
[2] Eph. 5:23.
[3] You can check my references to Greek words for yourself by using an interlinear Greek–English New Testament such as the one I used: Alfred Marshall, *The Interlinear Greek-English New Testament: The Nestle Greek Text with a Literal English Translation* (Grand Rapids, MI: Zondervan, 1975), or online at Interlinearbible.org, or an analytical concordance such as those by Strong or Young, which give all the translations of any given Greek word as well as listing all the biblical references where the word is used.
[4] κεφαλῇ (*kephalē*)

[5] Col. 1:18.

[6] Westminster Confession of *Faith,* 1.9; 2 Peter 1:20–21.

[7] John 10:7, 9.

[8] John 14:6.

[9] John 8:12.

[10] John 10:11.

[11] John 6:35, 48.

[12] John 1:29.

[13] 2 Pet. 1:20–21; 2 Tim. 3:16.

[14] Eph. 1:22–23.

[15] Eph. 4:12–15.

[16] Col. 1:18–20.

[17] Col. 1:15.

[18] John 1:14, 18.

[19] Col. 2:9–10.

[20] Matt. 10:40; 1 Cor. 12:27; 2 Cor. 2:14–16, 3:2–3, 17–18; 1 John 4:16–17.

[21] Eph. 4:15–16.

[22] Col. 2:19.

[23] Eph. 4:15–16.

[24] Col. 2:19.

[25] 1 Cor. 12:12; Eph. 4:2–5.

[26] Ps. 118:22.

[27] Matt. 21:42; Mark 12:10; Luke 20:17; Acts 4:11; 1 Pet. 2:7.

[28] 1 Pet. 2:4–5, 9.

[29] 1 Cor. 3:16; 2 Cor. 6:16; Heb. 3:6.

[30] The Greek word translated here as "chief cornerstone" (ἀκρογωνιαίου [*akrogōniaiou*]) may mean "top of the corner." The Greek word for "head" (κεφαλὴ [*kephalē*]) is not used in this verse. Young, Young's Analytical Concordance to the Bible, 203, Index–Lexicon to the New Testament, 58, 72.

[31] Could this have been what Jesus was referring to, at least in part, in John 2:18–21? When Christ completed his work, through his life, death, and resurrection, the worship of God would no longer be centered in a temple of stone. When Jesus died and rose again three days later, he both destroyed and rebuilt the temple, that is, God's dwelling place among his people. With the entrance of the new covenant, a physical building was no longer needed, but a spiritual one. (Eph. 2:19–22) The new temple, his body, the church, was a place where God could live by his spirit.

[32] Eph. 2:19–22.

[33] Eph. 1:22–23.

[34] Eph. 4:12–13, 15.

[35] Col. 1:18.

[36] Col. 2:19.

[37] In the Old Testament, it was the head of the sacrifices (Exod. 29:10, 15, 19; Lev. 1:4, 3:2, 8, 13, 4:4) and the head of the scapegoat (Lev. 16:8, 20–22) that symbolically carried all the sin of the people of Israel. Aaron, the high priest, was also to wear a gold plate on his forehead that bore the guilt of the people. (Exod. 28:36–38)

[38] Eph. 5:23.

[39] Col. 1:18.

[40] Eph. 1:22–23, 4:12–13; Col. 1:18–20, 2:9–10.

[41] Eph. 4:15–16; Col. 2:19.

[42] Ibid.

Chapter 6 – The Head of the Body: 1 Corinthians 11:3–16

[1] 1 Sam. 16:7.

[2] Gal. 2:6; James 2:1–4; 1 Pet. 3:3–4.

[3] Col. 1:18, 2:19; Eph. 1:22–23; 4:12, 13, 15.

[4] ἀνήρ (*anēr*) is translated "husband" in Eph. 5:23 and "man" in 1 Cor. 11:3. γυναικὸς (*gynaikos*) is translated "wife" in Eph. 5:23 and "woman" in 1 Cor. 11:3.

[5] 1 Cor. 11:3.

[6] Eph. 5:23.

[7] The Greek word ἀνδρὸς (*andros*) used for "man" in "every man" of 1 Cor. 11:3 usually accentuates the male meaning of *man* and comes from the same root Greek word ἀνήρ (*anēr*) used for "man" in "every man" of verse 4 and "the head of the woman is man" in verse 3. Its meaning may not always be as cut and dried as it first appears. This same Greek word, ἀνήρ (*anēr*), is used in Rom. 4:8 where Paul quotes Ps. 32:1–2. The Hebrew word, אָדָם (*'ā·ḏām*), used for "man" in these Old Testament verses means "human being," male and female, as it is used in Gen. 1:26–27 and 5:1–2.

Thus, at least at times, Paul himself, who was fluent in both languages, thought the Greek word he used in the phrase "every man" in both verses 3 and 4 meant every "human being."

[8] Gen. 1:27, 5:1–2.

[9] 1 Cor. 11:11–12.

[10] ἀνδρὸς (*andros*)

[11] 1 Cor. 11:3.

[12] Col. 1:18–20.

[13] Eph. 1:22–23, 4:12–15; Col. 2:9–10.

[14] Gen. 2:23.

[15] 1 Cor. 1:7.

[16] Col. 1:15.

[17] Col. l:19.

[18] John 1:14.

[19] Heb. 1:3; 2 Cor. 4:4–6.

[20] 2 Cor. 3:18; John 17:9–10.

[21] 1 Cor. 11:7.

[22] John Piper and Wayne Grudem, editors, *Biblical Manhood and Womanhood* (Wheaton, IL: Crossway Books, 1991), 130.

[23] The word *glory* is often attached to a crown in Scripture. Many times there is a crown of glory on the head or in the hand of Christ, the promised Messiah (Ps. 21:3–5, 132:17–18, Isa. 62:1–3; Zech. 9:16–17). Could this crown of glory be the church? (Ezek. 16:8–14 reminds me of Eph. 5:26–27.) And at least once, a wife is described as a crown on her husband's head (Prov. 12:4).

[24] John 14:7–11.

[25] 2 Cor. 3:2–3.

[26] 1 John 4:12.

[27] Ezek. 43:1–7.

[28] Eph. 2:19–22.

[29] 1 Cor. 12:27; 2 Cor. 4:7–11.

[30] Gen. 2:23.

[31] 1 Cor. 11:7, 9.

[32] πλήρωμα (*plērōma*).

[33] πεπληρωμένοι (*peplērōmenoi*).

[34] Col. 2:10 KJV.

[35] Eph. 1:10.

[36] Matt. 5:17–18; John 17:4; Acts 3:18; Eph. 3:10–11.

[37] John 1:18.

[38] John 1:4, 5, 9, 14.

[39] John 1:18.

[40] John 1:29, 41, 45.

[41] John 1:1.

[42] 1 John 2:5–6.

[43] 1 John 4:12.

[44] 1 John 4:16–17.

[45] John 17:4.

[46] Gen. 2:18.

[47] 1 Cor. 11:9.

[48] Gen. 1:31.

[49] Gen. 1:27.

[50] Matt. 5:14–16; John 12:36; Rom. 13:12, 14; 2 Cor. 4:4–6; Eph. 5:8, 13–14; Phil. 2:14–16; 1 Pet. 2:9–10; 1 John 2:7–8.

[51] Luke 1:78–79; John 1:4, 9; 8:12; Rev. 21:22–24; 22:5.

[52] 1 Cor. 11:8, 12.

[53] 1 Cor. 11:7–8.

[54] Eph. 4:15–16; Col. 2:19.

[55] 1 Cor. 11:3.

[56] 1 Cor. 3:23.

[57] 1 Cor. 11:7–8.

[58] Gen. 2:23.

[59] Gen. 2:24.

[60] Col. 3:10.

[61] Doesn't "the head of every man is Christ" (1 Cor. 3:11) and "Christ is the head of the church, his body" (Eph. 5:23) remind you of "I am the vine and you are the branches" (John 15:5)? Read John 15:1–17 for Christ's words on how to be his fullness? Jesus finishes God's work by harvesting fruit for eternal life (John 4:34–36), by dying with Christ, the church bears fruit to God (Rom. 7:4), and with the completion of mankind, male and female, they are fruitful and fill the earth (Gen. 1:28). The union of head and fullness produces fruit.

[62] Col. 2:9–19.

[63] John 8:42, 7:29, 6:32–33.

[64] John 17:18.

[65] John 17:1–5.

[66] John 17:6–19.

[67] 1 Cor. 11:11–12.

[68] Matt. 19:4–6.

[69] Definition of *incarnate*: a. invested with bodily and especially human nature and form; b. made manifest or comprehensible: embodied (http://www. merriam-webster.com/dictionary/incarnate).

[70] John 1:14, Col. 2:9.

[71] Eph. 5:28–29.

[72] 1 Cor. 11:3.
[73] Col. 2:10; Eph. 1:22–23, 4:12–13.
[74] 1 Cor. 11:7; 2 Cor. 3:17–18; Gen. 1:27, 5:1–2.
[75] 1 John 2:5–6, 4:12, 16–17.
[76] Gen. 2:23.
[77] Gen. 2:23; 1 Cor. 11:7.
[78] 1 Cor. 11:9; Gen. 2:18, 1:27, 31.
[79] Col. 2:9, 1:19.
[80] Col. 1:15; John 1:14; Heb. 1:3.
[81] Matt. 5:17–18; John 1:29, 41, 45, 17:4; Eph. 3:10–11; Acts 3:18.
[82] Col. 2:9–10; 1 Cor. 11:12; John 17:18.
[83] Cor. 11:11–12.
[84] 1 Cor. 11:8; Gen. 2:23.
[85] Matt. 10:40; John 8:42, 17:18.
[86] 1 Cor. 11:7.
[87] Ibid.
[88] 1 Cor. 11:8.
[89] 1 Cor. 11:9.
[90] 1 Cor. 11:10.
[91] My own illustration of sign of authority is found on pages x-xi at the front of the book.
[92] 1 Cor. 11:4–5.
[93] Gen. 3:16.
[94] ἐξουσίαν (*exousian*).
[95] Eph. 3:12.
[96] I first read this in Faith Martin's book, *Call Me Blessed* (Grand Rapids, MI: Eerdmans, 1988), 176.
[97] ἀγγέλους (*angelous*).
[98] Thanks to Renwick Wright, Professor Emeritus, Reformed Presbyterian Theological Seminary, Pittsburgh, PA.
[99] For example, Luke 7:24 and 9:52.
[100] Josh. 2:1.
[101] If I had been reading this letter as the original Corinthian recipients did from start to finish without any chapter or verse delineations, it would not have surprised me that this passage is about the new freedom believers have in Christ and the issues of Christian liberty. Paul introduces this subject with the words "Now for the matters you wrote about:" in 1 Cor. 7:1 and sums it up in 1 Cor. 10:23–33 that directly precedes this particular passage we are here discussing.
[102] Gal. 2:4–5.
[103] Luke 20:20.
[104] Gal. 5:1, 13, 14.
[105] Gal. 5:13.
[106] Gal. 3:26.
[107] Eph. 2:19; 1 Tim. 3:15.
[108] Perhaps the men were also exercising their new freedom in Christ. "Every man who prays and prophesies with his head covered dishonors his head." (1 Cor. 11:4) Where did Paul get this idea? In the Old Testament, the priests had to cover their heads when they performed the duties of worship (Exod. 28:36–38, 29:6; Lev. 8:9, 21:10; Ezek. 44:18). A man's head covering was also a sign of humility before God (Ezek. 29:18; Jer. 14:3–4, 2:37; Amos 8:10) and respect toward him (Lev. 19:27, 21:5–6, 10:6).

Could Paul have been calling upon the men to exercise their new freedom in Christ by approaching God through Christ alone rather than through the Jewish laws, customs, and traditions of the Old Testament, thus honoring Christ by their uncovered heads since it was Christ who fulfilled all these Old Testament laws (Eph. 3:12; Heb. 10:19–23)?

Why did men and women express their freedom with their head coverings in such opposite ways? Because the head coverings of men and women had different meanings. A man's head covering was necessary to fulfill the law and tradition of ceremonial worship. A woman's head covering had nothing to do with these Old Testament worship laws and customs; it simply signified modest dress.

[109] Gal. 5:2.
[110] Gal. 2:5, 5:1.
[111] 1 Cor. 7:22.
[112] Eph. 3:12.
[113] 1 Cor. 9:1.
[114] 1 Cor. 10:29.
[115] 1 Cor. 8:9.
[116] 1 Cor. 9:19.
[117] 1 Cor. 10:31–11:1.
[118] Matt. 12:3–8, 23:23; 1 Pet. 1:23–25.
[119] Distinguishing between issues and biblical principles is not the cultural relativism that undermines the authority of the Bible. Rather it is sound biblical interpretation that allows the truth of the Bible to be universally applied to ***all*** cultures throughout ***all*** times and in ***all*** places.

[120] 1 Cor. 11:11–12.
[121] Josh. 2:1.
[122] Gal. 2:4–5; Luke 20:20.
[123] Gal. 2:5, 5:1.
[124] Gal. 5:2; 1 Cor. 7:36.
[125] Gal. 5:13.
[126] Gal. 5:13–14; 1 Cor.8:9.
[127] Gal. 5:1.
[128] Gal. 2:5; 1 Cor. 9:19.
[129] Gal. 2:4.
[130] Gal. 5:13–14.
[131] 1 Cor. 11:4–5.
[132] 1 Cor. 11:16.
[133] Τοιαύτην (*toiautēn*).
[134] 1 Cor. 11:16.
[135] 1 Cor. 10:31–33.
[136] 1 Cor. 7:12–40.
[137] 1 Cor. 8:1–13.
[138] 1 Cor. 9:1–27.
[139] 1 Cor. 11:3–16.
[140] 1 Cor. 11:17–34.
[141] 1 Cor. 11:33.
[142] 1 Cor. 1:10.
[143] 1 Cor. 3:1–3.
[144] 1 Cor. 3:4–9.
[145] Ibid.
[146] 1 Cor. 6:1.
[147] 1 Cor. 7:25–11:16.
[148] 1 Cor. 12:1–11, 14:1–40.
[149] 1 Cor. 12:12–31.
[150] 1 Cor. 13:1–13.
[151] 1 Cor. 15:1–58.
[152] 1 Cor. 16:1–24.
[153] 1 Cor. 15:57–58.
[154] 1 Cor. 4:20.
[155] 1 Cor. 10:23–11:2.
[156] 1 Cor. 7:12–40.
[157] 1 Cor. 8:1–13, 10:1–33.
[158] 1 Cor. 9:1–27.
[159] 1 Cor. 11:3–15.
[160] 1 Cor. 11:17–34.
[161] 1 Cor. 3:1–3.
[162] 1 Cor. 3:4–9.
[163] 1 Cor. 5:1.
[164] 1 Cor. 6:1.
[165] 1 Cor. 7:25–11:16.
[166] 1 Cor. 12, 14:1–25.
[167] 1 Cor. 12.
[168] 1 Cor. 13.
[169] 1 Cor. 14.
[170] 1 Cor. 15.
[171] 1 Cor. 16.
[172] 1 Cor. 1:10, 12:24–25, 16:14.

Chapter 7 – The Head of the Body: Ephesians 5:22–33

[1] Gen. 3:15; Rom. 16:20; Gal. 3:13–14.
[2] Eph. 4:1.
[3] Eph. 5:1–2.
[4] 1 John 3:16.
[5] 1 John 4:10–12.
[6] 1 John 4:16.
[7] 1 Cor. 13:4–8, 13.
[8] Eph. 5:21.
[9] Phil. 2:5–8.
[10] Eph. 5:2.
[11] Rom. 12:1.
[12] Eph. 5:22.
[13] Eph. 5:25.
[14] John 13:34; Eph. 4:2, 5:21.
[15] Eph. 5:23.
[16] Eph. 5:21.
[17] Eph. 5:33.
[18] Mark 8:34–35; Rom. 12:1.
[19] Phil. 2:5–8; Heb. 5:4–10.
[20] Eph. 5:21.
[21] Eph. 5:22, 33.
[22] Eph. 5:1–2, 25.
[23] Eph. 5:25; 1 John 4:19.
[24] Eph. 5:1–2; 1 John 3:11, 4:21.
[25] Eph. 5:25.
[26] Eph. 5:22, 24.
[27] Christ is perfect, without sin, and husbands are not. So wives are faced with the possibility of having to submit to evil. This is a difficult issue, but one the church and wives in particular must face. Please refer to chapter 4 "Servanthood: Serve One Another in Love," the sections entitled "Authority Instituted among Men," "The Weaker Partner," and "Trusting the Just Judge."
[28] Eph. 5:23.
[29] Phil. 2:6–7.
[30] 1 John 3:16.
[31] Phil. 2:3.
[32] 1 Cor. 10:33.

33 Rom. 12:10.
34 Matt. 7:12.
35 Matt. 22:39–40; Eph. 5:33.
36 Eph. 5:31–32.
37 Gen. 2:24.
38 Matt. 19:4–6.
39 Eph. 5:23, 31, 32.
40 Eph. 5:23, 28–33.
41 Eph. 5:28b–29.
42 Eph. 5:29b–30.
43 Eph. 2:19–22; 1 John 4:13.
44 Col. 3:4.
45 Matt. 19:4–6.
46 Gen. 2:23–24.
47 Eph. 5:29–32.
48 Eph. 5:26–27.
49 Rom. 3:20–26; 1 Tim. 2:5–6; Titus 2:13–14; Heb. 10:10–14.
50 Eph. 2:15.
51 Gen. 2:18; Exod. 12:5; Song of Sol. 4:7; Heb. 9:14; 1 Pet. 1:19; Rev. 21:2.
52 1 Cor. 5:17; Eph. 2:15.
53 1 Cor. 7:14–15.
54 Heb. 10:24; 1 Pet. 4:10.
55 Eph. 4:1–5.
56 Gen. 1:26–27, 2:24.
57 Eph. 2:14–15, 5:32.
58 2 Cor. 5:17; Gal. 6:15; Eph. 2:12–22, 4:20–25.
59 1 Cor. 15:45–50.
60 Isa. 62:5; John 3:29; 2 Cor. 11:2; Eph. 5:28–29; Rev. 21:2, 9–10.
61 John 17:20–26.
62 Rev. 19:7–8, 21:1–22:6.
63 Rev. 22:3; Gen. 3:16.
64 Eph. 5:31–32.
65 Also called The Song of Solomon.
66 Song of Sol. 1:16; Ps. 27:4: Rev. 5:12, 21:22–23.
67 Song of Sol. 4:7; Ps. 45:11; Col. 3:12–14; Rev. 19:7–8, 21:2, 9–11.
68 Song of Sol. 2:4.
69 Song of Sol. 3:4.
70 Song of Sol. 2:16, 6:3; 1 Cor. 6:19; Eph. 5:2; 1 John 3:16.
71 Song of Sol. 7:10; Eph. 5:22, 25; 1 John 4:16–18; Gen. 3:16, Rev. 22:3.
72 Song of Sol. 8:6–7; John 3:16; 1 Cor. 13:13; Rev. 21:3–4.
73 Eph. 4:23–24.
74 Eph. 5:1–2.
75 Eph. 5:29–32.
76 Eph. 4:1–6.
77 Eph. 4:3–4, 5:1–2, 21.
78 Eph. 5:1–2.
79 Eph. 5:1–2, 25.
80 Ibid.
81 Eph. 5:21.
82 Eph. 5:24.
83 Eph. 5:21, 24.
84 Eph. 5:25.
85 Ibid.
86 Ibid.
87 Eph. 5:22.
88 Eph. 5:24.
89 Ibid.
90 Eph. 1:9–10, 13.
91 Eph. 2:13.
92 Eph. 2:15–16; Hosea 2:16, 23.
93 Eph. 2:19–22.
94 Eph. 3:6.
95 Eph. 2:15.
96 Eph. 4:1–6.
97 Eph. 6:9.
98 Eph. 6:10.
99 Eph. 6:20.
100 Eph. 3:6, 2:19.
101 Eph. 5:2, 21.
102 Eph. 3:8–11.
103 Eph. 3:14–19.
104 When we expose Scripture to the rule that our interpretations must be in harmony with the light of the gospel, everything becomes clear.
105 Eph. 4:1.
106 Eph. 1–3.
107 Eph. 2:13, 3:6.
108 Eph. 1:1, 5, 11, 2:13, 3:6, 6:24.
109 Eph. 1:13, 2:13, 3:6.
110 Eph. 2:19–22, 3:6.
111 Eph. 2:19, 3:6, 6:9.
112 Eph. 2:19, 3:6.
113 Eph. 2:15, 21, 3:6, 4:4, 5, 12, 25, 5:28–32.
114 Eph. 1:3–14, 2:18, 4:4–6, 5:18–20, 6:18, 23.
115 Eph. 4:1.
116 Eph. 4:1–6:9.
117 Eph. 4:2, 12, 29, 32, 5:2, 21, 22, 24, 25, 33, 6:1, 2, 4, 5, 9.
118 Eph. 4:3, 13, 16.
119 Eph. 4:32, 5:2, 8, 10, 25, 29.
120 Eph. 4:24, 32, 5:1, 2, 8, 9, 25, 28.
121 Eph. 1:22, 23, 4:15, 5:23, 30.

[122] Eph. 1:23, 3:14–21, 4:13, 30, 5:14, 18, 26, 27, 6:5–7, 10–18.

[123] Eph. 2:1, 2, 12, 4:17–19, 22, 5:8.

[124] Eph. 2:15, 4:23–24.

Chapter 8 – The Head of the Body: Oneness through Servanthood

[1] John 1:12.

[2] John 5:19, 17, 21, 23, 26, 6:32–33, 38, 57, 7:29, 8:19, 42, 10:30, 37, 38, 12:44–45, 14:7, 9, 10, 11, 15:23, 16:15, 17:1, 4–5, 10.

[3] 1 Cor. 11:3.

[4] John 10:30.

[5] John 14:12, 13:14, 15:12, 20, 16:15, 17:14, 16, 19; Rom. 8:29.

[6] 1 Cor. 11:3.

[7] Gal. 3:28.

[8] John 15:9–12, 5:21, 6:57, 10:14–15, 14:19, 20, 21, 23, 15:20, 21, 17:11, 18, 21, 22, 23, 24, 25, 26.

[9] John 1:1, 5:17–18, 10:30.

[10] John 1:14; Rom. 1:2–4; Heb. 2:14–18.

[11] John 14:6, 13, 14, 15:15, 17:8.

[12] Heb. 10:19–20.

[13] 1 Tim. 2:5–6.

[14] Col. 3:3.

[15] John 17:21-26.

[16] 1 Cor. 11:3.

[17] Deut. 6:4; John 10:30; 1 Cor. 8:4; Eph. 4:3.

[18] 1 Cor. 12:12; Rom. 12:4; 1 Cor. 6:17, 10:17; Eph. 4:4..

[19] Matt. 19:4–6; Gen. 2:23–24, 5:2; 1 Cor. 11:12.

[20] John 17:11.

[21] John 10:16.

[22] Rom. 12:2; 1 Cor. 2:7–16; Eph. 1:17.

[23] Philip Schaff, *The History of the Christian Church*, vol. 3 (Grand Rapids, MI: Eerdmans, 1910), 696.

[24] As originally written, the Latin word used was *omnipotens*.

[25] Schaff, *The History of the Christian Church*, vol. 3, 692–693, #13–20, 25–27.

[26] http://www.merriam-webster.com/dictionary/power.

[27] Westminster Larger Catechism, Questions 8 and 9.

[28] Schaff, *The History of the Christian Church*, vol. 3, 694, #33–34.

[29] Phil. 2:5–8.

[30] Gen. 1:26–27, 2:23, 5:1–2; Matt. 19:4–6; 1 Cor. 11:11–12.

[31] John 1:1–2; Acts 5:3–4.

[32] Schaff, *The History of the Christian Church*, vol. 3, 693, #21–27.

[33] Isa. 40:10–31, 55:8–9.

[34] John 14:7–11, 26.

[35] Search the Internet for "Subordination, Trinity, Women" for numerous in-depth discussions on this topic.

[36] Eph. 3:3–5.

[37] Rom. 8:30.

[38] John 17:11, 22; Rom. 12:4; 1 Cor. 12:12; Gal. 3:28; Eph. 4:4.

[39] Gen. 1:27, 2:24, 5:1–2; Matt. 19:4–6; 1 Cor. 11:12.

[40] John 1:1, 14, 17:11, 22.

[41] John 16:13–14, 17:1–5.

[42] John 3:35.

[43] John 14:31.

[44] John 16:13–14.

[45] 1 John 3:16.

[46] John 1:18, 10:38, 14:7–11; Heb. 1:3.

[47] Phil. 2:1–5; 1 John 4:7, 8, 10, 16, 19.

[48] 1 John 4:6.

[49] Luke 22:42.

[50] Heb. 4:15.

[51] Also John 10:17–18, 12:27–29.

[52] John 1:14; Matt. 1:23.

[53] Matt. 20:28.

[54] Phil. 2.

[55] John 13:3–5; 1 Tim. 5:9–l0.

[56] Matt. 7:7–12, 5:42–48.

[57] John 14:13–14.

[58] 1 Cor. 12:4–11.

[59] Rom. 12:4–5.

[60] Rom. 12:1–21.

[61] Matt. 5:38–48.

[62] Eph. 2:15.

[63] Matt. 20:24–28.

[64] Gal. 5:13.

[65] Matt. 9:16–17; Eph. 4:22–24; Rom. 7:6.

[66] Eph. 5:32.

[67] Eph. 3:3.

[68] Eph. 4:1–6.

[69] Phil. 2:9; John 3:35, 10:17, 15:9, 17:23, 24, 26.

[70] John 5:30, 14:31; Phil. 2:6–7.
[71] John 16:13–14; Rom. 15:30.
[72] Deut. 7:8; Matt. 20:26–28; John 1:18, 3:16, 10:38, 14:7–11; 2 Cor. 13:14; Heb. 1:3; 1 John 3:16, 4:7, 8, 10, 16, 19.
[73] Matt. 5:38–48; 1 John 3:16, 4:7.
[74] Rom. 12:4–13, 15:5–7; 1 Cor. 12:4–7, 24–25; Eph. 4:1–5; Phil. 2:2–5.
[75] Matt. 7:7–12, 20:28; John 13:3–5; Rom. 15:8–9.
[76] John 14:19, 15:13; Rom. 5:8; Gal. 2:20; Eph. 5:25.
[77] John 14:13–14; Eph. 3:20.
[78] John 14:11–12, 16, 21.
[79] John 3:16, 13:1, 14:23, 15:9; Rom. 8:35–39; 1 Tim. 1:14; 1 John 3:16; 1 John 4: 10, 19.
[80] Mark 8:34–35; Eph. 5:24; Col. 3:17.
[81] Deut. 6:5, 11:1, 13, 22, 30:6; Ps. 18:1; Matt. 22:37; John 14:21; 1 John 4:16–18, 5:1–3.
[82] Rom. 12:1–21; 1 Cor. 11:33, 12:7, 25, 13:1–13; Gal. 5:13, 6:2–3; Eph. 4:1–3, 32, 5:21; Col. 3:12–14; Heb. 13:1; 1 Pet. 1:22, 4:8–11; 1 John 3:11–24, 4:7–21.
[83] Lev. 19:18, 34; Matt. 19:19, 22:39; John 13:34–35, 15:12; Rom. 13:8–10; Gal. 5:14; Eph. 5:1–2; Phil. 2:2; 1 Thess. 3:12; 1 John 4:11; 2 John 5.
[84] Eph. 5:29–31.
[85] Eph. 5:22, 24; 1 Cor. 7:3, 4, 10, 13; Col. 3:18; 1 Pet. 3:1.
[86] John 13:34; Eph. 5:1–2; Titus 2:4.
[87] Eph. 5:25, 28, 29; Col. 3:19; 1 Pet. 3:8.
[88] Eph. 5:21; 1 Cor. 7:3, 4, 11, 12; Gal. 5:13; Phil. 2:3; 1 Pet. 2:21–24, 3:7.

Chapter 9 – The Head over Everything: You Have Only One Master

[1] In these four scriptures, Paul refers to the head/body metaphor five times (Eph. 1:23, 4:15–16; Col. 1:18, 24, 2:19), and "head over"/"under everything" three times (Eph. 1:10, 22,; Col. 2:10).
[2] Col. 1:18.
[3] Eph. 1:22.
[4] Charles McIlhenny, "Letter From the left Coast: Feminism and Gayism," *The Christian Statesman,* (July–August, 1992), 38.
[5] Eph. 1:10.
[6] Eph. 1:22.
[7] Col. 2:10.
[8] Col. 1:16.
[9] Col. 1:17.
[10] Eph. 1:23, 4:10.
[11] Col. 1:16.
[12] Col. 1:17.
[13] Eph. 1:22.
[14] Col. 1:18.
[15] Ibid.
[16] Col. 1:15–16.
[17] Eph. 1:21; Col. 1:16.
[18] Eph. 1:21.
[19] Eph. 1:10; Col. 1:16.
[20] Col. 2:13–15.
[21] Eph. 1:22–23.
[22] Eph. 1:22.
[23] Ibid.
[24] Rom. 16:20; Ps. 144:2; Isa. 49:23, 60:13–14.
[25] Eph. 1:19–21.
[26] Eph. 2:6–7.
[27] Eph. 1:18–19.
[28] Eph. 1:19–20.
[29] Heb. 7:16.
[30] Eph. 1:17–18.
[31] Ps. 139:6.
[32] Eph. 2:5.
[33] Col. 1:27.
[34] Eph. 1:20–21; Heb. 8:1, 12:2.
[35] Col. 2:10.
[36] Col. 1:18.
[37] 1 Tim. 6:15; Matt. 2:6; John 18:37; 1 Cor. 15:24.28; 1 Tim. 1:17; Rev. 1:5–6, 11:15, 19:11–16.
[38] Eph. 1:5, 12, 19; Col. 1:12, 27, 2:2.
[39] Luke 8:21; Rom. 8:14–17; 2 Cor. 6:18; Gal. 3:26–28, 4:4–7; Heb. 2:14–18.
[40] Col. 1:18–20.
[41] John 5:22; Acts 10:42, 17:31; 2 Tim. 4:1; Rev. 19:11–16.
[42] Eph. 2:14–16, 1:19–20; Col. 1:21–23.
[43] Eph. 3:8–13, 2:6; Col. 1:24–29.
[44] Gen.1:27–28.
[45] 2 Cor. 5:18–20.
[46] Col. 2:10.
[47] Matt. 28:18–20.
[48] John 17:4.
[49] John 14:10–14, 4:37.
[50] Col. 1:20.

[51] 1 Cor. 15:20–28.
[52] 2 Cor. 5:18–20.
[53] Eph. 2:14–18, 3:9–11; Col. 1:26–27, 2:9–15.
[54] Eph. 4:1–6, 5:1–2, 21; Col. 3:12–15.
[55] Matt. 19:28; 1 Cor. 6:2; Rev. 21:2, 22:5
[56] Eph. 1:10, 22; Col. 2:10.
[57] Col. 1:18.
[58] Col. 1:17.
[59] Eph. 1:10, 20–22; Gen. 3:15; Rom. 16:20; 1 Cor. 15:25–27.
[60] Col. 1:15–16.
[61] Eph. 1:21.
[62] Col. 1:16.
[63] Eph. 1:21.
[64] Col. 1:16.
[65] Eph. 1:10; Col. 1:16.
[66] Col. 2:13–15.
[67] Col. 1:15.
[68] Col. 1:16.
[69] Ibid.
[70] Col. 1:17.
[71] Col. 1:18.
[72] Col. 1:15.
[73] Col. 1:18; Eph. 1:20.
[74] Col. 1:20, 2:15; Eph. 1:10, 2:21–22; 2 Cor. 5:18.
[75] Col. 2:14–15; Eph. 1:7, 2:13–14; 2 Cor. 5:21.
[76] John 5:22; Acts 10:42, 17:31; 2 Tim. 4:1.
[77] Rom. 5:9–11; Col. 1:22, 14, 2:11–14; Eph. 2: 13–18; 2 Cor. 5:18.
[78] 2 Cor. 5:18–21; Eph. 1:13, 2:5, 6, 10, 19–22, 3:6, 17, 4:4–5; Col. 1:27, 2:10, 13, 19, 3:3–4, 11.
[79] Eph. 2:1–3, 11–22, 4:1, 17–24 , 5:8; Col. 1:10, 3:5–11.
[80] Eph. 1:13–14, 17, 2:18, 3:16, 4:30, 5:18.
[81] Eph. 1:19, 3:17–18, 20; Col. 1:11, 2:12.
[82] Eph. 2:19; Col. 1:12–13.
[83] Eph. 1:5, 2:19, 3:15.
[84] Eph. 3:8, 16, 2:7; Col. 1:27, 2:2.
[85] Eph. 1:14, 18, 3:6; Col. 1:12.
[86] John 14:10–14; 2 Cor. 5:18–19.
[87] Luke 22:29; Rom. 5:17, 8:17; Eph. 1:22, 2:6; 2 Tim. 2:12.
[88] Eph. 3:8–10; Col. 1:26–2:3; 2 Cor. 5:18–21; Matt. 28:18–20.
[89] Eph. 2:14–18, 3:9–11; Col. 1:26–27, 2:9–15.
[90] 1 Cor. 6:2; Matt. 19:28.
[91] Col. 3:1–17; Eph. 2–5.
[92] Rom. 12; 1 Cor. 12–13; 2 Cor. 5, 8; Gal. 5–6; Phil. 2–4; 1 Thess. 4; 2 Thess. 2:13–17, to list only a few.
[93] Col. 3:1, 3, 4, 11.
[94] Col. 3:5–9.
[95] Col. 3:11.
[96] Col. 3:10–14.
[97] Eph. 4:8, 11–13.
[98] Col. 3:16.
[99] Matt. 7:12, 22:39; Mark 12:31; Luke 6:31; John 13:34, 15:12; Rom. 12:3, 10; Phil. 2:3–4; Gal. 5:13; Eph. 5:21; Heb. 13:1; 1 Pet. 4:8, 10, 5:5 the short list.
[100] Col. 3:10; Eph. 4:23–24.
[101] Col. 3:1, 3, 4, 15, 16; Eph. 1:17, 3:16–17.
[102] Col. 3:16.
[103] Col. 3:17.
[104] Col. 3:14.
[105] Col. 1:17, 2:19; Eph. 4:16.
[106] Col. 3:14.
[107] 2 Cor. 5:14.
[108] Col. 3:15.
[109] Col. 3:14–15; Rom. 8:35–39, 13:8–10; 1 Cor. 13:1–14:1; 2 Cor. 13:11–12; Eph. 3:17–19, 5:1–2; 1 John 3:11–24, 4:7–12, to list only a few.
[110] Eph. 2:4–5, 21, 4:4–5; Col. 1:27, 3:3.
[111] Eph. 1:17–20, 23, 3:17–19, 4:4–6, 13, 15–16, 25; Col. 2:2–3, 9–10, 3:17.
[112] Eph. 2:14, 4:3; Col. 3:15.
[113] Col. 3:16.
[114] Eph. 1:17, 2:18, 3:16, 4:30, 5:18.
[115] Eph. 4:2–3, 15–16, 28, 29, 32, 5:1, 2, 21; Col. 2:2, 3:12–14.
[116] Eph. 4:8, 11–13.
[117] Eph. 5:19–20; Col. 3:16.

Chapter 10 – Brothers: You Are All Brothers

[1] Young, *Young's Analytical Concordance to the Bible*, 124.
[2] Matt. 23:8.
[3] John 3:5–8; Gal. 4:28–29; 1 Pet. 1:23.
[4] John 1:12–13.
[5] Col. 3:11; Eph. 4:4–5.
[6] Gal. 3:28.
[7] Acts 10:9–23, 15:9.
[8] Acts 10:34–35.
[9] Acts 10:47, 15:8.
[10] Rom. 10:10.
[11] Ibid.
[12] Rom. 10:12–13; Acts 15:11.
[13] Rom. 15:7.
[14] Acts 1:13–16.
[15] Matt. 23:8.
[16] This figure was calculated by listing all those believers who were contemporary with each New Testament letter writer that the writer either mentioned or directly addressed. Of the eighty-seven people who qualified for this list from Romans through Jude, twenty-six were women, or 29.8 percent of the total.
[17] 1 Cor. 1:2, 10.
[18] Rom. 1:7, 13.
[19] Eph. 1:1, 6:23–24.
[20] 1 Pet. 1:1–2, 22; 2 Cor. 1:1, 8; Col. 1:2; 1 Thess. 1:1, 4; 2 Thess. 1:1, 3; James 1:2; 2 Pet. 1:10; 1 John 2:7.
[21] Phil. 1:1, 12.
[22] Rom. 16:14, 15; Col. 1:2.
[23] Rom. 1:6–7.
[24] Acts 8:3, 9:1–2, 13, 26:10.
[25] Matt. 23:8.
[26] Matt. 23:13.
[27] Matt. 23:5.
[28] Matt. 23:2–3.
[29] Matt. 23:4, 15.
[30] Matt. 23:5–7.
[31] Matt. 23:25–28.
[32] Matt. 23:16–22.
[33] Matt. 23:29–36.
[34] Matt. 23:37.
[35] Matt. 23:8–12.
[36] Matt. 20:23.
[37] Matt. 12:48–50; John 6:29.
[38] Matt. 25:40.
[39] Heb. 2:10–11, 14–3:1.
[40] Acts 10:9–23, 34–35, 15:9; Rom. 1:17, 3:21–26, 5:18–19; Rev. 7:14.
[41] Acts 10:47, 11:15–17, 15:8; 1 Cor. 2:9–10; Eph. 1:13–14.
[42] 2 Tim. 2:11–12.
[43] 2 Cor. 5:18–20; Eph. 2:6–7.
[44] Eph. 1:7; Col. 1:20, 22; Heb. 9:12–22; 1 Pet. 1:18–19; 1 John 1:7; Rev. 1:5–6, 5:9.
[45] Rom. 6:8; 2 Cor. 5:14; Col. 2:20, 3:3.
[46] Rom. 6:8; Col. 2:12, 3:1, 4.
[47] Rom. 3:21–26, 4:5–8, 5:9, 18–19; 1 Cor. 1:30; 2 Cor. 5:21; Gal. 2:16; Phil. 3:8–9.
[48] Heb. 10:19–22.
[49] Rom. 3:22–23.
[50] John 14:6.
[51] John 6:63, 14:17; Acts 2:38–39; 1 Pet. 3:18.
[52] Rom. 8:16.
[53] Rom. 8:9–11; Gal. 5:22; 2 Thess. 2:13; 1 Pet. 1:2.
[54] John 14:17, 16:13; 1 Cor. 2:9–10; 1 John 3:24.
[55] 2 Tim. 3:16–17.
[56] Matt. 23:10; John 13:13.
[57] John 14:26, 16:14.
[58] 2 Cor. 3:18.
[59] Rom. 8:17; Eph. 2:6.
[60] Ps. 47:2–3; Matt. 19:28; Luke 22:29–30; Rom. 5:17, 8:17; 2 Tim. 2:12; Rev. 1:6, 3:21, 5:10, 22:5.
[61] 2 Cor. 5:18–19.
[62] Matt. 28:18–20; 2 Cor. 5:20.
[63] Eph. 2:14–16, 4:1–6.
[64] John 13:35, 17:23.
[65] Acts 1:13–16.
[66] Matt. 23:1, 8.
[67] Matt. 12:48–50; 1 Cor. 1:2, 10; 1 Pet. 1–2, 22.
[68] 1 Cor. 1:2, 10.
[69] Rom. 1:7, 13.
[70] Eph. 1:1, 6:23–24.
[71] Eph. 6:23–24.
[72] 1 Pet. 1:1–2, 22.
[73] 1 Pet. 1:2, 22.
[74] Eph. 1:7; Col. 1:20, 22; Heb. 9:12–22, 13:12; 1 Pet. 1:18–19; 1 John 1:7; Rev. 1:5–6, 5:9.
[75] Isa. 45:25; Jer. 33:16; Rom. 3:21–26, 4:5–8; 5:9, 18–19; 1 Cor. 1:30; 2 Cor. 5:21; Gal. 2:16; Phil. 3:8–9.

[76] Rom. 8:1–4; 1 Pet. 3:18–22.
[77] John 3:5–8; Acts 2:17–18; John 14:16–17; 2 Cor. 3:17–18; Eph. 3:16–17.
[78] John 14:25–27, 15:26, 16:13–15; Eph. 1:17.
[79] Ps. 37:31, 40:8; Jer. 31:33, 32:40; Rom. 2:15, 7:22; 2 Cor. 3:3, 12–18; Col. 3:16; Heb. 8:10.
[80] Rom. 8:5–14, 26–27; Gal. 5:16.
[81] Luke 8:21; 2 Cor. 6:18; Heb. 2:14–18.
[82] Rom. 8:14–17; Gal. 3:26–28, 4:4–7.
[83] Ps. 47:2–3; Matt. 19:28; Luke 22:29–30; Rom. 5:17, 8:17; Rev. 1:6, 3:21, 5:10, 22:5.
[84] Matt. 5:3–10; Rom. 5:11, 15:14–16; 2 Cor. 5:18–20; Eph. 2:16; Col. 1:20–22.
[85] Rom. 8:15–30; Eph. 1:5, Gal. 4:5 KJV.

Chapter 11 – The Head over Everything: Rule through Reconciliation

[1] 1 Cor. 12:18–20.
[2] 1 Cor. 13:1, 13.
[3] 1 Cor. 13:1, 2, 8.
[4] 1 Cor. 13:1–3.
[5] Col. 3:14.
[6] 1 Cor. 14:1.
[7] Cor. 12:7.
[8] Eph. 4:7.
[9] Eph. 4:12–13.
[10] Rom. 1:11–12.
[11] 1 Cor. 14:12.
[12] 1 Pet. 4:10.
[13] Rom. 12:6–8.
[14] 1 Cor. 12:7, 11; 1 Pet. 4:10.
[15] Eph. 5:21.
[16] Rom. 12:5.
[17] 1 Cor. 12:14–20.
[18] 1 Cor. 12:8.
[19] Ibid.
[20] 1 Cor. 12:9, 13:13.
[21] 1 Cor. 12:9, 28, 29.
[22] 1 Cor. 12:10, 28, 29.
[23] Rom. 12:6; 1 Cor. 12:10, 28, 29, 14:1; Eph. 4:11.
[24] 1 Cor. 12:10, 28, 29.
[25] 1 Cor. 12:10, 29.
[26] 1 Cor. 12:28, 29; Eph. 4:11.
[27] Rom. 12:7; 1 Cor. 12:28, 29; Eph. 4:11.
[28] 1 Cor. 12:28.
[29] Ibid.
[30] Rom. 12:9; 1 Cor. 13:1–13.
[31] 1 Cor. 13:13.
[32] Rom. 12:7.
[33] Rom. 12:8.
[34] Ibid.
[35] Ibid.
[36] Ibid.
[37] Eph. 4:11.
[38] Ibid.
[39] Gal. 5:22–23.
[40] John 3:3.
[41] John 3:6.
[42] 1 Cor. l2:1.
[43] John 6:63; Rom. 8:9–11.
[44] 1 Cor. 12:21–26.
[45] 1 Cor. 12:25–26.
[46] 1 Cor. 12:4–7; Eph. 4:4–7, 11–13.
[47] Eph. 5:21–22.
[48] 2 Cor. 13:10.
[49] Col. 1:25; Acts 20:24.
[50] Rom. 1:11–12, 16:4, 23; Gal. 2:1–3, 4:13–14; Phil. 2:25, 4:14–16.
[51] Titus 2:15; 1 Thess. 4:2.
[52] Matt. 23:10.
[53] John 15:15.
[54] 1 Cor. 3:11–13; 1 Tim. 4:6, 6:3; 2 John 9.
[55] 1 Tim. 3:1.
[56] Rom. 12:8.
[57] Titus 1:9; 1 Tim. 1:10.
[58] 1 Pet. 5:1–4; 1 Thess. 2:6–12.
[59] 1 Pet. 5:5–6.
[60] Matt. 20:23.
[61] Heb. 13:17; 1 Thess. 5:12–13.
[62] Rom. 12:6–8; 1 Tim. 4:14; 2 Tim. 1:6.
[63] Matt. 25:14–30.
[64] Rom. 12:6–8; 1 Pet. 4:11.
[65] 1Tim. 5:14; 2 Tim. 1:6.
[66] Col. 1:25; Acts 20:24; 1 Cor. 12:7, 11.
[67] Acts 6:5–6, 13:3; 1Tim. 4:14.
[68] 1 Cor. 16:15–16.
[69] Heb. 13:17.
[70] 1 Cor. 12:4–11, 24–27.
[71] Gen. 2:18.
[72] Gal. 3:28.
[73] 1 Tim. 3:15.
[74] 1 Cor. 12:21.
[75] 1 Cor. 12:28.
[76] 1 Cor. 12:22–23.

[77] 1 Cor. 13:13.
[78] 1 Cor. 12:31.
[79] 1 John 4:7–21.
[80] John 13:12–17.
[81] Matt. 7:29, 23:10.
[82] Matt. 18:1–4.
[83] Matt. 11:11.
[84] Eph. 3:8; 1 Cor. 15:9; 2 Cor. 12:11; 1 Tim. 1:15.
[85] James 5:17.
[86] Col. 3:16; Eph. 5:19.
[87] John 4:23, 14:6.
[88] 1 Pet. 2:4–5, 9.
[89] Rom. 12:1; Luke 9:23–24.
[90] John 4:23.
[91] Rom. 12:2; 2 Cor. 3:18; Eph. 4:23–24.
[92] John 4:23–24, 14:6.
[93] Phil. 2:5–11.
[94] Heb. 8:1–13, 9:14; Phil. 3:3–11.
[95] John 14:6; Gal. 5:7–12; 1 Tim. 2:5.
[96] Gal. 5:4; Eph. 2:8–9; 2 Tim. 1:9; Titus 3:5.
[97] Heb. 7:23–8:13, 10:10.
[98] John 14:6; 1 Tim. 2:5.
[99] Gal. 2:19–21.
[100] 1 Cor. 3:5–8.
[101] Heb. 10:19–25.
[102] Heb. 10:35.
[103] Rom. 11:33–36.
[104] R. B. Kuiper, *The Glorious Body of Christ* (Grand Rapids. MI: Wm. B. Eerdmans, 1967), 129.
[105] Ibid.
[106] 1 Cor. 1:18–31; 2 Cor. 13:4.
[107] Eph. 1:13–14.
[108] Rom. 8:29–31; Heb. 9:11–15.
[109] Gal. 2:5, 5:1.
[110] Heb. 2:1–4.
[111] 2 Cor. 3:4–6.
[112] Rom. 6:1–14.
[113] 1 Cor. 15:1–2, 9–10; 2 Cor. 4:4–6.
[114] Heb. 4:14.
[115] Heb. 6:15–20.
[116] 1 Cor. 6:2–3.
[117] Matt. 23:8.
[118] Eph. 1:22.
[119] Col. 1:18.
[120] John 14:16, 25–26, 15:26.
[121] 1 Cor. 12:7–11.
[122] 1 Cor. 12:31–13:13.
[123] 1 Cor. 12:14–20.
[124] 1 Cor. 12:21–26.
[125] 1 Cor. 12.
[126] 1 Cor. 12:4–6.
[127] Col. 1:17, 2:19, 3:14
[128] 1 Cor. 12:7.
[129] 1 Cor. 12:7, 21, 26.
[130] John 17:20–21; 1 Cor. 12:4–6, 11;; 2 Cor. 1:20–22; Gal. 3:27; Col 1:27, 3:3–4.
[131] Eph. 5:23.
[132] Heb. 2:11.
[133] Matt. 20:27.
[134] Matt. 20:28.
[135] Phil. 2:9; Rom. 14:9–13, 17.
[136] Matt. 5:3–10.
[137] Rom. 12:5, 10, 14:13, 15:7; Gal. 5:13–14; Eph. 4:7, 32, 5:19–20; Col. 3:12–14, 16; 1 Thess. 5:11–15; Heb. 10:24–25; James 5:16; 1 Pet. 3:8, 4:10–1l; 1 John 4:11–12.
[138] Rom. 12:3, 9–13; 1 Cor. 13:1, 4–7, 14:1, 16:15–16; Gal. 6:1–10; Eph. 4:1–6, 5:21; Phil. 2:1–16; Col. 2:1–2, 3:12–14; Heb. 13:1–3; 1 John 3:11–4:21.
[139] John 13:35, 17:23: Eph. 3:10.
[140] Rom. 10:11–13; Eph. 2:14–18, 4:1–4, 16; Col. 3:10–11.
[141] Eph. 4:7–13; 1 Cor. 12.
[142] Rom. 12:6; 1 Cor. 12:1, 4, 7–11; Eph. 4:7.
[143] 1 Cor. 12:7, 25–26, 14:12; 2 Cor. 13:10; Rom. 1:11–12.
[144] Eph. 4:11–12.
[145] 1 Pet. 4:10.
[146] Eph. 4:7; 1 Cor. 12:7, 11; 1 Pet. 4:10.
[147] John 13:12–17; Eph. 4:16; 1 Thess. 2:6–12; 1 Pet. 5:1–4.
[148] Col. 1:24–25; Acts 20:24; 1 Cor. 3:5, 12:7, 11; 2 Tim. 1:6–7.
[149] Heb. 13:17; Matt. 25:14–30; Rom. 12:6–8, 14:12; 1 Cor. 3:8.
[150] 1 Cor. 16:15–16; 1 Thess. 5:12–13; Heb. 13:7.
[151] Rom. 12:6; Eph. 4:7; 1 Pet. 4:10.
[152] John 4:23–24; Eph. 5:19; Col. 3:16.
[153] John 4:23–24.
[154] John 14:6; Eph. 3:10–12; 1 Tim. 2:5; Heb. 7:23–8:13, 10:10, 19–25.
[155] Rom. 12:1; Luke 9:23–24; Gal. 2:20; Phil. 2:5–11.
[156] Rom. 8; Heb. 4:14–16; 1 Pet. 2:4–5, 9.
[157] Rom. 8:9–11; 1 Cor. 3:16; 1 John 4:13, 5:6.
[158] John 14:25–27, 15:26, 16:13–15; Eph. 1:17.

[159] Rom. 8:5–14, 26–27; Gal. 5:16–26.

[160] Rom. 12:6; 1 Cor. 12:7; Eph. 4:7; 1 Pet. 4:10.

Chapter 12 – The Exceptional Women of the Bible: Proof of the Rule

[1] Exod. 15:20–21: Mic. 6:4: 1 Cor. 11:5, 14:26; Col. 3:16.
[2] Judg. 4:4–5; Acts 1:14–15, 26; Col. 3:15.
[3] 1 Sam. 1:22, 27–28, 3:19–21; Exod. 2:1–4: Prov. 31:16, 27; 1 Cor. 7:15.
[4] 2 Kings 22:14–20; Luke 2:36–38; Acts 21:9; 1 Cor. 11:5.
[5] Ruth 4:11–14; Eph. 1:13, 2:19–22, 3:6; Josh. 6:25; Heb. 11:31; James 2:25.
[6] Esther 4:14–16.
[7] Esther 7:3–6.
[8] Esther 8:3–9:32.
[9] Rom. 8:29–31; 2 Cor. 5:18–20.
[10] Luke 1:46–55; 2 Tim. 3:16.
[11] Acts 18:26; Luke 2:36–38; Prov. 31:26; 1 Cor. 14:26; Col. 3:16.
[12] John 14:6.
[13] Acts 4:12.
[14] 1 John 1:9.
[15] Acts 2:38.
[16] Rom. 3:23.
[17] 1 John 1:8.
[18] 1 Sam. 21:1–9.
[19] Lev. 24:9.
[20] Luke 6:3–4.
[21] Lev. 24:5–9.
[22] Hosea 6:6.
[23] Matt. 12:7.
[24] Matt. 12:5–6.
[25] Isa. 59:1.
[26] Acts 17:24–25.
[27] Heb. 1:8–9.
[28] Exod. 16:1–4, 31; 1 Kings 17:1–6; Matt. 14:13–21.
[29] Matt. 9:11–13.
[30] Matt. 23:23.
[31] John 14:8–11.
[32] John 6:35.
[33] Matt. 12:14.
[34] Exod. 3–4.
[35] Acts 9:1–31.
[36] Luke 1:26–33, 42, 2:6–7; Gal. 4:4–5.
[37] Luke 2:36–38.
[38] Matt. 28:8.
[39] John 4:7, 27.
[40] Mark 1:30–31, 5:25–34, 7:25–30; Luke 13:11–13.
[41] Mark 5:35–43.
[42] John 4:7–42.
[43] Mark 5:34, 7:29, 14:6.
[44] Luke 2:7, 8:3.
[45] Luke 10:38.
[46] Luke 7:44.
[47] Matt. 26:7–13; Luke 23:55–56.
[48] Luke 23:27; John 20:11.
[49] Luke 23:49.
[50] John 4:39–42, 20:17–18; Luke 2:36–38, 24:10.
[51] Mark 12:41–44, 14:9; John 10:42.
[52] Matt. 26:6–13; Mark 14:3–11; Luke 7:36–50; John 12:1–8.
[53] John 11:2, 12:3.
[54] John 4:24.
[55] Mark 14:6.
[56] Luke 7:50.
[57] Matt. 26:10; Luke 7:44–47.
[58] Matt. 26:13.
[59] Matt. 20:26–27.
[60] Acts 1:13–14, 23–26.
[61] Rom. 16:1; Phil. 4:3.
[62] Rom. 16:2, 3, 6, 12, 15.
[63] Acts 16:14–15, 40; Rom. 16:7; 1 Cor. 16:19; Col. 4:15.
[64] Acts 21:8–9.
[65] Acts 18:26; 2 Tim. 1:5, 3:14–15.
[66] Luke 8:1–3, 23:27, 55, 24:22; Acts 1:14.
[67] Acts 5:14, 8:3, 12, 9:2, 16:13, 14, 40, 17:4, 12, 34, 22:4.
[68] Gen. 1:26–28.
[69] Ps. 144:12.
[70] Ps. 68:11 NASB.
[71] Prov. 31:11, 28 as contrasted to Gen. 3:16. My thanks to Faith Martin, who first brought these contrasting verses to my attention.
[72] Isa. 43:1, 5–7.
[73] Isa. 49:22–23.
[74] Acts 1:14, 2:1, 4.
[75] Acts 2:17–18; Joel 2:28–29.
[76] Mark 10:6–9.
[77] 1 Cor. 7:4; Song of Sol. 6:3.
[78] 1 Cor. 11:11–12.
[79] 1 Pet. 3:7.
[80] 2 Sam. 7:14.
[81] 2 Cor. 6:18.

[82] Gal. 3:26–29.
[83] Matt. 12:3, 5, 7.
[84] Matt. 12:4.
[85] Matt.12:7; Hosea 6:6.
[86] Matt. 23:23.
[87] Matt. 12:5–7.
[88] Exod. 15:20–21.
[89] Judg. 4:4–5.
[90] Judg. 4:14–24.
[91] Ruth 4:11–14.
[92] 1 Sam. 1:22, 27–28, 3:20–21.
[93] 2 Kings 22:14–20.
[94] Esther 4:14–16, 7:4–6, 9:29–32.
[95] Luke 1:46–55.
[96] Luke 2:36–38.
[97] Acts 16:14–15, 40.
[98] Acts 18:26, Rom. 16:3–5.
[99] Rom. 16:1–2.
[100] Rom. 16:7.
[101] Mark 16:1–7, 9–11.
[102] Judg. 4:4–6; Mark 16:5–7; Luke 1:28; John 4:21–26; Gal. 4:4.
[103] Exod. 15:20–21; Luke 1:48, 2:37–38; Mark 14:6–9.
[104] Judg. 4:4–6; Esther 9:29–32; Acts 1:13–15, 23–26.
[105] Judg. 4:4–6; Exod. 15:20–21; 2 Kings 22:14–15; Luke 1:46–55.
[106] Acts 18:26; Rom. 16:3–5.
[107] Gen. 1:26–28; Num. 27:6–7; 2 Sam. 7:14 and 2 Cor. 6:18; Ps. 68:11, 144:12; Isa. 43:1, 5–7, 49:22–23; Joel 2:28–29 and Acts 2:17–18; 1 Cor. 7:4, 11:11–12; 1 Pet. 3:7.
[108] Gen. 3:16; Gal. 3:13–14; Prov. 31:11, 28; Hosea 2:16, 23; Eph. 2:17–20.

Chapter 13 – Must She Be Silent?: 1 Corinthians 14:26–40

[1] Ps. 119:105.
[2] 1 Cor. 14:26–40.
[3] 1 Tim. 2:1–15.
[4] 1 Cor. 14:34–35.
[5] 1 Cor. l:2.
[6] 1 Cor. 14:26.
[7] 1 Cor. 14:39.
[8] 1 Cor. 14:26.
[9] Ibid.
[10] Acts 2:38–39, 3:26; Rom. 14:12, 15:2.
[11] 1 Cor. 14:3l.
[12] Ibid.
[13] 1 Cor. 11:5.
[14] 1 Cor. 14:33.
[15] 1 Cor. 14:33 KJV.
[16] 1 Cor. 14:33 NASB.
[17] 1 Cor. 14:33–34.
[18] 1 Cor. 14:34–35.
[19] 1 Cor. 14:26.
[20] 1 Cor. 14:31.
[21] 1 Cor. 12.
[22] 1 Cor. 12:21–27.
[23] 1 Cor. 12:7; Eph. 4:7.
[24] 1 Cor. 11:5.
[25] 1 Cor. 11:11–12.
[26] 1 Cor. 14:35.
[27] 1 Cor. 1:10.
[28] 1 Cor. 16:19.
[29] 1 Cor. 1:4.
[30] 1 Cor. 1:2.
[31] Acts 10:15, 11:9, 15–17; Exod. 28:36–38; Lev. 20:25–26, 21:8; 2 Cor. 7:1; Eph. 5:26; 1 John 1:7.
[32] I believe Paul wrote what is written here in the Bible. But I do not believe he originated this idea. I believe he is here quoting another source.
[33] *ἤ (ē)*. I first read of this Greek word in *Beyond Sex Roles* by Gilbert Bilezikian (Grand Rapids, MI: Baker Book House, 1985), 151.
[34] I have chosen the lightning bolt symbol (ϟ) to represent ē in illustration of and to emphasize the way Paul used this small and often overlooked Greek word with rhetorical questions to forcefully and explosively refute and reject false ideas.
[35] 1 Cor. 14:36.
[36] 1 Cor. 1:12–13, 17.
[37] 1 Cor. 6:1–3, 7–9, 11.
[38] It is interesting to note that some translators disagree about when to use quotation marks to indicate that Paul is quoting an idea from another source. In 1 Cor. 6:12 and 10:23, Paul quotes a saying that was evidently commonly known to the Corinthians. Paul then goes on to modify and clarify its meaning as applied to the Christian life. Yet the translators disagree as to whether this idea should be written

in quotation marks or not. The NIV puts the phrase "Everything is permissible" inside quotation marks to show clearly that Paul is quoting someone else. But the KJV and the NASB do not use quotation marks for this phrase.

The original Greek language evidently does not make it explicitly clear, through some sort of punctuation as in English, when Paul is quoting another source. Consequently, it must be deduced from the context whether Paul is quoting an external idea he himself did not originate or stating his own idea.

39 1 Cor. 6:15–20.
40 1 Cor. 9:3–12.
41 1 Cor. 10:20–22.
42 1 Cor. 11:20–22.
43 1 Cor. 11:26–34.
44 1 Cor. 14:33–40.
45 1 Cor. 14:26, 31–33.
46 Paraphrase of 1 Cor. 14:34–35.
47 Paraphrase of 1 Cor.14:34–36.
48 Paraphrase of 1 Cor. 14:34–38.
49 Paraphrase of 1 Cor. 14:34–40.
50 1 Cor. 14:34.
51 1 Cor. 4:6–7.
52 1 Cor. 15:9–10.
53 Rom. 4:1–25, 7:4–6; Gal. 3:1–14, 5:1–4.
54 Rom. 7:6.
55 1 Cor. 14:34.
56 Gal. 2:16, 5:1–4.
57 1 Cor. 9:20.
58 1 Cor. 15:54–56.
59 Rom. 2:17–23; Matt. 23:13–36.
60 1 Cor. 14:37–38.
61 1 Cor. 14:26–27, 29–31, 39.
62 1 Cor. 14:37.
63 1 Cor. 14:39–40.
64 1 Cor. 14:13, 14, 19, 22, 23.
65 1 Cor. 14:26, 39–40.
66 1 Cor. 14:26, 31.
67 1 Cor. 14:28–31.
68 1 Cor. 14:33.
69 1 Cor.14:36 KJV.
70 1 Cor. 14:36–38.
71 Eph. 2:8–9.
72 Phil. 3:10–16.
73 1 Cor. 13:12.
74 2 Cor. 12:7–9.
75 James 1:2–4.
76 James 1:4; Rom. 5:3–5; Eph. 4:11–13.
77 1 Cor. 12:26.
78 Heb. 5:8.
79 Job 19:25–27.
80 1 Cor. 2:2.
81 1 Cor. 15:57–58.
82 Rom. 8:28.
83 Phil. 3:10–11.
84 2 Tim. 1:12.
85 1 Cor. 14:34–35.
86 1 Cor. 7:2–3, 4, 5, 10–11, 12–13, 14, 15, 16.
87 1 Cor. 1:10, 3:16–17.
88 Rom. 3:22–27; Eph. 2:8–10; 1 Cor. 15:1–2, 10.
89 1 Pet. 1:23–25.
90 Rom. 16:3–5; 1 Cor. 1:11, 16:19.
91 1 Cor. 1:2, 4:17, 6:4, 7:17, 10:32–33, 11:16, 18, 22, 12:28, 14:4, 5, 12, 19, 23, 28, 33, 15:9, 16:1, 19.
92 1 Cor. 15:9–10.
93 1 Cor. 12.
94 Ps. 119:105.
95 2 Pet. 1:19; 1 John 1:6–7; Rom. 11:33–36; Eph. 3:14–21.
96 1 Cor. 12:21–27.
97 1 Cor. 14:26, 39.
98 1 Cor. 1:2.
99 1 Cor. 14:26, 31, 39.
100 1 Cor. 14:26.
101 1 Cor. 14:26, 31.
102 Ibid.
103 1 Cor. 14:26, 27, 39.
104 1 Cor. 14:26.
105 1 Cor. 14:31, 39.
106 1 Cor. 14:26.
107 1 Cor. 14:31.
108 1 Cor. 14:40.
109 1 Cor. 14:31.
110 1 Cor. 14:27.
111 1 Cor. 14:30.
112 1 Cor. 14:33.
113 Ibid.
114 1 Cor. 13.
115 1 Cor. 12.
116 Ibid.
117 1 Cor. 1:10, 3:3, 6:6, 8:9–13, 10:29–32, 11:16, 19, 22, 33.
118 1 Cor. 14:34.
119 1 Cor. 14:35.
120 Ibid.
121 1 Cor. 14:26, 31, 39.

122 1 Cor. 14:31.
123 1 Cor. 14:39.
124 1 Cor. 1:10, 11:17–19, 12:12–13, 24–25; Eph. 4:3–7.
125 1 Cor. 14:26, 31, 39, 11:5.
126 1 Cor. 14:26, 31.
127 1 Cor. 14:39.
128 1 Cor. 14:34.
129 Rom. 7:6.
130 1 Cor. 9:20.
131 1 Tim. 1:9.
132 1 Cor. 15:56.
133 Ibid.
134 1 Tim. 1:9–10.
135 1 Cor. 1:2, 10–11.
136 1 Cor. 14:26, 31.
137 Ibid.
138 Ibid.
139 1 Cor. 14:39.
140 1 Cor. 1:13, 6:2, 9, 15, 16, 9:6, 10:22, 11:22.
141 1 Cor. 1:12–17, 4:18–21, 6:1–3, 7–11, 15–20, 9:3–12, 10:21–22, 11:20–34.
142 1 Cor. 1:17, 6:3, 11, 19–20, 9:11–12, 11:26–34.
143 1 Cor. 14:36.
144 Ibid.
145 1 Cor. 14:39–40.
146 1 Cor. 14:37.
147 1 Cor. 14:38.
148 1 Cor. 14:26, 31, 39.
149 1 Cor. 11:11–12.
150 1 Cor. 11:3–16.
151 1 Cor. 7:1–16.
152 1 Cor. 15.
153 1 Cor. 15:1.
154 1 Cor. 15:10.
155 1 Cor. 15:1.
156 1 Cor. 15:2.
157 1 Cor. 12, 1:10, 3:16–17.
158 1 Cor. 1:12–17, 24, 3:5–7, 4:6–7, 11:11–12, 12:4–7, 16: 19–20.
159 1 Cor. 13, 15:58.
160 1 Cor. 1:2, 10, 11, 26, 2:1, 3:1, 4:6, 6:5, 8, 7:24, 29, 8:12, 9:5, 10:1, 11:2, 33, 12:1, 14:6, 20, 26, 39, 15:1, 6, 50, 58, 16:11, 12, 15, 20.
161 1 Cor. 6:11, 11:23–26, 15:3.
162 1 Cor. 1:4–9, 2:10–16, 6:11, 12:11.
163 1 Cor. 6:2–5.
164 1 Cor. 16:22.

Chapter 14 – Must She Be Silent?: 1 Timothy 2:8–15

1 1 Tim. 2:12.
2 αὐθεντεῖν *(authentein).*
3 1 Tim. 2:12.
4 1 Cor. 11:11–12.
5 1 Tim. 1:2.
6 1 Tim. 1:18–19, 6:12.
7 1 Tim. 4:6–16, 5:23, 6:11–12, 20–21.
8 1 Tim. 4:14, 6:20.
9 1 Tim. 3:15.
10 1 Tim. 2:1–15, 3:1–16, 5:1–22, 6:1–2, 6–10, 17–19.
11 1 Tim. 5:21; James 2:8–9.
12 1 Tim. 5:1–21.
13 1 Tim. 1:3–11, 19–20, 4:1–5, 6:3–5, 20–21.
14 1 Tim. 3:3.
15 1 Tim. 1:7.
16 1 Tim. 1:4.
17 1 Tim. 1:5.
18 1 Tim. 1:7–11.
19 1 Tim. 1:10.
20 1 Tim. 1:11.
21 1 Tim. 6:3.
22 1 Tim. 1:11, 14–17, 2:3–6, 3:16, 4:3–4, 9–10, 6:11–16.
23 1 Tim. 1: 11–12.
24 1 Tim. 1:13–16.
25 1 Tim. 2:7.
26 1 Tim. 3:15.
27 1 Tim. 2:2.
28 1 Tim. 2:1–4.
29 1 Tim. 2:5–6.
30 1 Tim. 2:8.
31 1 Cor. 11:5.
32 1 Tim. 2:1; 1 Sam. 2:1; Ps. 32:6, 66:20, 102:17; Isa. 56:3–8; Matt. 6:5–13; Luke 21:36; Acts 4:23–30, 12:12; Rom. 15:30; Eph. 6:18; Phil. 1.6; Col. 4:2–4; 1 Thess. 5:17, 25.
33 Ps. 28:2, 63:4.
34 Ps. 143:6–8, 24:7–10, 25:1, 86:4, 119:48; Luke 21:28; Acts 4:24.
35 Matt. 5:23–24; Eph. 4:1–6, 5:21; Col. 3:15–16; Heb. 10:24–25, 13:15–16.
36 1 Tim. 1:6, 6:3–5.

[37] 1 Tim. 2:9–10.
[38] Matt. 5:27–29; Gal. 5:19; Eph. 5:3–4; Col. 3:5; 1 Thess. 4:3–8; Heb. 13:4.
[39] 1 Tim. 5:2.
[40] Matt. 5:16; John 15:16; Gal. 5:22–25; Eph. 2:10; Titus 2:13–14; Heb. 10:24, 13:16.
[41] 1 Tim. 2:3.
[42] 1 Tim. 6:17–18.
[43] 1 Tim. 2:11.
[44] Ibid.
[45] Deut. 5:1.
[46] Deut. 31:13; Ps. 34:11; Isa. 28:23; Mark 4:9; John 6:45; Rom. 10:14.
[47] 2 Tim. 3:6–7.
[48] 2 Tim. 2:2, 24.
[49] ἀνθρώποις *(anthrōpois).*
[50] 1 Tim. 2:3–4.
[51] 1 Tim. 6:15–16.
[52] Heb. 5:12.
[53] Luke 8:14; Titus 1:1.
[54] Rom. 15:14; 2 Tim. 2:2, 24; Titus 2:1.
[55] Gal. 5:13.
[56] Rom. 14:9–13.
[57] Gal. 5:1.
[58] Rom. 7:6, 10:4: Gal. 3:10–14.
[59] Rom. 6:1–2, 8.
[60] Rom. 6:15, 18.
[61] Rom. 1:17; Hab. 2:4.
[62] Rom. 6:22–23.
[63] 1 Tim. 3:16.
[64] Heb. 11:1.
[65] Rom. 8:28–39.
[66] 1 Tim. 1:10–11.
[67] Rom. 1:17.
[68] 1 Tim. 1:4.
[69] 1 Tim. 1:3–4, 6:20.
[70] Rom. 7:6.
[71] Gal. 5:16.
[72] 1 Tim. 2:12–13.
[73] Gen. 27:1–40, 32:26–28.
[74] Gen. 28:13–15.
[75] Rom. 9:13–15.
[76] 1 Sam. 16:7.
[77] Matt. 19:30.
[78] Matt. 20:27.
[79] John 8:42, 31–59.
[80] Matt. 3:9.
[81] 1 Cor. 1:26–31; Deut. 7:6–8.
[82] Col. 1:15.
[83] James 1:18.
[84] Matt. 11:28; John 1:16, 3:16, 6:45, 17:21; Rom. 3:22, 10:12; Col. 3:11.
[85] 1 Tim. 5:21.
[86] Acts 10:15, 34.
[87] 1 Tim. 2:4, 6, 4:10.
[88] 1 Tim. 1:11.
[89] 1 Tim. 2:14.
[90] Gen. 6:5; 1 Kings 8:46; Ps. 53:3; Isa. 53:6, 64:6; Matt. 7:2; Rom. 3:10, 20, 23; 1 John 1:8.
[91] James 2:10.
[92] Prov. 14:21, 21:4; Jer. 17:9; Rom. 14:23; James 4:17; John 3:4, 5:17.
[93] Gen. 2:17; Ezek. 18:4; Rom. 5:12, 6:23.
[94] Isa. 53:5; 2 Cor. 5:21; Rom. 5:1–11; 1 Pet. 2:24.
[95] 1 Tim. 2:5–6.
[96] 1 John 1:9; Ps. 103:12; Isa. 1:18.
[97] 2 Cor. 11:3–4, 13–15.
[98] John 8:44–45; 2 Cor. 4:2–4; 2 Thess. 2:7–12.
[99] 1 Cor. 1:20–30, 3:18–23.
[100] Rom. 3:9–31.
[101] 1 Tim. 1:10–17, 2:3–6, 3:15–16, 4:4–6, 9–10, 5:21, 6:3, 11–16.
[102] Eph. 2:14–16.
[103] Eph. 3:6–12.
[104] Eph. 4:1–6.
[105] Eph. 6:19–20.
[106] Rom. 5:12–21; 1 Cor. 15:21–22, 45–49.
[107] Rom. 12:3.
[108] Phil. 2:3.
[109] Rom. 14:10–13; Eph. 6:9.
[110] Matt. 23:8–10.
[111] NEB, The *New English Bible,* Oxford University Press, 1970.
[112] 1 Cor. 12:7.
[113] 1 Tim. 2:15.
[114] John 3:16; Eph. 2:8–9.
[115] 1 Tim. 2:5–6.
[116] Heb. 2:15.
[117] Gen. 3:16.
[118] John 11:25–26; 1 Cor. 15:51–56; Heb. 11:4, 33–40.
[119] Eph. 2:8–10.
[120] Eph. 1:13–14.
[121] Rom. 8:29; 2 Cor. 3:18.
[122] Col. 1:22–23.
[123] 1 Tim. 5:20.
[124] Rom. 3:22–23.
[125] Gen. 3:16.

[126] Rom. 8:1–2; Gal. 3:13–14.
[127] Gal. 5:22–26; Col. 3:1–2.
[128] Phil. 1:3–11; Rom. 15:14.
[129] 1 Tim. 1:16.
[130] 1 Tim. 1:15.
[131] Gal. 5:13.
[132] Matt. 20:24–28; Eph. 5:1, 2, 21; Phil. 2:3–8.
[133] Matt. 23:8–10; 2 Cor. 3:3–6.
[134] Deut. 7:7–9.
[135] 1 Tim. 1:4, 5, 14, 19, 2:15, 3:13, 6:11, 12.
[136] 2 Tim. 3:16-17; Acts 2:38-40, 15:15.
[137] Can another New Testament example be found of a prohibition directed to a specific person or group within the Christian community that cannot in principle be extrapolated to apply to all believers? Three examples of prohibitions directed to specific people that apply to all believers are 1 Tim. 1:3–4: "Command certain men not to teach false doctrines"; 1 Tim. 6:17: "Command those who are rich . . . not to be arrogant nor to put their hope in wealth"; Eph. 6:9: "masters, . . . Do not threaten them." The reason we may see the prohibition directed to "a woman" in 1 Tim. 2:12 in a different light may be because we see "having authority over" as a virtue, rather than a characteristic of the old life and thus a prohibition for all believers. Yet Christ taught us differently in Matt. 20:25–28. He has all authority and his authority is applied to the church through each believer as each one is united to Christ and his truth through the Spirit. The reason no other examples can be found is that God's standard for his followers is exactly the same for all.
[138] Eph. 1:13–14.
[139] Gal. 5:13–16.
[140] 1 Tim. 1:3–20, 4:1–16, 6:3.
[141] 1 Tim. 2:1–3:15.
[142] 1 Tim. 5:1–21.
[143] 1 Tim. 2:1; 1 Cor. 11:5; 1 Sam. 2:1; Ps. 32:6, 66:20, 102:17; Isa. 56:3–7; Matt. 6:5–13; Luke 21:36; Acts 4:24–30, 12:12; Rom. 15:30; Eph. 6:18; Phil. 4:1, 6; Col. 4:2–4; 1 Thess. 5:17, 25.
[144] Ps. 28:2, 63:4, 143:6–8.
[145] Matt. 5:23–24; Gal. 5:14–16; Eph. 4:1–6, 5:21; Col. 3:15–16; Heb. 10:24–25, 13:15–16.
[146] 1 Tim. 2:9–10, 5:2: Matt. 5:27–29; Gal. 5:19; Eph. 5:3–4; Col. 3:5; 1 Thess. 4:3–8; Heb. 13:4.
[147] 1 Tim. 2:3, 10, 6:17–18; Matt. 5:16; John 15:16; Gal. 5:22–25; Eph. 2:10; Titus 2:7, 13–14; Heb. 10:24, 13:16.
[148] 1 Tim. 2:3, 10; John 12:26; Gal. 6:2, 10; Eph. 6:7; Col. 3:17, 23; Titus 3:8; James 2:17–18; 1 Pet. 2:12.
[149] 1 Tim. 2:11; Deut. 4:10, 31:12; Ps. 119:7; Isa. 1:17; Matt. 11:29; John 14:31; 1 Thess. 4:4.
[150] 1 Tim. 2:11; Deut. 5:1, 31:13; Ps. 34:11; Isa. 28:23; Mark 4:9; John 6:45; Rom. 10:14; 2 Thess. 3:11–12.
[151] Eph. 4:23–24; Phil. 1:9–11, 3:15; Col. 4:12; Heb. 5:14, 6:1; James 1:4.
[152] Deut. 4:9; Rom. 12:7, 15:14; Eph. 4:11; 2 Tim. 2:2, 24; Titus 2:1; Heb. 5:12.
[153] 1 Tim. 2:12; Matt. 7:12; 1 Cor. 1:26–31, 4:6–7, 12:21, 25; 2 Cor. 10:17–18; Jude 16.
[154] Rom. 12:3.
[155] Phil. 2:3.
[156] Rom. 14:10–13.
[157] Matt. 23:8–12.
[158] Gal. 5:13.
[159] John 15:15; 1 Cor. 3:11–13; 2 Cor. 3:3–6; 1 Tim. 4:6, 6:3; 2 John 9.
[160] Matt. 23:8–12.
[161] 1 Tim. 2:13; Matt. 3:9, 19:16–30, 20:27; John 8:42, 31–59; Rom. 3:27, 9:13–15; 1 Cor. 3:5–9, 4:6–7.
[162] 1 Tim. 2:14; Gen. 6:5; 1 Kings 8:46; Ps. 53:3; Isa. 53:6, 64:6; Matt. 7:2; Rom. 3:10, 20, 23; 1 John 1:8.
[163] Rom. 3:9, 19; James 2:10, 4:17; 1 John 3:4, 5:17.
[164] Gen. 2:17; Ezek. 18:4; Matt. 25:41; Rom. 5:12, 6:23; 2 Thess. 1:8–9.
[165] 1 Tim. 1:4, 5, 14, 19, 2:15, 3:13, 6:11, 12; John 3:16; Rom. 1:17, 3:26; Eph. 2:8–9; Col. 1:23, 2:12.
[166] Isa. 53:5; 2 Cor. 5:21; Rom. 5:1–11; 1 Tim. 2:5–6; 1 Pet. 2:24.
[167] Rom. 6:22–23; Eph. 1:13–14; Phil. 1:9–11; Gal. 5:22–26; Col. 1:22, 3:1–2.
[168] Rom. 8:29; 2 Cor. 3:18.
[169] Gal. 3:26–28.
[170] 1 Tim. 1:3–11, 19–20, 4:1–5, 6:3–5, 20–21.
[171] 1 Tim. 1:6–8.

[172] 1 Tim. 1:4–5, 10–11, 6:3.
[173] 1 Tim. 1:10–11, 14–17, 2:3–6, 3:16, 4:3–4, 9–10, 6:3, 11–16.
[174] 1 Tim. 3:15.
[175] Ibid.
[176] 1 Tim. 5:21.

Chapter 15 – The Middle of the Road: How Safe Is It?

[1] Gen. 2:18.
[2] עֵזֶר (*'ê·zer*).
[3] Exod. 18:2–4.
[4] Deut. 33:7, 26, 29.
[5] Ps. 20:1–2.
[6] Ps. 38:22.
[7] Hosea 13:4, 9.
[8] Exod. 18:4; Deut. 33:7, 26, 29; Ps. 20:2, 33:20, 70:5, 89:19, 115:9, 10, 11, 121:1, 2, 124:8, 146:5; Hosea 13:9.
[9] Gen. 2:18.
[10] Ibid.
[11] Gen. 2:24.
[12] Gen. 1:27.
[13] Gen. 1:31.
[14] Gen. 3:16.
[15] Gen. 3:16–19.
[16] Gen. 2:17.
[17] Gen. 2:24; Matt. 19:4–6.
[18] Gen. 1:31.
[19] Gen. 3:19.
[20] 1 Cor. 15:54–57.
[21] Gal. 3:13–14.
[22] Rom. 4:25; Heb. 2:9, 14–15.
[23] 2 Tim. 1:10.
[24] Rom. 5:10.
[25] Eph. 1:22.
[26] Matt. 20:28.
[27] Col. 1:20.
[28] Gen. 2:18.
[29] Gen. 5:1–2.
[30] Matt. 22:37–40; Deut. 6:5; Lev. 19:18.
[31] Gal. 5:13–14; Col. 3:14.
[32] Young, *Young's Analytical Concordance to the Bible*, 744–745.
[33] Col. 3:14 KJV.
[34] Col. 3:14 NIV.
[35] 1 John 4:16
[36] Deut. 6:4.
[37] John 17:23 KJV.
[38] John 17:23 NIV.
[39] Exod. 18:4; Deut. 33:7, 26, 29; Ps. 20:2, 33:20, 70:5, 89:19, 115:9, 10, 11, 121:1, 2, 124:8, 146:5; Hosea 13:9.
[40] Exod. 18:2–4; Ps. 20:1–2.
[41] Matt. 28:19–20.
[42] Acts 17:30; Rom. 15:2–4; Col. 1:23.
[43] Rom. 12:7; 1 Cor. 12:28.
[44] 2 Tim. 3:16; Heb. 4:12–13.
[45] 2 Pet. 1:19–21.
[46] 1 Tim. 4:12.
[47] 1 Tim. 4:11.
[48] 1 Tim. 4:13.
[49] 1 Cor. 14:34.
[50] 1 Tim. 2:12.
[51] 1 Tim. 3:1.
[52] 1 Tim. 3:2.
[53] 1 Tim. 3:12.
[54] Rom. 16:1.
[55] As in notes to 1 Tim. 3:11 in both the NIV and NASB translations.
[56] Eph. 5:22–23.
[57] A similar argument is set forth by George W. Knight III in *Recovering Biblical Manhood and Womanhood: A Response to Evangelical Feminism* (Piper and Grudem, 169. "The two concepts mutually explain one another." That's circular reasoning.
[58] Col. 3:16–17; Rom. 15:14.
[59] Col. 1:2.
[60] Col. 4:15.
[61] Eph. 5:19.
[62] Eph. 5:15, 18.
[63] Eph. 5:20, 21.
[64] Luke 8:21; Rom. 7:4, 8:29; Col. 1:2; Heb. 2:11, 3:1.
[65] Rom. 15:14; 1 Cor. 14:26, 39.
[66] Rom. 1:7; 1 Cor. 1:2; Col. 1:2.
[67] 1 Cor. 6:2–3.
[68] John 3:3, 5, 6:50.
[69] 1 Tim. 3:1, 5; 1 Pet. 4:11.
[70] Acts 2:38; 1 Cor. 12:7, 11; 2 Cor. 5:10; 1 Pet. 4:10.
[71] 1 Cor. 14:26.
[72] John 17:21; Rom. 3:22–24.
[73] 1 Cor. 14:31.
[74] Gen. 1:26–27; Eph. 2:15; 1 Tim. 2:4–5; 2 Tim. 3:17.

75 1 Cor. 14:34–35; 1 Tim. 2:12; 2 Tim. 2:2.
76 Rom. 15:2, 4; 2 Tim. 3:14–17.
77 Matt. 28:19–20; 1 Tim. 4:13; Col. 3:16.
78 Matt. 28:19; Rom. 15:14; 1 Cor. 14:26; Col. 3:16–17; 1 Tim. 4:11, 13; 2 Tim. 2:2.
79 1 Tim. 4:13.
80 Col. 3:16–17.
81 Matt. 28:19.
82 1 Cor. 14:39.
83 James 5:16.
84 Piper and Grudem, *Recovering Biblical Manhood and Womanhood,* 76.
85 Women may give in to the ungodly use of manipulation, although here it seems to be Taylor who is yielding to it. It is ungodly because it is both deceitful and self-centered. Manipulation has often been a temptation to those who are either afraid of or denied open and honest participation in the decision making process, but still want their own way.
86 Why was Priscilla's teaching "unofficial" when God used it not only for the instruction of Apollos, but also to spread the gospel throughout Asia (Rom. 16:3; Acts 18:26–28; 1 Cor. 3:5)?
87 Piper and Grudem, *Recovering Biblical Manhood and Womanhood,* 85.
88 Ibid., 76.
89 Ibid., 69–70.
90 Ibid., 88.
91 Rom. 12:8.
92 1 Cor. 12:7, 11.
93 1 Cor. 12:7.
94 1 Pet. 4:10.
95 1 Cor. 14:34–35.
96 Piper and Grudem, *Recovering Biblical Manhood and Womanhood,* 89, and Appendix 2: Danvers Statement Rationale #8 and #9: 469.
97 Ibid., 257.
98 Matt. 12:9–12.
99 Mark 7:9–13.
100 Matt. 23:16.
101 Rom. 1:17; 11:36; Eph. 1:23; Heb. 13:8; Rev. 1:8.
102 Matt. 22:37–40.
103 Matt. 7:12.
104 Mark 7:8–9.
105 Rom. 1:17, 11:36; Eph. 1:23; Heb. 13:8; Rev. l:8.
106 Matt. 22:37–40; Lev. 19:18; Matt. 19:19; Gal. 5:14.
107 Matt. 7:12; Luke 6:31.
108 Mark 7:8–9; Matt. 15:6; Col. 2:8.
109 Gal. 3:28.
110 Piper and Grudem, *Recovering Biblical Manhood and Womanhood,* #26 A, 71.
111 This answer obfuscates the true meaning of Galatians 3:28 and seems to purposely promote confusion as to its value as a call to equality within God's family. Galatians 3:28 is not written in the context of marriage or sexual morality, nor can it be applied to these issues or as a biblical principle upon which Christian marriage and sexual morality are based. There are plenty of other scriptures that speak directly to these things. Galatians 3:28 is about who is included in God's family as sons.
112 1 Cor. 12; Rom. 12; Eph. 4.
113 Rom. 12:3–5.
114 The purpose of this statement is to "set forth the Biblical view of the relationship between men and women, especially in the home and in the church." It was "prepared by several evangelical leaders at a Council on Biblical Manhood and Womanhood meeting in Danvers, Mass., in December 1987," and "was first published in final form by the CBMW in November, 1988." (Piper and Grudem, *Recovering Biblical Manhood and Womanhood,* 470, 471.
115 Ibid., 470.
116 Ibid.
117 Rom. 1:18–32.
118 Gen. 1:27, 31.
119 Gen. 2:24; Matt. 19:4–6; Eph. 5:28–33.
120 Gal. 5:19–21.
121 1 Cor. 6:9–10; Eph. 5:3–7.
122 John 3:3–8.
123 1 Cor. 5:9–13; Eph. 5:3.
124 Acts 5:12–14, 16:13–15, 40; 1 Cor. 1:2; Heb. 2:11–3:1.
125 Eph. 2:19; 1 Pet. 2:5.
126 1 Tim. 3:15.
127 1 John 1:9.
128 Eph. 5:3–14: Gal. 5:16–26.
129 Gal. 5:24–25.
130 Eph. 2:19.
131 Rom. 8:17.

[132] Rom. 12:6.
[133] Rom. 3:22–24, 10:11–13.
[134] 1 Cor. 12:14–25.
[135] Rom. 8:29; Eph. 1:5, 11.
[136] Rom. 8:30; Eph. 4: 1.
[137] Acts 16:31; Rom. 10:9.
[138] Acts 2:38–39; 1 John 1:9.
[139] Rom. 3:24–26, 5:9, 8:30; Eph. 1:7.
[140] Eph. 3:12; Heb. 4:14–16.
[141] Luke 9:23; John 10:4.
[142] Acts 2:38–39; Eph. 1:13–14.
[143] 1 Cor. 12:7, 11; Eph. 4:7.
[144] John 1:12–13.
[145] Heb. 2:11–3:1.
[146] 2 Cor. 5:16–21.
[147] Matt. 19:28; 1 Cor. 6:2.
[148] 1 Cor. 6:2–5.
[149] Matt. 23:8; 1 Cor. 1:2, 10, 12:1, 12–13, 27.
[150] Eph. 5:1, 2, 21; Gal. 5:13–14.
[151] 2 Cor. 5:16, 20; Eph. 2:14–22.
[152] Rom. 12:4–16; Gal. 5:13–14; Eph. 4:1–11.
[153] 1 Pet. 4:10.
[154] Eph. 4:12–13.
[155] Eph. 4:13 KJV.
[156] Eph. 4:13; Marshall, *The Interlinear Greek-English New Testament*, 767.
[157] Matt. 7:12
[158] Eph. 4:3–5.
[159] Eph. 5:3–15.
[160] I have been careful to distinguish the homosexual person from homosexual behavior. If there are believers who might consider themselves homosexual in identity but live chaste lives without any sexual immorality, either in action or thought, then they are without sin in this regard. However, this person may experience a greater burden of aloneness and separation, as may any believer who is sexually moral but single. The homosexual believer, like his or her single heterosexual "brother" must then find and experience God's recreation and redemption of oneness in the church (Isa. 56:3–8; Matt. 19:11–12).
[161] Gen. 2:24.
[162] 1 Cor. 11:11–12.
[163] Gen. 2:24; Matt. 19:4–6; Eph. 5:28–33.
[164] 1 Cor. 6:9.
[165] Rom. 1:18–32.
[166] 1 Cor. 6:9–10; Gal. 5:19–21; Eph. 5:3–7.
[167] John 3:3–8.
[168] 1 Cor. 5:9–13; Eph. 5:3.
[169] Acts 5:12–14, 16:13–15, 40; 1 Cor. 1:2; Heb. 2:11–3:1.
[170] Eph. 2:19; 1 Tim. 3:15; 1 Pet. 2:5.
[171] Eph. 5:3–14; Gal. 5:16–26.
[172] Gal. 5:24, 25.
[173] Rom. 8; Eph. 2:11–22; Col. 3:1–17; Gal. 3:26–4:7.
[174] Matt. 23:8; Rom. 3:22–24, 8:17, 10:11–13, 12:6; 1 Cor. 12:24–25; Eph. 2:19.
[175] 1 Cor. 14:34.
[176] 1 Tim. 2:12.
[177] Rom. 12:1–2.
[178] Luke 9:23–24.
[179] Matt. 7:21, 12:50; Luke 12:47–48; Col. 4:12.
[180] Acts 16:31.
[181] 1 Cor. 4:6; 1 Tim. 1:10–11, 3:15, 6:3.
[182] Gal. 5:1.
[183] John 16:13; Eph. 1:17–18.
[184] Rom. 1:17, 3:21–31, 15:7.
[185] John 8:32.
[186] Heb. 8:10; Jer. 31:33.
[187] Luke 24:45.
[188] When I read *How I Changed My Mind About Women in Leadership,* I felt the confirmation I sought and became convinced it was time to publish this study. (Alan F. Johnson, editor, *How I Changed My Mind About Women in Leadership* [Grand Rapids, MI: Zondervan, 2010].)
[189] 2 Cor. 12:10.
[190] 1 Cor. 2:2–5.
[191] Rom. 1:17, 3:21–31, 15:7.
[192] Rom. 12:1–2.

Chapter 16 – Sons: You Are All Sons

[1] Rom. 8:14, 29; Eph. 1:5
[2] Rom. 8:14–15; Gal. 3:26, 4:7, and so on.
[3] Gal. 4:7.
[4] Ibid.
[5] Gal. 4:4 paraphrased.
[6] Gal. 1:1, 4:2, 6 paraphrased.
[7] Gal. 4:6 paraphrased.
[8] Gen. 3:16.
[9] Gal. 4:6.
[10] Rom. 8:17.
[11] John 1:12–13; 1 John 3:1.
[12] Eph. 2:19, 1 Tim. 3:15.
[13] Rom. 8:14–17; Gal. 4:4–7.
[14] Gal. 3:26–29, 4:5; 2 Cor. 6:18.
[15] Gal. 3:28.
[16] John 8:36; Ps. 118:5.
[17] 1 Pet. 4:10.
[18] Rom. 10:13–15.
[19] Gal. 1:6.
[20] Gal. 2:14.
[21] Gal. 1:7.
[22] Gal. 1:9.
[23] Gal. 3:1, 3.
[24] Gal. 3:6–7, 26, 4:4.
[25] Gal. 3:3, 6–7, 25.
[26] Gal. 3:12.
[27] Gal. 2:16, 3:10–11.
[28] Gal. 3:22, 23.
[29] Gal. 5:1.
[30] Gal. 5:4.
[31] Gal. 5:2–4.
[32] Gal. 1:7.
[33] Gal. 5:1.
[34] Gal. 2:4–5.
[35] Gal. 3:19.
[36] Gal. 3:24–25; Rom. 3:20, 5:20–21.
[37] Rom. 7:6.
[38] Rom. 8:1–4.
[39] 1 Tim. 1:10–11.
[40] Matt. 5:17
[41] Heb. 4:15.
[42] Rom. 8:2.
[43] Heb. 10:1–14.
[44] James 1:25.
[45] Gal. 3:26; Luke 15:11–32; John 8:31–36.
[46] Gal. 4:4–5; Heb. 2:9–11.
[47] Gal. 3:27.
[48] Gal. 3:28.
[49] Gen. 17:7.
[50] Gal. 3:8.
[51] Gen. 17:4–8; Gal. 3:6–7.
[52] Gen. 17:23.
[53] Gen. 17:21; Gal. 4:21–31.
[54] Acts 2:38–39.
[55] 1 Pet. 2:9–10; Rev. 5:9–10.
[56] Rom. 2:29; Col. 2:11.
[57] Col. 2:17; Heb. 8:5–6, 10:1, 10.
[58] Gen. 3:l5, 17:21; Acts 13:23, 32–33; 2 Cor. 1:20.
[59] Gal. 4:26, 31.
[60] Gal. 3:6–9.
[61] Gal. 4:28.
[62] Gal. 4:1–3.
[63] Rom. 8:14–16; Eph. 1:13.
[64] Gal. 3:26–29, 4:4–7.
[65] Col. 1:27; Heb. 6:11, 19, 11:1.
[66] Gal. 3:6–7, 4:3; Col. 2:8.
[67] John 1:12–13.
[68] Gal. 2:12.
[69] Gal. 5:2.
[70] Gal. 2:14.
[71] Gal. 5:16, 25.
[72] Gal. 6:15–16.
[73] Col. 3:10–11.
[74] Gal. 6:15–16; 2 Cor. 5:16–17.
[75] Paul was addressing the issue of circumcision in Galatians, but the principle was "what counts is a new creation" (Gal. 6:15). "The only thing that counts is faith expressing itself through love" (Gal. 5:6). "The life I live in the body, I live by faith in the Son of God, who loved me and gave himself for me. I do not set aside the grace of God" (Gal. 2:20–21). Issues may change, but not biblical principles (1 Pet. 1:23–25). Today we face the issue of the role of women in the family and church. The principle remains the same.
[76] Eph. 4:17, 21–24.
[77] Eph. 5:8.
[78] Phil. 1:21.
[79] Phil. 1:27.
[80] Col. 2:6.
[81] Col. 2:8.
[82] Col. 3:1–3.
[83] 1 John 1:6–7.

[84] 1 John 2:6.
[85] 1 John 2:28.
[86] Gal. 3:26–28.
[87] 1 Tim. 1:10–11, 3:15; Eph. 2:19; Phil. 1:27; Gal. 2:14.
[88] 1 John 3:18.
[89] Gal. 5:7.
[90] Gal. 5:16; Rom. 8:11–12.
[91] Rom. 7:6.
[92] Matt. 6:10.
[93] 2 Cor. 13:11.
[94] Rom. 1:17.
[95] Gal. 3:23–25.
[96] Gal. 2:19.
[97] Gal. 2:20–21.
[98] John 15:12.
[99] Rom. 15:7.
[100] Rom. 16:2.
[101] Philem. 17.
[102] Gal. 4:14.
[103] Matt. 25:40.
[104] Gal. 3:28.
[105] James 1:22–25.
[106] 1 Tim. 3:15.
[107] Eph. 3:6.
[108] Gal. 3:7, 29.
[109] Gal. 4:3–7; Rom. 6:22.
[110] Gal. 3:26, 4:6.
[111] Gal. 3:28.
[112] Gal. 4:3; 1 John 2:16–17.
[113] Gal. 4:5.
[114] υἱοθεσίαν *(huiothesian).*
[115] Rom. 9:4–5.
[116] Eph.1:4–14.
[117] Eph. 1:1, 6:23–24.
[118] Eph. 5:22.
[119] 1 John 3:1; Matt. 7:11; Eph. 2:4–5.
[120] Rom. 9:4.
[121] Gal. 3:7, 26, 29; Rom. 9:22–26; Eph. 1:4–5, 11; 1 Pet. 2:9; Ps. 105:6, 42–45, 106:4–5; Isa. 43:16, 19–21.
[122] Gal. 4:6; Eph. 1:13–14; Rom. 8:14–16.
[123] Rom. 8:13–14; Luke 20:36, 38; Gal. 5:25; Eph. 2:4–5; 1 Pet. 3:7.
[124] Gal. 4:7, 26, 31, 5:1; Rom. 8:15, 21; Heb. 1:14.
[125] Gal. 4:7; Rom. 4:13–15, 8:17; Deut. 4:20; Dan. 7:18, 27; Matt. 25:34; Acts 20:32; Eph. 1:18; Col. 1:12, 3:23–24; 1 Pet. 3:7.
[126] Rom. 8:17; Eph. 1:13–14, 3:6.
[127] Rom. 8:17; Phil. 1:29; 2 Thess. 1:5; 2 Tim. 2:12; Heb. 13:12–13; 1 Pet. 2:21, 4:1–2.
[128] Heb. 12:7.
[129] Heb. 12:7–10.
[130] Eph. 1:4–5; Acts 20:32; Gal. 2:21, 5:5; 2 Cor. 6:14–18; Phil. 2:15; 1 Thess. 5:5; 1 Pet. 1:13–16; 1 John 3:10.
[131] 1 John 3:2; Rom. 8:29; 2 Cor. 3:17–18.
[132] Rom. 8:17, 4:13, 9:4; Matt. 19:28; Eph. 2:6; Col. 1:12; 2 Tim. 2:12; Heb. 2:10; Rev. 5:10.
[133] Gal. 3:26, 28; John 11:52, 17:22–23.
[134] 1 Pet. 1:4.
[135] Eph. 1:18.
[136] Gal. 4:4–5.
[137] Gal. 3:26.
[138] Gal. 4:7.
[139] Rom. 8:2.
[140] Eph. 2:19.
[141] Gal. 4:7.
[142] Heb. 1:2.
[143] 1 Cor. 2:7, 9; Isa. 64:4.
[144] Gal. 2:21, 5:2–4.
[145] Gal. 3:23.
[146] Gal. 5:6.
[147] Gal. 6:15.
[148] Gal. 1:15, 2:15–16, 20, 3:8–9, 11, 14, 18, 22, 24, 25, 26, 5:6.
[149] Gal. 3:6, 5:5, 16, 24.
[150] Gal. 3:7–8, 11–14.
[151] Rom. 3:21–31.
[152] Rom. 5:1–2.
[153] Gal. 2:20.
[154] Gal. 3:28.
[155] Gal. 3:3; 1 John 2:16.
[156] Gal. 3:11.
[157] Gal. 3:28.
[158] Gal. 2:21, 5:4.
[159] Gal. 3:18, 4:28.
[160] Gal. 3:21–22.
[161] Gal. 3:11, 5:6.
[162] Gal. 3:17, 22.
[163] Gal. 3:6–9.
[164] 1 John 5:1–5.
[165] Rom. 2:28–29.
[166] Gal. 4:3–5; Rom. 6:22.
[167] Col. 2:11, Rom. 2:29.
[168] Gal. 3:26, 4:7.
[169] Acts 17:24; 2 Cor. 6:16; Eph. 2:21–22; 1 Pet. 2:4–5.

[170] Gal. 3:28.
[171] Acts 17:28.
[172] 1 Cor. 12:13.
[173] Col. 3:10–11.
[174] 1 Cor. 8:6.
[175] Eph. 4:1–6.
[176] Rom. 11:33, 36.
[177] Gal. 3:7.
[178] Gal. 4:28–29.
[179] Gal. 3:14.
[180] Ibid.
[181] Gal. 3:26.
[182] Gal. 4:7.
[183] Gal. 4:7; Rom. 4:13–15, 8:17; Deut. 4:20; Dan. 7:18, 27; Matt. 5:3–12, 25:34; Acts 20:32; 1 Cor. 3:19–23; Eph. 1:18; Col. 1:12, 3:23–24; 1 Pet. 3:7.
[184] Heb. 12:10.
[185] Eph. 1:4–5; Acts 20:32; Gal. 2:21, 5:5; 2 Cor. 6:14–18; Phil. 2:15; 1 Thess. 5:5; 1 Pet. l:13–16; 1 John 3:10.
[186] 1 John 3:2; Rom. 8:29; 2 Cor. 3:17–18.
[187] Rom. 8:17; Eph. 1:13–14, 3:6.
[188] Rom. 8:17; Phil. 1:29; 2 Thess. 1:5; 2 Tim. 2:12; Heb. 13:12–13;1 Pet. 2:21, 4:1–2.
[189] Heb. 12:7.
[190] Rom. 8:17, 4:13, 9:23–24; Matt. 19:28; Eph. 2:6; Col. 1:12; 2 Tim. 2:12; Heb. 2:10; Rev. 5:10.
[191] Heb. 1:2.
[192] Gal. 4:5.
[193] 1 John 3:1; Matt. 7:11; Eph. 2:4–5.
[194] Gal. 3:29; Rom. 9:22–26; Eph. 1:4–5, 11; 1 Pet. 2:9; Ps. 105:6, 42–45, 106:4–5; Isa. 43:16:19–21.
[195] Gal. 4:6; Eph. 1:13–14; Rom. 8:14–16.
[196] Rom. 8:13–14; Luke 20:36; Gal. 5:25; Eph. 2:4–5; 1 Pet. 3:7.
[197] Gal. 4:7, 26, 31, 5:1; Rom. 8:15, 21; Heb. 1:14.
[198] Gal. 3:28.
[199] Gal. 3:6, 22.
[200] Gal. 3:26.
[201] Gal. 3:6, 9, 27, 5:5.
[202] Gal. 3:12.
[203] Gal. 3:3.
[204] Gal. 3:10.
[205] Gal. 5:6.
[206] Gal. 3:11; Hab. 2:4.
[207] Gal. 2:20.
[208] Gal. 2:14.
[209] Rom. 8:11–12; Gal. 5:16, 25; Rom. 7:6.
[210] Gal. 6:15–16.
[211] 1 Tim. 1:10–11, 3:15; Eph. 2:19; Phil. 1:27.
[212] 1 John 3:18; Gal. 5:16.
[213] 1 Cor. 13:11.
[214] Rom. 1:17; Gal. 2:20–21, 3:26, 5:6.
[215] John 15:12.
[216] Rom. 15:7, 16:2; Gal. 4:14; Philem. 17.
[217] Eph. 2:13–22, 3:6; Gal. 4:28.
[218] KJV and NASB.
[219] Gal. 3:26–29, 4:3–7.
[220] Gal. 6:15–16.

CPSIA information can be obtained at www.ICGtesting.com
Printed in the USA
BVOW08s1314230616

453028BV00003B/134/P

9 781457 520006